Environmental Education

Environmental Education

An Interdisciplinary Approach to Nature

edited by
MATTHEW ETHERINGTON

Foreword by Amba J. Sepie

WIPF & STOCK • Eugene, Oregon

ENVIRONMENTAL EDUCATION
An Interdisciplinary Approach to Nature

Wipf & Stock
An Imprint of Wipf and Stock Publishers
199 W. 8th Ave., Suite 3
Eugene, OR 97401

www.wipfandstock.com

PAPERBACK ISBN: 978-1-6667-3190-3
HARDCOVER ISBN: 978-1-6667-2494-3
EBOOK ISBN: 978-1-6667-2495-0

09/18/23

To

This book is dedicated to my marvelous family who are far more precious than jewels, and to all my past, present, and, indeed, future outdoor educators.

Contents

Foreword

Rekindling our Ecological Relations

AMBA J. SEPIE

It would seem that the time is upon us for becoming very honest when it comes to the collective reality we are presently birthing—to ponder deeply the quality of the relationships we are cultivating and the learnings we pass on to the generations who will inherit the future. Sometimes I am *genuinely* hopeful that we are doing well with this, but sometimes—like you, I am sure—the call to responsibility feels weighted with an imperative that is gathering at the level of our collective soul. As conflicts continue between warring cultures, climate change looms over us with mounting uncertainty, and we feel threatened by the possibility of socio-ecological ruin, the impetus to act, and act appropriately, is ever more keenly felt. These are difficult days.

This book, borne from the collective efforts of those who are taking up this mantle of hope, of critique, of ecological contemplation and solution, comes into being at this moment of change, where we will determine what our relationship with Earth will be as the incoming generations follow our footsteps into our shared future. We could ask how we might locate the fire necessary to burn away the old ways of doing things. Where we will look for the bones, the structure upon which we can build a tomorrow that will *hold* what we need it to. How we will awaken our hearts and minds to the memory of how to live here in true relationship. And what worldview we could carry forwards with us as we traverse the path ahead.

In my work of collecting the voices, advice, and sentiment of global Earth elders, generally from traditional and Indigenous communities, it has become evident that there is somewhat of a plan afoot, if we might remain open toward the foundational knowings that are at the heart of this plan. The invitation is clearly stated and pitched without hesitation to those of us who feel they have lost track of their connection with Earth. The invitation, first put forward in the 1970s by the Haundenosaunee Confederacy to the United Nations, encourages the "western human" to become as if a younger brother to the elder wisdom of traditional peoples and follow their lead when it comes to how we might decolonize from many centuries of war-oriented and self-serving thinking. History documents the uncomfortable reality that, on its first pass, this invitation led to cultural appropriation and legions of westernized humans attempting to claim Native ways of being for themselves. An unfortunate misfire. Thankfully, the second attempt to invite the junior players into council is now here, and if we pause for but a moment, we may actually discover that the worldview being offered here is asking for a shift in our perception and a value change—to a kinship system of relationship that has been sustaining generations of Earth-oriented humans for a very long time.

To put it plainly, we are being encouraged to accept that Earth is a conscious, sentient being, fully agential and maternal with respect to all life birthed on this planet. We are further advised that these "gaps" between us, this air we imagine as empty, is not only information-rich, but full of Earth's consciousness. That we humans are, in fact, *internal* to the consciousness of a sentient Earth. We are being asked to realize that we are all receivers and transmitters, dancing within consciousness, rather than distinct individuals with a consciousness that lives only inside our heads. How radical an idea, to conceive of ourselves as nodes of a living Earth who is becoming conscious of herself through us. It is not radical at all to generations of elders, healers, and wisdom-keepers, across many continents, who consult not just with Earth directly but also with the invisible realms of spirit and ancestors and with other species. We are being asked to surrender our doubt when it comes to the instinctual and intuitive nature of the human being, who is *at core* intimately connected to an Earth who has been minimised and side-lined via an unhealthy and destructive cultural complex. We need to recognize that westernized thinking, in whatever form (colonization, globalization, modernization, and so on), is in urgent need of a values overhaul.

Our net of kin relations has been severed by generations of people who have denied our spiritual and biological relationship with Earth, and rejected traditionally sustaining notions of spirit, to the point of warring over how spirit would be defined. Whether we think of spirit as a movement and motion that communes with Earth, across geographies and time, to be named as Great Spirit, or Holy Ghost, or as the breath of God speaking the world into existence, there is a partnership here. There is no secularity in the worldview upheld by Indigenous Earth-oriented people, but it isn't quite monotheistic either. The whole world comes alive, every species, every person, every place, with the spirit-borne consciousness of Earth herself, within which we live our lives. There is a grace here that demands our attention. We are being encouraged to cast off the unhealthy habit of separation thinking, whereby we insist we are encircled, literally, by an environment that we remain disconnected from.

The notion that we are interwoven with a multitude of interconnected ecologies is hardly new, but this has not yet been merged with the efforts to reconsider the nature and extent of consciousness, albeit via the wisdom of Indigenous and traditional thinking or within conventional neuro-philosophical or physics laboratories. The ecological networks within which we are embedded, from microbial to interplanetary, are generally considered to be distinctly physical, whilst, simultaneously, we can see there is a global movement to confer personhood to rivers, mountains, and so forth—to extend consciousness to Earth, her geological features, and to other animal kin with whom we share our places of being. Can the two be brought together in a manner that harvests the very best of Indigenous knowledge, ecological thinking, and religio-cultural understandings to remedy our planetary and social distress?

As is also known across Turtle Island (and elsewhere), Earth is not merciful when it comes to ecologies of which we are a part but oversees an ongoing, cyclic process of regeneration which is antithetical to the privilege felt by human beings when it comes to preserving oneself. We are challenged by the notion that humans are the "most special" animal amongst all those inhabiting Earth, as it displaces our sense of being in charge. Oren Lyons, faithkeeper of the Turtle Clan of the Onondaga Nation, is rather famous for his reminder that Earth has no mercy, only law and laws to which we are beholden despite any objections we might raise in this matter. The worldview he speaks to here is based on the recognition of not only Earth's consciousness but cross-species kinship and a value system that includes relationship, reciprocity, reverence, redistribution, regeneration, and ultimately, responsibility. The central teaching is that a return to a traditional kinship-based value structure will, over time, recalibrate our relationships with one another, with other animals, plants, the tiniest creatures upon which we depend, and with Earth herself. We are not being asked nor encouraged to take up the *specific* symbolic architecture that vitalizes traditional communities, but we *are* being asked to modify our frenzied and progressive Western production, our technologies, and our modes of community building, education, and healthcare by incorporating a value system that recognizes Earth. The request is that we strip away the dysfunctional aspects of what "the westernized human" has created and retain only what is useful, repurposing our creative endeavours so as to cohere with the value system that has sustained our (and other) species over millenia. To look, feel into, and appreciate the places where we are now, to learn from the places directly, is a forgotten art within these westernized worlds, and yet the healing that might be gifted by the land itself is ongoing.

As we survey the contributions to education, comments on its organization, its curricula, its engagement (or lack thereof) with traditional and Indigenous modes of learning, sharing, and being, we might take a moment to venture outside our comfort zone and into consideration of worldview *in toto*. To pause, as the contributors here encourage, and stretch our perception toward embracing how the learnings herein might collectively push us towards a recalibrated and rekindled (as in kin, kinship, or *ki,* to borrow from Robin Wall Kimmerer of the Potawatomi Nation) system of environmental education that takes traditional values to heart and inscribes these in the minds and actions of those who come next.

Contributors

Dr. Amba J. Sepie: Amba J. Sepie is a transdisciplinary author, teacher, and community collaborator working at the nexus of cultural ecology, human geography, anthropology, and Indigenous studies. She is the author of numerous publications which profile socioecological transformation, decolonization, and worldview, as guided by traditional and Indigenous Earth-oriented teachings and cosmology. She is a MBIE Science Whitinga Fellowship recipient, currently based at Te Kunenga ki Pūrehuroa and Te Whare Wānanga o Waitaha in Aotearoa, New Zealand.

Dr. Douglas D. Karrow: Associate professor in the department of educational studies, Brock University. He has been active in the field of environmental and sustainability education (ESE) throughout his career. He teaches in the undergraduate, teacher education, master's, and doctoral programs. Research interests include ESE, i.e., teacher education, curriculum, pedagogy, and policy (provincial, national, and international), the applied philosophy of continental philosophers to education, e.g., Martin Heidegger, and alternative philosophies of education and education theory. He is a former co-chair of the Canadian Network for Environmental Education and Communication's (EECOM) standing committee on ESE-teacher education.

Dr. Sharon R. Harvey: First founding faculty member for the start-up location of Arizona State University at Lake Havasu. She directs the general education/general studies program and teaches philosophy, religion, and sustainability courses. Her research interests are primarily in environmental philosophy and environmental education. She holds a master's degree in religious studies from McGill University, a master's degree in philosophy from Washington State University, and a doctorate in environmental science from University of Idaho. In her free time, Sharon enjoys swimming, playing the piano, and taking walks with her dog.

Dr. Ben McFarland: PhD in biomolecular structure and design from the University of Washington. He has taught and researched immunoprotein biochemistry at Seattle Pacific University since 2003. Ben's current interests also include how chemistry organized natural history and influenced art history. The McFarland research group tests protein-antibody binding both in biochemistry laboratory courses and through independent research. He has delivered the 2009 SPU Weter Award lecture "The Chemical Constraints on Creation," written the 2016 book *A World from Dust: How the Periodic Table Shaped Life* (OUP), and contributed to the 2021 book *30-Second Biochemistry* (Quarto).

Professor Bruce Pardy: Executive director of Rights Probe (rightsprobe. org) and professor of law at Queen's University. He is one of Canada's few classically liberal legal academics. A critic of legal progressivism and the expansive managerial state, he has written on a range of pressing legal subjects at the front lines of the civil war inside the law, including environmental governance, climate change, energy policy, human rights and freedoms, professional and university governance, property and tort theory, free markets, and the rule of law. He has taught at law schools in Canada, the United States, and New Zealand, practiced civil litigation at Borden Ladner Gervais LLP in Toronto, served as adjudicator and mediator on the Ontario Environmental Review Tribunal, and is senior fellow at the Fraser Institute.

Kirsty Jackson: Doctoral research student and tutor within the school of education at the University of Queensland, Australia. Her bachelor of education honors thesis (2019) focused on sustainability and primary-school children's activist identities. Her doctoral research concerns children's relationship with the more-than-human world with a focus on digital mediation and literate practices. To theorize her research, she deploys the Vygotskian concept of *perezhivanie* that foregrounds the integration of emotional, cognitive, and enactive modes of learning. She is committed to addressing the challenges of the Anthropocene through creative educational initiatives that enable children's agency and activism.

Dr. Peter Renshaw: Emeritus professor of education at the University of Queensland. He has collaborated with Ron Tooth to research place pedagogies since 2009 and currently is leading a research project investigating children's relationship with the more-than-human world. He has drawn upon Vygotskian theory for three decades to investigate children's learning and recently began deploying *perezhivanie* to theorize learning as an emotionally engaging and holistic process. He collaborates with scholars in Finland and Hong Kong to consider how educators might address the environmental crises of the Anthropocene.

Melanie Burgess: Grade 7 student beginning high school this year in Brisbane. Since 2019, she participated in the research project on the more-than-human world conducted by the University of Queensland and Pullenvale Environmental Education Centre. She is a keen bush walker and is also very interested in art and creative writing. Melanie has used her art and writing to communicate her belief in equality between humans and the more-than-human world and hopes to change how other people understand themselves as part of the living systems of the Earth.

Dr. Ron Tooth: Founding principal of the Pullenvale Environmental Education Centre. Ron has a doctorate from the University of Queensland where he is also an adjunct professor in the school of education. Ron has an extended history of professional engagement with teachers and students through the Pullenvale Environmental Education Centre as well as through his scholarly inquiry into the different forms of narrative and place-responsive pedagogy. Ron collaborates closely with Peter Renshaw and is currently a partner investigator on their Australian Research Council Discovery project.

Harriet Mortlock: Primary school teacher in New South Wales, Australia. She is a committed environmental educator and advocate. During the research project reported in this chapter, Harriet worked at Pullenvale Environmental Education Centre (PEEC) as a program leader and also was a research assistant on the project. She contributed significantly to all aspects of the project. Harriet is active in advocating for the environment through local community-based organizations and networks.

Dr. Matti Erpestad: Instructor and undergraduate program coordinator of environmental and outdoor education at the University of Minnesota Duluth, located on the westernmost tip of Lake Superior. Before teaching undergraduate and graduate students, Matti worked as a naturalist, environmental educator, and canoe and kayak guide on wilderness trips throughout northern Minnesota in a variety of non-profit organizations as well as accredited schools. Matti also studied outdoor education in Niittylahti, Finland, and holds certification as a professional wilderness and nature guide, skills which he incorporates into his outdoor guiding business, Day Tripper of Duluth. In his free time, he is currently training two four-and-a-half-year-old boys and a two-year-old girl to love the outdoors.

Dr. Matthew Etherington: Professor in the school of education at Trinity Western University, British Columbia, Canada. He has a PhD in the philosophy of education from Macquarie University in Sydney, Australia. Matthew is the director of the Institute of Indigenous Issues and Perspectives (IIIP) and vice president of the Association for the Advancement of

Scandinavian Studies in Canada (AASSC). His primary interests are in the philosophy of education, environmental and outdoor learning, Indigenous sovereignty, elderhood and worldview analysis. He writes on a diversity of topics in education, philosophy, and spirituality.

Dr. Ken Badley: Research professor of education at Tyndale University in Toronto, Ontario. He has taught at all levels from secondary through doctoral and has worked in both Canada and the United States, as well as working extensively with teachers and professors in Kenya and the Philippines. Aside from academic work, Ken works as a finishing carpenter, and he takes extended canoe trips annually. Ken lives in Edmonton, Alberta.

Dr. David I. Smith: Professor of education, director of the Kuyers Institute for Christian Teaching and Learning, and coordinator of the de Vries Institute for Global Faculty Development at Calvin University in Grand Rapids, Michigan, USA. He serves as editor of the International Journal of Christianity and Education.

Brynjarr Þór Eyjólfsson (Julian Mendoza): Master's student in comparative literature at the University of Iceland and the University of Helsinki. He completed his bachelor's degrees in Icelandic as a second language at the University of Iceland and English literature at the University of Manitoba. His current research focuses on aesthetics, affect theory, and ecopoetics in Icelandic literature. He has worked on various translations projects and is currently editing an online interactive language platform for learners of Old Norse through texts from the Poetic Edda. The research on his article is funded by the Canadian Initiative for Nordic Studies.

Dr. Melanie Simpson: Visiting professor in the faculty of education at York University. As course director and practicum facilitator in the Deaf and Hard of Hearing Teacher Education Program, she has developed collaborative relationships with over twenty-five school boards across Canada. Her current research focuses on bilingual spoken language and literacy development in deaf learners, early intervention, cochlear implants, and inclusive education.

Dr. Grant Havers: Chair of the department of philosophy (with a cross-appointment in the department of political studies) at Trinity Western University (Canada). He has published and lectured widely on political philosophy and the history of philosophy. Havers is the author of *Lincoln and the Politics of Christian Love* (University of Missouri Press, 2009) and *Leo Strauss and Anglo-American Democracy: A Conservative Critique* (Northern Illinois University Press, 2013).

Doug Weir: Research and policy director, Conflict and Environment Observatory (CEOBS). Doug has undertaken research and advocacy on the polluting legacy of armed conflicts and military activities since 2005, founding CEOBS in 2017. He has contributed to a wide range of domestic and international initiatives, currently focusing on the development of the legal framework protecting the environment in relation to armed conflicts.

Dr. Kim Franklin: Kimberly Franklin has spent a lifetime learning about educational practice at both the K-12 and post-secondary levels. She was an associate professor and dean of education at Trinity Western University in Langley, BC, from 2007 to 2017, a unique teacher education program that intentionally connects educational practice with the rich tradition of Christian understandings of teaching and learning. During her tenure, she and her colleagues were focused on advancing educational research and educational practice that nurtures wisdom, compassion and care for all, integral and ethical ways of understanding the world and others, and transformation of learners and communities.

Dr. Jenna Coughlin: holds a PhD in Scandinavian languages and literatures from the University of California, Berkeley. Her research focuses on representations of environmental change in Nordic literature and media, as well as international perceptions of the Nordic countries as environmental leaders. She teaches Norwegian language at St. Olaf College, as well as courses on nature in Nordic culture and Arctic literature. She is the director of an undergraduate research project on international responses to Greta Thunberg and the school strikes for climate movement.

Cullen Hauck: is an undergraduate student at St. Olaf College where he is double majoring in environmental studies and biology with a concentration in Nordic studies. While studying abroad in Stockholm, Sweden, through Rotary Youth Exchange, he witnessed Greta Thunberg's movement come to fruition and gained first-hand knowledge of Swedish language and youth culture. Cullen has a varied resume of ecological research and international non-profit work and brings an interdisciplinary enthusiasm for global discussions on climate change.

Introduction

This book has a single motif and a dual purpose. Its motif is the portrayal of influential authors within an environmental framework and worldview. The motif is not to be exhaustive but is presented in different ways in which environmental understandings might be plumbed. The purposes are to engender in the reader a broad knowledge of some of the ideas and problems inherent in a discussion of nature and the environment and to stimulate the reader to go further into the sources of their tradition and worldview in search of meaning and insights that are uniquely relevant to their philosophy.

The selection of chapters for this endeavor turned out to be much more difficult that I had anticipated. Any hope of presenting a symmetrical, quantitatively balanced body of selections was defeated by the fact that some writers are generally consistent and can be epitomized fairly in one or two passages, whereas others are more complex and various and have many hues and tones that need to be caught. I dealt with these problems by abandoning any attempt at symmetry and allowing each writer to "speak" according to their idiosyncratic style. Thus, there is a taste of author range and diversity as well as an attempt to encircle the core of the discussion topic.

BEGINNINGS

In the fall of 2021, at a small Canadian university located in British Columbia, I commenced teaching the very first outdoor environmental education course within a teacher education program. Seven spirited teacher education students were the first to enroll in the thirteen-week outdoor education course. These students anticipated a healthy, durable, and authentic outdoor experience.

The opportunity to run an outdoor class was a relief to the isolation and lack of human interaction from two plus years of COVID in-person restrictions. Not unlike other educators, at the start of the fall semester 2021, I was skeptical that in-person classes would return, perhaps ever again. And so, in January 2022 when the university cautiously commenced classes, the first two weeks were to be taught online. This was not a great start to an outdoor course, and so when an exemption was granted for any "experimental" classes that could not be delivered online to begin in-person, I was thrilled. And so, my first outdoor education class was given the green light for face to face teaching.

Prior to teaching the outdoor course, each Friday I had been observing my children prepare for and take part in forest school activities at a variety of outdoors areas in the locality. The forest school field trips began at the end of summer and went right through the winter finishing in the middle of spring. I watched my family and many other families brave the Canadian winter to play in the great outdoors. This was very different to the outdoors in Australia, where the weather was generally friendlier and where I had spent much of my childhood and adult years. The Canadian winters were cold, snowy, or wet, and often all three, yet no one complained. The children seemed oblivious to the conditions and were keen to immerse themselves fully in the outdoors no matter the weather. I knew that many adults and educators would perceive the cold and wet weather to be intolerable for learning and yet these children had no qualms playing for hours in the winter forests. Moreover, to my amazement, our children did not get ill once during this time. I assumed that being outside in the cold would make you ill.

Of course, the health benefits of being outdoors in nature have long been known and promoted around the world. Time spent in the outdoors can strengthen the autoimmune system and build resistance to allergies. Various studies have shown that children who are active outdoors in nature have the best overall health. A stronger immune system leads to less illness and less use of antibiotics. The Japanese practice of spending time outdoors, called "forest bathing," which is being in the company of trees, has been an important part of community health programs in Japan since the 1980s. The "shinrin-yoku" plan, which in Japanese means forest (*shinrin*) and bathing (*yoku*), refers to showering or basking in nature.

We know that architecture and design can influence our beliefs and behavior. Similarly, nature as architecture also shapes us, forming who we become and value. Even empty spaces in nature, i.e., *terra nullius,* the term a Latin term meaning "land belonging to no one", was not truly empty. St. Hilary, the fourth-century bishop and patron snake against snake bites wrote, "Everything that seems empty is full of the angels of God."[1] Terrence Kardong, a monk at an abbey in North Dakota, describes the Great Plains, which is a large region which is generally flat and found in the central United States and central Canada, as a "school for humility." Our identity is shaped through our connection and relationship to the environment. As Kardong writes, "if you take us somewhere else, we lose our character, our history—maybe our soul."[2] I pledge to appreciate, respect, and care for the land I live upon and recognize all of nature as a gift.

I conclude with a tribute to the authors of this book. I pay homage to my environmental students for tolerating my experimentations during those first few outdoor education classes and inspiring me to continue this good and worthwhile journey.

Matt Etherington

1. Norris, *Dakota: A Spiritual Geography*, 11.
2. Norris, *Dakota: A Spiritual Geography*, 9.

1

Nature as Teacher

MATTHEW ETHERINGTON

INTRODUCTION

How can we address the challenges inherent in the role and delicate relationship humans have with nature? I say "we" because I hold the view that it requires a "village" of people with a kin-centric worldview that will acknowledge their utter interdependence with each other and nature. How should we relate to nature in the third and fourth decade of the twenty-first century? Should we leave nature completely alone or should we involve ourselves in nature like never before? The first action is to recognize nature as a teacher. A teacher is essentially one who imparts wisdom to others. Of course, a teacher does not have to be human; there are many non-human teachers. Nature gifts human beings with a wisdom-pedagogy that teaches a de-centering of learning. Nature teaches us to surpass human-body boundaries and to better understand the "more-than-human world" of plants and animals.[1] The "more-than-human world" offers "ecological epistemologies,"[2] that is, knowledge to better understand the world and our place in it.

1. Carvalho et al., "Learning from a More-Than-Human Perspective," 145–47.
2. Carvalho et al., "Learning from a More-Than-Human Perspective," 147.

NATURE AS TEACHER

During times of uncertainty, pandemics, war, and tragedies, nature has been a good and reliable teacher. In times of crisis people have looked to nature for guidance, wisdom, and hope, and nature has delivered, offering joy, and general wellbeing, even when sadness and heartache abounds. One example is during a two-year period, from July 6, 1942 to August 4, 1944, when Anne Frank, a girl of fifteen, confined to a hidden annex in Amsterdam, found solace and hope as she looked through the attic window at a horse-chestnut tree.[3] Anne wrote about the tree in her diary three times, the last time was May 13, 1944.[4] The tree became a symbol of life and possibility. The resilience of trees can support a confidence that life will go on, noticed or unnoticed.[5] We meet trees in their context, they are our neighbors and mentors, they provide company when we are alone, and they shape our landscape.[6]

Another example of how nature can offer relief is during the coronavirus setback of 2020 and 2021which unveiled, among other things, the condition of our human-nature relations. During the height of the virus, a larger than normal number of people travelled to forests. This was particularly evident in England during February 2021 where forests and parks experienced a 40 percent increase from visitors.[7] Also, in Vermont, in the United States, residents expanded their outdoor activities, while outdoor equipment and products sales surged.[8] Human-nature relationships are important during times of uncertainty, hopelessness, pandemics, and disaster.

CHILDREN AND NATURE

Children's concepts of nature are influenced by their place of residence in shaping how they think about the natural world. In Western culture there is a prevailing humanist paradigm consumed with the development of the *individual* child within their socially exclusive context. Children inherit beliefs about the right to own, buy, rent, and sell nature and to place boundaries around nature as a protection from outsiders.

The English philosopher and political theorist John Locke, from whom these ideas descend, established private property as essential for

3. Choukas-Bradley, *Resilience*, 12.
4. "Chestnut Tree."
5. Kaza, *Conservations with Trees*, 19.
6. Kaza, *Conservations with Trees*, 38.
7. "How Has Lockdown Changed Our Relationship with Nature?"
8. Morse et al., "COVID-19 and Human Nature Relationships," 16.

liberty. Nature should be privately owned by individuals.[9] Accordingly, it is of no surprise that people have few regrets clear-cutting, mining, polluting, and even poisoning nature as an end goal. As a producer-consumer, nature is perceived in terms of what it can offer which often leads to a lifestyle of consumption and overproduction.

In the groundbreaking book, *Last Child in the Woods*, Richard Louv comments that children today, especially children living in urban environments, have very little communication with nature.[10] Moreover, adults often relate their childhood nature experiences to their children in overly sacred, romanticized, or even unhealthy ways.

In relation to romanticized and precarious notions of nature, Bourdeau expressed some future challenges:

> Nature can be seen as beautiful and harmonious, but it also inspires fear in man who has had to fight it in order to survive. Now, nature is threatened by man who has become detached from it. Technology has endowed humans with the power of a major geological agency, which may act on a continental or even planetary scale (e.g., acid rain, photochemical smog, radioactive contamination, stratospheric ozone depletion, climate change).[11]

Consequently, children become adults who perceive nature as irrelevant, or associate nature with fear and catastrophe, or else sentimentalize it. We like to trap nature in the flatness of our computer screens and Google maps. We read reviews of parklands and forests determining how many conveniences are available. Consequently, other than the neighborhood park, children today have a curious relationship with nature. Children learn to fill their time with computer games and social media notifications rather than with human-nature experiences. Louv discussed these realities back in 2008, and since then, research suggests a decrease in nature connectedness, especially with seven- to fifteen-year-olds.[12]

WHAT IS NATURE?

What is nature, and what does *valuing* nature mean? These two questions are important because knowledge and value is shaped by epistemology.

9. Morse et al., "COVID-19 and Human Nature Relationships," 28.
10. Louv, *Last Child in the Woods*, 145.
11. Bourdeau, *Man-Nature Relationship*, 9.
12. Richardson et al., "Measure of Nature Connectedness."

For example, science is one way to know about nature however is largely unfinished, and so philosophical knowing can commence and make its contribution.[13] Philosophical knowing is not about "rightness"—philosophy is non-judgmental; that is, philosophy pursues wisdom, essence, and truth, and so the philosophical enterprise is a manifestation of being a thoughtful inquiring person. We need the *is* of science for knowing *about* nature and the *ought* of philosophy for knowing how we *should* interact with nature.

"Nature" has several different meanings. For example, nature can refer to the essence of something as we muse over the *meaning* of a deer, a mountain, or a valley. Alternatively, nature can refer to a person's character, e.g., "Jody has an aggressive nature." In addition, nature can be a physical force, e.g., "the firefighters were at the mercy of nature."

Nature can also embody the cosmos. Consider the thoughts from the English philosopher John Stuart Mill:

> "Nature," Mill construed, is "the sum of all phenomena, together with the causes which produce them; including not only all that happens, but all that is capable of happening; the unused capabilities of causes being as much a part of the idea of Nature as those which take effect."[14]

In other words, the birds and animals, the land, the wind, insects, sky, the oceans, rain, sun, and hurricanes are nature. This correlates with the beliefs of many Indigenous people, as nature encompasses all water, earth, and air and refers not only to a geographic place but "gestures to the ways that discourses within places, inform and are informed by our beliefs, pedagogies, and teaching practices."[15]

To compare the beliefs of nature held by Europeans and Indigenous peoples, two generally distinct worldviews become evident. According to Kohak, author of *The Green Halo: A Bird's Eye View of Ecological Ethics*, the original Indigenous Australians interpreted nature very differently to Europeans. Nature was not about *interpretation* but rather *perception*. The Indigenous Peoples of Australia perceived and valued nature not as raw materials but as laden with spirit, energy, and meaning.[16]

What nature *is* and *how* nature is *perceived* is important.[17] In the book *Braiding Sweetgrass,* Robin Kimmerer considers an Indigenous worldview

13. Sokolowski, *Introduction to Phenomenology*, 201.
14. Mill, *On Nature*, 8.
15. Styres et al., "Towards a Pedagogy of Land," 4.
16. Kohak, *Green Halo*, 54.
17. Kohak, *Green Halo*, 57.

of nature. There is nothing in nature, e.g., trees, berries, the land, etc., which can be bought or sold, instead they are an expression of nature's gift economy, and a gift is always offered freely except when a gift carries obligations for the receiver. Kimmerer notes wild strawberries as a gift from nature, and when perceived as a gift, an ongoing relationship begins, that is, "the receiver now has a responsibility to the gift giver."[18] Similarly, Kohak mentions anthropologists discovering the gift economy of hunter-gatherer people and their spiritual interactions with nature. They understand and receive the gifts of nature but do not manipulate or farm nature. They are in partnership with nature and live together in harmony. They understand that nature transcends the human being because humans are always dependent on nature.

To people of the European conceptual heritage, the scientific explanation of nature *is* objective, that is, nature as it "really" is.[19] However, David Barnhill explains the relationship-forming understanding of nature.[20] Our relationship to the earth is radical; that is, it lies at the root of our perception and our culture and any sense of a rich life and right livelihood.

And yet, largely understood as a property right, a Eurocentric worldview contrasts an Indigenous worldview of nature where nature is sentient and when experienced as a gift from the creator, and humans are but one part of a greater harmonious being and obliged to respectfully participate. Therefore, nature cannot be owned. Rather, nature is inherited and shared.

Interpretations and Perceptions of Nature

The important insight is not necessarily how nature is *interpreted* but how nature is *perceived* and *experienced*. The lived experience of nature encourages human beings to recognize our interdependent relationship.

Consequently, there are problems with distinguishing "nature" from so called "unnatural" environments.[21] Nature becomes a place people "go" to and not something they are intrinsically part of—in relationship with. By implying that nature is "over there" affirms a commitment to Cartesian dualism, where everything is separated and non-related.

Cartesian dualism keeps alive the conceptual and perceptual human/nature industrial divide.[22] As a result, the very concept of "nature" being

18. Kimmerer, *Braiding Sweetgrass*, 26.
19. Kimmerer, *Braiding Sweetgrass*, 54.
20. Barnhill, cited in hooks, *belonging*, 61.
21. Fletcher, "Connection with Nature," 228.
22. Zylstra et al, "Connectedness as a Core Conservation Concern," 221.

"out there" "ironically, impedes a proper relationship with the earth and its lifeforms."[23] We rarely look to our ancestors to learn how they lived in harmony with the natural world and with its changing seasons. Nature, as our ancestors understood and experienced, is everywhere, it is not just where we live or go to; it is the very reason we are alive.

The more time we spend with nature can help us better understand that nature is so vast, and we are so small and dependent. Nature is not to be divided and conquered; rather our lives are contingent with nature. We can value, respect, and cherish nature or we can ignore, exploit, and even harm nature.[24] We have that choice.

WORLDVIEW AND NATURE

The concept of worldview offers a foundational approach to explore nature. For the purpose of clarity, a worldview approach to nature is best explained by Sepie as an origin story:

> Worldview is . . . a total ordering system, extending from cosmology (charter myths or origin stories) as the first principle, which informs ontology, epistemology, axiology, and practices (including those practices we call culture, religion, and identity).[25]

Worldview always begins with *cosmology* because cosmology appears through our origin stories, i.e., how we came to be, and explains where we came from. Cosmology can adopt a theological, cultural, spiritual, or scientific origin story.

The second aspect of worldview is *ontology*. This entails classifying or grouping things in various ways which demonstrates their uniqueness. For example, the tree has a distinct color, shape, and even a spatial relation such as being "on-top-of."

The third component of worldview is *epistemology* which requires revealing the source or type of knowledge we draw upon to make sense of nature. This can entail scientific, theological, or cultural knowledge.

The fourth component of worldview is *axiology* which involves the values that we consider important to defend. This could be honesty, respect, gratitude, purity, tenacity, and commitment.

23. Morton, *Ecology without Nature*, 2.

24. hooks, *belonging*, 115.

25. Sepie, "Tracing the Motherline," 8.

The final aspect of worldview is *practice* which involves how one *ought* to behave. A worldview accepts but also rules out other types of knowledge, values, and behavior. A worldview understanding can help to explain how our origin stories guide us to perceive and interact with the natural world.

Finally, worldview is the main methodology we use to investigate the world. A person adopts a worldview and presupposes philosophical, scientific, and metaphysical principles about themselves and the world.

Environmental Worldviews

Now we know what characteristics make up a worldview, there are four major environmental worldviews that people live by according to their espoused philosophy. While people may know *where* they lie on the spectrum of worldviews previously described, people may not know where they lie on the spectrum of *environmental* worldviews.

Environmental worldviews are important to realize because, as recent approaches in environmental and animal history indicate, "analyzing education in purely social and cultural terms may be a shortcoming stemming from a persistent and dominant worldview that only addresses humankind."[26]

The four worldviews offered by Robert Elmore explain how human beings relate to nature and behave on the earth.[27] After reading the descriptions of each one, which of these most closely echoes your environmental worldview?

1. the anthropocentric or human-centered worldview
2. the geocentric or earth-centered worldview
3. the acentric (all equal) worldview
4. theocentric (God-centered) worldview.

The *anthropocentric* or *human-centered* worldview. This assumes the interests of humans should take precedence *over* the interests of nonhumans. In other words, a focus primarily on the needs and wants of people. The advantage is that maintaining the environment for human material benefit is often the greatest motivation for nature protection.[28] One example of the *anthropocentric* worldview is Gifford Pinchot who was a young forester who eventually became the first chief of the U.S. Forest Service.

26. Caruso et al., "Education and Nature," 5.
27. Elmore, *Our Relationship with the Ecosystem*, 43.
28. Norton, *Environmental Ethics and Weak Anthropocentrism*, 131–48.

Pinchot's *anthropocentric worldview* compelled him to experience nature as a resource that ought to be shared among the most people possible.[29] For example, Pinchot believed that someone could have "multiple uses" of national parks, allowing for hunting, fishing, grazing, forestry, watershed protection, and the preservation of wilderness values.[30] Generally speaking, human interests take priority over the concerns of nature. This is sometimes referred to as the tragedy of the commons. Elmore suggests that there is a "tragedy" of the commons when an anthropocentric experience develops, and the sharing of nature becomes unsustainable.[31] William Forster Lloyd also called this "the tragedy of the commons."[32] Consider any national park which is open to all without limit. It is to be expected that people use the park any day and hour of the week. Visits or traffic to the park increase as people arrive in greater numbers and with more visits over time. The national park has some free parking available however, this causes people to park there all day, thereby stopping others who could also share in the park. The number of people increase, pollution increases, wildlife decrease, and the destruction of plants and vegetation becomes more evident over time. Eventually the park has to close down to regenerate. This is one example of the tragedy of the commons.

The *geocentric* or *earth-centered* (biocentric) worldview is focused on individual species, the entire biosphere, or some level in between. The *earth-centered* worldview assumes that "because humans and all forms of life are interconnected parts of the earth's life-support system, it is in our own self-interest not to act in ways that impair the overall system."[33]

The acentric (all equal) worldview believes that everything is one and part of one essence with no major difference between species or things. All is one, and everything is interconnected.

Finally, the theocentric (God-centered) worldview acknowledges a higher authority exists in conjunction with people and the ecosystem—specifically God as creator of nature—who also created people in part as stewards of creation. Wilderness should be conserved because it possessed, if not embodied, spiritual value beyond what humans could comprehend.[34] John Muir, who was a famous naturalist in American history, is an example of someone who held to a *theocentric worldview.* He perceived nature as

29. Keel, "Frenemies."

30. Hoffman and Sandelands, "Getting Right with Nature," 7.

31. Elmore, *Our Relationship with the Ecosystem*, 43.

32. Lloyd, *Two Lectures*, 37.

33. "What Are Some Major Environmental Worldviews," 665.

34. Hoffman and Sandelands, "Getting Right with Nature," 7.

God and understood that nature is best preserved from the interference of human beings.

Gifford Pinchot and John Muir revealed a *biocentric* and *theocentric* or *earth-centered* worldview. Pinchot and Muir both held to a *biocentric worldview* meaning that all of life matters, not just human life, although they diverged in how their worldviews should be applied.[35] Muir and Pinchot represent two contrasting worldviews of nature, and these environmental perspectives tend to resonate with most people at some level. When it comes to the environment, we tend to be either a Pinchot (we should engage with nature but do it responsibly) or a Muir (leave nature completely alone).

There are also four environmental worldview applications of nature shown in figure 1:

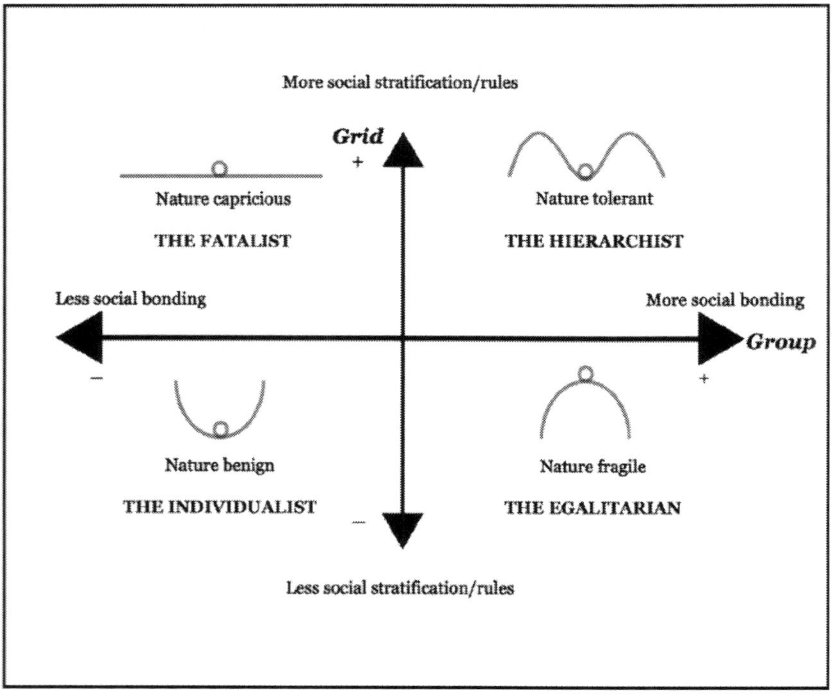

Figure 1: The Four Worldviews and Views of Nature Described in the Cultural Theory of Risk (Figure adapted from McNeeley and Lazrus 2014).[36]

The *individualist* worldview involves weak social bonds and minimal social structure, while the *fatalist* worldview perceives nature as capricious

35. Anthonya et al., *Surveying Environmental Perspectives*, 138.

36. McNeeley and Lazrus, "Cultural Theory of Risk," 506–19.

and fundamentally random and unpredictable. The *hierarchist* worldview believes nature is manageable and tolerant of some human-induced changes and will thus accommodate human action to a point, which is identified and planned by scientific experts. The *egalitarian* worldview believes nature is fragile and in a precarious balance with humanity.[37]

Human culture is born in the wild; we draw our food there. It is, as Henry Thoreau described,[38] "the salvation of civilization" which means no climbing every mountain "because it is there"; that is, the wild should stay wild.[39] Whichever worldview one finds most compelling, and the worldviews are important for understanding the beliefs and behaviors of people, what often unites environmental worldviews, and in particular, *earth centered* and *theocentric* worldviews, is the teaching responsibility of nature. We now turn to the teaching role of nature.

NATURE AS TEACHER

Nature is our original teacher since human beings developed in the wild. In fact, nature continues to be perceived as an educative tool in itself. For instance, "natural environments for learning have been reclaimed as being a counterbalance of the artificial environment of education. Here, green playgrounds, school gardens, the contemplation of forests and landscapes, the use of purportedly 'responsive' animals in education and therapy are some of the remedies."[40]

The following six analogies illustrate the *teaching* role of nature.

Nature as Teacher: *Solitude*

Nature is a teacher of solitude. Nature can be a threat to one's existence and an attraction to contemplation. Think of the barren spaces of an empty desert or the feeling of looking over a cliff top. The solitude often invokes an undistracted communication between something that is greater than we are. People speak of being lost in a dark cloud on a mountain top, and the experience of losing their separate identity, stripped of self, and becoming one with the cloud offering an awareness of the existence of an existential greatness.[41]

37. Thompson et al., *Cultural Theory.*
38. Thoreau, *Reflects on Nature*, 117–21.
39. Jenkinson, *Come of Age*, 172.
40. Caruso et al., "Education and Nature," 5.
41. Lane, *Exploring the Desert Solace*, 6.

A few summers ago, I visited the town of Jasper, Alberta, in the Rocky Mountains of Canada and spent a whole day hiking up one of the mountains. I still remember pausing on the mountain as a dark cloud of cold and mist slowly embraced my whole being. The feeling of isolation, together with the silence and the peace I experienced in those brief few minutes, offered an existential reality that I knew was greater than me. The focus was no longer on me, or time, my breathing, hunger, or thirst. It was a teaching moment of patience and humility which I never will forget.

Nature as Teacher: *Responsibility*

Nature teaches us responsibility. We interact with nature as nature provides for that relationship; however, like any relationship, we frequently take advantage of what is given to us. And so, a child climbing a tree or building a tree house disturbs the tree; yet it may be that the greater good is to understand the obligations we now have to that tree. We are in a co-relationship with the tree, entangled with each other. The "tree of life," the human-nonhuman connection. The lesson is that the tree and I are enmeshed with each other, and human beings have an obligation to cooperate with and learn from those with whom we are entangled.

This raises questions about our entanglement and mutual responsibilities with each other in these challenging ecological times.[42] For example, ant behavior can move us away from our heroic individual human narrative of rescue and recovery. Ant encounters demonstrate the folly of treating the world only on a human stage and seeing ourselves as the only actors in it. The individual is not really an individual but part of interacting ecologies of interdependent relationships; consequently, the ideal of the autonomous individual is a Western cultural myth.[43]

In fact, human lives are dependent on the lives of others—much smaller, often overlooked, and sometimes invisible creatures. In an interview with author Oliver Milman, Davies suggests three-quarters of the world's flowering plants and about a third of the world's food crops depend on important pollinators such as bees, wasps, and flies, at some stage. Without these creatures, we would be without apples, cranberries, melons, almonds, broccoli, blueberries, cherries, spices, curries, and alfalfa. [44]

42. Styres et al., "Learning with Insects," 3.

43. Bowers, *University Reform*, 127.

44 See interview with Oliver Milman by Davies, "World's Insect Population."

We often extend a sense of ethical responsibility to animals with appealing big eyes (like ours) and a cute face (like ours). It is not so easy to be responsible to those life forms which have no face at all.[45]

Nature as Teacher: *Exploitation*

The world is not just about us, and we are not its only learners, scriptwriters, actors, movers, makers, and shapers. Simply put, we are not separate from the rest of the world. Although human beings are exceptional, we exploit what we are given, what is shared, and risk anthropocentric hubris. We forget or ignore the reality of the choices we make and the lives we live are entangled with in nature.

We explore the wisdom teachings of nature and the consequences for not caring. One way to recognize how humans have depicted the exploitation of nature is to observe how nature and human interaction is portrayed in the movie industry. The iconic movie monsters from the 1950s provide a sequence of consequences for humans who exploit the environment. Murray and Heumann refer to the 1954 film *Godzilla*, as a cautionary account of the costs associated with mistreating the natural world—monstrous nature on the attack. Godzilla provides a space in which to explore the complexities of a monstrous nature that humanity both creates and embodies. Arrogance is seen in those who think they can control and subdue nature.[46] In *Avatar* (2009), forests are decimated, biodiversity is demolished, carbon released into the atmosphere, and the Indigenous peoples are slowly weakened and destroyed.

The lesson for humans is that arrogance, injustice, and exploitation are not virtues.

Nature as Teacher: *Revenge*

The notion of nature's revenge is another theme unveiled in the movies. For example, in *The Wizard of Oz* (1939) and the *Lord of the Rings* trilogy, trees transform into "monsters" seeking revenge against the human world of oppressors that exploit them, which not only highlight the power of nature, but also suggests how nature will ultimately fight back. As Murray and Heumann remark, in *The Lord of the Rings* trees fight back against humans,

45. Taylor and Pacini-Ketchabaw, "Learning with Children," 9.

46. Murray and Heumann, "Monstrous Nature," xi.

becoming monstrous nature as Sam watches the attack from the branches of one of the surrounding trees.

In *The Wizard of Oz* trees become animated when their apples are stolen. In *The Two Towers*, trees ultimately seek vengeance against Saruman and his army when their leader sees a section of Fangorn Forest that Saruman has destroyed to feed his iron forges.[47] The lesson involve the consequences that come with exploitation and disrespect.

Nature as Teacher: *Healer*

Nature teaches us to slow down, that life need not be rushed, consequently, people seek the remedial health benefits and healing advantages of nature. The psychological benefits of nature are so obvious that many doctors prescribe to their patients what has been dubbed "nature therapy." This involves extended time with nature to help alleviate anxiety and depression.

In nature, we engage delicately in the "primary experience" of seeing, feeling, tasting, hearing, and smelling.[48] Our attention is gently drawn to the details of the surrounds and to the larger experience of where we find ourselves. I remember a few years ago, a schoolteacher who had recovered from a near-death experience, told me that she now gives her attention and appreciation to the tops of trees because, as she explained, the treetops have weathered the storms and challenges of life and survived. The treetops have made it through life, especially the harsh winters. This teacher was in her own season of winter, but the treetops gave her hope with an uncertain future.

People often bring their pain, losses, and heartaches to nature. Nature accepts us just as we are, and so we are in a good place with nature; it does not judge us either in our good times or bad.

Nature as Teacher: *Conserve*

Scientists and engineers are working on technological solutions to reduce greenhouse gases, but we are also being told to keep consuming as economic growth is equally important.[49] Yet, nature teaches that overconsumption is dangerous. Nature shows what happens when "we take from the planet more than we're regenerating. [It's] a particular strand of overconsumption,

47. Murray and Heumann, "Monstrous Nature," xiv.

48. Louv, *Last Child in the Woods*. . ., 65.

49. Bowers, *University Reform*.

where we purchase things, not to fulfil our basic needs, but to fill some void in our lives and make social statements about ourselves."[50] Political scientist Robert Putman argues that we are paying the ultimate price for our consumeristic tendencies with the loss of friendships and fragile communities that are less supportive and trusting.[51]

As we consume more and conserve less, we disregard the cultural values and behaviors that placed limits on environmentally polluting activities.[52] The old traditions that formed communities such as the sharing of natural resources, skills, and knowledge, are breaking down, if not extinct already. As a result, people experience individualistic and lonely worlds together with more consumeristic and dependent lives.

Consumerism increases the extraction of nature's resources, as industries operate at higher levels due to consumer demand. There is a loss of quality of natural resources such as the dumping of waste into rivers and oceans. Nature teaches us that there are consequences for not conserving.

In Grassy Narrows, northwestern Ontario, Canada, for over fifty years the Asubpeeschoseewagong First Nation community has suffered food and water contamination from the mercury dumped into the river system from the pulp and paper mill industries. As a result, nearly 90 percent of Grassy Narrows community members suffer from symptoms of mercury poisoning.

The natural world is, for the reasons presented, a teacher, but what are its lessons for an impatient humanity? Nature teaches that everything is accomplished in just the way it should be and at the right time. Nature *is* a teacher, and we ought to listen and learn because nature is self-sufficient and older than us. We should fear its demise and respect its existence.

NATURE CARE AND FOLLOWING THROUGH

When encountering a tree in the forest, we do not see the tree merely as timber; rather we regard its being, its attributes of strength, size, beauty, resilience, or magnificence.[53] We value the tree for its "tree-ness" but also refer to its absent properties. We perceive what is not obvious to the eye, thinking in its absence we transcend the immediate environment.[54] If humans value what is seen and what is not seen, why are we not awakened to the value

50. Leonard, *Story of Stuff*, 65.
51. Putnam, *Bowling Alone.*
52. Bowers, *University Reform.*
53. Rolston, "Value in Nature," 14.
54. Sokolowski, *Introduction to Phenomenology*, 45.

and potential of nature? If humans are unique, they must behave uniquely. Williams and Parkman explain the dilemma:

> Without adequate predation, deer left to graze and reproduce soon find themselves in the midst of an ecological crisis of their own making. Without "higher consciousness" deer simply cannot choose to eat less and have fewer offspring. It is part of their instinctual hardwiring simply to do what deer do. Humans, on the other hand, have the intellectual ability to make choices and to solve problematic circumstances. While humans can theoretically resolve the largescale ecological problems they cause, they generally do not, and in many cases see no reason to be concerned about such matters.[55]

Humans can value but we do not follow through on those values. One reason is that we are disconnected from nature. Nature is "out there" somewhere. There is urbanization which swallows up natural areas and cuts people off from natural surroundings. Our urban lifestyles do not require us to care much about nature. In the year of 2015, 53.9 percent of the world's population lived in cities, and this percentage is forecasted to grow to 62.5 percent in the year 2050.[56] Consequently, we are experiencing less time with nature, let alone having experiences working the land for our sustenance or survival. In a study by Kesebir and Kesebir, they determine the increasing disconnection of nature is more likely city living, technological change, and in particular the burgeoning of indoor and virtual recreation options such as television and video games."[57]

The 1872 painting below by Winslow Homer's *Snap the Whip* shows children playing in wide open green fields. The lived and shared experience of joy and connection to nature is evident in these children. The energy passes between them and this place, which has become an expression of their lives. It is easier to care for and appreciate nature when we interact with nature as these children are doing.

55. Williams and Parkman, "On Humans and Environment," 453.

56. "Proportion of Population in Cities Worldwide."

57. Kesebir and Kesebir, "How Modern Life Became Disconnected."

"Snap the Whip": Winslow Homer, 1872

Robin Kimmerer appreciates the relationship of land with people. In response to human care and protection, she reports that the land gives back to people, in a kind of shared bi-directional relationship. One example is the local garden. Many people care deeply for their gardens. They lovingly return to the soil something of its gifts in the form of compost.[58]

Kimmerer illuminates:

> She [the garden] loves us with beans and tomatoes, with roasting ears and blackberries and birdsongs. She provides for us and teaches up to provide for ourselves. That's what good mothers do. The ultimate reciprocity, loving and being loved in return.[59]

We give, and in return the garden, the land, gives back. This resembles the ancient image of the educator as a gardener. Yet with more condensed city living, people are minimally connected and less dependent on the land. We rarely think about where our food comes. And yet, the importance we place on nature immediately awakens when droughts, floods, forest fires, or crop failure ruin the land. We think only of independence because that is what we have been taught to value and promote, but natural disasters are a reminder of our fragility and dependence. Sadly, it often takes a natural emergency such as a flood or drought resulting in crop failure and possible

58. Kohak, *Green Halo*, 55.

59. Kimmerer, *Braiding Sweetgrass*, 122.

food shortages to reawaken us to care more about nature as our revered presence and partner in life.

Environmental Education: What Should Be the Focus?

Although formal schooling is one influences that shape people's environmental values and attitudes, our behaviors and desires are also shaped by social and mainstream media, friends, family, and our political associations. Therefore, when we speak of environmental education everything must be included—formal schooling, social media, politics, and so forth—that is, all that affects what we know, practice, and love.

Although climate change, deforestation, and other realities are always a pressing concern, education about the environment can frequently be taught in a gloomy and fatalist way. If education is largely a social process, as noted by philosopher and educator John Dewey, then learning about the environment is not a preparation for life but *life itself*.[60] If we apply this thought to environmental education then educators and learners can set aside their anxieties about the environment and revel in this opportunity for wisdom, for this is, in fact, life itself.

This approach would embody the *ethical* aspects of our relationship with the environment including our habits and decision-making. For example, a fisherman takes as much as he needs for his family's sustenance but no more. In *Braiding Sweetgrass*,[61] Kimmerer explains our relationship with nature by way of indigenous wisdom. To be wise is to understand and practice a habit of generosity. Kimmerer notes that cedars can teach us generosity because of all they provide, from canoes to capes. The focus is on reciprocal care and observance and a move away from the mindset and habit of being preoccupied by consumption which also includes autonomous individualism, indubitable rationality, and technology.

Environmental education could encourage a hopeful outlook on nature. People are inspired to involve themselves in meaningful experiences with nature and to imagine what a careful balancing of land use and human involvement might look like. Problem solving in education must not always pursue the "experts" as the solution to environmental problems because resorting only to the "experts" and relying only on technological solutions hands the problem solving over to others and neglects the wisdom and responsibility that individuals could learn on a local level and perspective.

60. Dewey, *Democracy and Education.*

61. Kimmerer, *Braiding Sweetgrass.*

THINKING LIKE A MOUNTAIN: CRITICAL THINKING

Naturalist and ecophilosopher Aldo Leopold, sometimes recognized as the father of wildlife ecology, wrote about the interconnectedness of nature within the entire ecosystem. His theme of "thinking like a mountain" described nature in terms of the whole ecosystem and not just one species or phenomena, in other words, thinking about the mutual dependence of everything in nature. The following thoughts from Leopold as he witnesses the last few minutes of a dying wolf's life illustrates his ecosystem thinking:

> We reached the old wolf in time to watch a fierce green fire dying in her eyes. I realized then, and have known ever since, that there was something new to me in those eyes—something known only to her and to the mountain.[62]

What was this unknown? If "we" are to survive the Anthropocene,[63] Leopold maintained, human beings must not think in terms of individual value, such as the life of the wolf, but in terms of the entire balance of life. For example, the mountain only cares about the balance of life—that is, the entire ecosystem.[64] So the lesson for human beings is a role change, that is, from conqueror of nature to plain member and citizen of it.[65] When we do that, we can surpass our individual wants and needs, and increase the ability to think long-range, collectively, and unselfishly.

If we can "think like a mountain," that is, in terms of the whole ecosystem, how would recycling, for example, factor into the entire ecosystem? We know that recycling can reduce the demand for new mining; however, recycling does not address the greater challenge to nature—today's hyper-consumerism.[66] Hyper-consumerism is a far greater threat to the entire balance of life and the ecosystem. One recent example is the electric car industry. Although fossil fuels have their own environmental problems there are numerous environmental complications with the electric vehicle industry. If we consider the lithium batteries that power electric vehicles, these are made

62. Leopold, *Sand County Almanac*, 129–33.

63. Anthropocene is the period during which human activities have had an environmental impact on the Earth regarded as constituting a distinct geological age.

64. Kohak, *Green Halo*, 88.

65. Leopold, *Sand County Almanac*, 240.

66. Capitalism began as a system for meeting the real human needs of consumers; however, today more people are buying goods that they don't need, i.e., hyper-consumerism. This is a distortion of the original intent of capitalism. For more, see Benjamin R. Barber's book, *Consume: How Markets Corrupt Children Infantilize Adults And Swallow Citizens Whole.*

from nonrenewable materials. A 2019 report[67] by Mark Mills revealed more than 500,000 pounds of earth must be dug and moved to garner enough lithium, cobalt, nickel, graphite, and copper ore for just *one* 1,000-pound electric vehicle battery. Making one car battery requires digging up, moving, and processing more than 500,000 pounds of raw materials.

Consider for a moment Congo, home to 70 percent of the world's cobalt. The extraction of cobalt involves child labor, harsh working conditions, pollution, and increasing birth defects.[68] Also consider Tesla, the world's best-known battery maker. Mills claims that $200,000 worth of Tesla batteries, which collectively weigh over 20,000 pounds, are needed to store the energy equivalent of just one barrel of oil.[69]

The Sydney-based Institute for a Sustainable Future[70] admits the technology needed for electric vehicles is increasingly problematic as it attempts to solve one environmental problem by creating another environmental problem. The Institute cautions that a global "gold rush" for minerals could take miners into "some remote wilderness areas [that] have maintained high biodiversity because they haven't yet been disturbed." Better strategies, they note, would be to reduce demand and consumption, such as improved public transport and car sharing. Although car sharing can potentially reduce the number of privately-owned cars, they may be used more intensively which could shorten battery life, and there is limited evidence to suggest that car sharing schemes have resulted in a significant reduction in car ownership.

Are we thinking in terms of the entire balance of life? Is this a good example of environmental stewardship that meets the needs of people and considers the preservation of the ecosystem or just an example of novelty and hype, i.e., hyper-consumerism?

Ecosystems are complex, and strategies such as individual recycling and expanding the electric vehicle industry are low hanging fruit. *Thinking like a mountain* is a reminder that decisions about the environment must not be made at an individual level, but in terms of how our actions can alter the entire balance of life.

67. Mills, ""New Energy Economy,"" 1–24
68. Mills, ""New Energy Economy,"" 1–24.
69. Mills, ""New Energy Economy,"" 11.
70. "Are Electric Cars as Sustainable as They Sound?"

CONCLUSION

The popularity of community gardens, people buying locally, and a greater awareness of Indigenous wisdom suggest there is a change in the wind. People are beginning, albeit slowly, to let go of their modern values of hyper-consumption. We are beginning to lose our taste for the industrial prepacked and canned. Although a generation of children were raised in a world where ketchup and french fries were counted as vegetables and still are, we are increasingly snubbing fast food and moving in the direction of *slow* food. We want to know where our "stuff" comes from.[71] Bigger, faster, cheaper is not always better. In a similar way, our environmental worldviews are changing, as we engage with nature and begin to understand how organically beautiful, wise, sensual, patient, and spiritual it is.

When nature is experienced as a gift, we live together responsibly. We engage with nature and do it maturely. Alternatively, we can leave nature completely alone. However, I think a relationship with nature which acknowledges and learns from its "teachings," without cannibalizing what we learn and inherit helps to furnish humility, a much needed virtue in a world of individualistic values and practice. Humility opens our hearts and minds to a truth that we are not the creators of nature; rather, we are only tenants.

Nature teaches us to be attentive, to notice what non-humans notice, and to question what we care about and why. The natural world is, for these reasons, a good and wise teacher. Formal education is necessary for shaping environmental values and attitudes but alone it is insufficient. We must experience and be involved with nature because all healthy relationships require active participation.

Finally, if we are to survive the Anthropocene, individual rights and needs are secondary to the entire ecosystem. It is the difference between individual and collective responsibility transcending a contemporary culture of wanting more. We should never place individual autonomy, progress, or novelty over the wellbeing of other living entities which includes all of nature. Nature has much to teach humanity, but the question remains: will we be attentive, and are we ready to learn from our non-human teachers?

71. Fields, *Spirit of Food*, xxii.

QUESTIONS FOR DISCUSSION AND DEBATE

1. Does nature exist to only serve humans? Should we be nature-independent, nature-dependent, or nature-interdependent?
2. Must we leave nature completely alone or regularly engage with nature?
3. What is meant by the statement "nature is valuable"? Think in terms of worldviews.
4. What do you believe is more valuable: wild forests, parks, gardens, or farms?
5. How might the notion of "thinking like a mountain," alter the way you relate to nature?
6. Which worldview do you associate with in relation to nature? The anthropocentric or human-centered, the geocentric or earth-centered, the acentric (all equal), or the theocentric (God-centered) worldview?
7. Do you think the ecological crisis has its roots in religious or secular traditions?

BIBLIOGRAPHY

Anthonya, Brendon M., et al. "Surveying Environmental Perspectives among Faculty at an Institution of Christian Higher Education." *Journal of Research on Christian Education* 29 (2020) 137–55. https://www.tandfonline.com/doi/abs/10.1080/10656219.2020.1800539?journalCode=urce20.

"Are Electric Cars as Sustainable as They Sound?" UTS. https://www.uts.edu.au/news/health-science/are-electric-cars-sustainable-they-sound.

Arendt, Hannah. *The Human Condition*. Chicago: University of Chicago Press, 1985.

Ardoin, Nicole M., and Joe E. Heimlich. "Environmental Learning in Everyday Life: Foundations of Meaning and a Context for Change." *Environmental Education Research* 27 (2021) 1681–99. https://www.tandfonline.com/doi/full/10.1080/13504622.2021.1992354.

Berger, P., and A. Zijderveld. *In Praise of Doubt: How to Have Convictions without Becoming a Fanatic*. New York: HarperOne, 2009

Bourdeau, P. H. "The Man-Nature Relationship and Environmental Ethics." *Journal of Environmental Radioactivity* 72 (2004) 9–15.

Bowers, Chet A. *The False Promises of Constructivist Theories of Learning: A Global and Ecological Critique*. New York: Lang, 2005.

———. *University Reform in an Era of Global Warming*. Eugene, OR: Eco-Justice Press, 2011.

Caruso, Marcelo, et al. "Education and Nature." *Paedagogica Historica* 56 (2020) 1–8.

Carvalho, Isabel Cristina de Moura, et al. "Learning from a More-Than-Human Perspective: Plants as Teachers." *Journal of Environmental Education* 51 (2020) 144–55.

"The Chestnut Tree." https://www.annefrank.org/en/anne-frank/front-section/chestnut-tree/.

Choukas-Bradley, Melanie. *Resilience: Connecting with Nature in a Time of Crisis*, 2020, Washington: ChangeMaker Books.

Darian, Steven. *Understanding the Language of Science*. Austin, TX: University of Texas Press, 2003.

Davies, Dave. "The World's Insect Population Is in Decline—and That's Bad News for Humans." NPR, Feb 24, 2022. https://www.npr.org/sections/goatsandsoda/2022/02/24/1082752634/the-insect-crisis-oliver-milman.

Dewey, John. *Democracy and Education: An Introduction to the Philosophy of Education*. New York: Free Press, 1966.

Elmore, R. W. "Our Relationship with the Ecosystem and Its Impact on Sustainable Agriculture." *Journal of Production Agriculture* 9 (1996) 42–45. https://doi.org/10.2134/jpa1996.0042.

Fields, Leslie Leyland, ed. *The Spirit of Food*. Eugene, OR: Wipf & Stock, 2010.

Fletcher, Robert. "Connection with Nature Is an Oxymoron: A Political Ecology of 'Nature-Deficit Disorder.'" *Journal of Environmental Education* 48 (2017) 226–33. https://doi.org/10.1080/00958964.2016.1139534.

Gehlen, Arnold. *Man, His Nature and Place in the World*. New York: Columbia University Press, 1988.

Hoffman, Andrew, and Lloyd Sandelands. "Getting Right with Nature: Anthropocentrism, Ecocentrism and Theocentrism." *Organization & Environment* 18 (2004) 141–62.

hooks, bell. *belonging: a culture of place*. New York: Routledge, 2009.

"How Has Lockdown Changed Our Relationship with Nature?" https://www.ons.gov.uk/economy/environmentalaccounts/articles/howhaslockdownchangedourrelationshipwithnature/2021-04-26.

Institute for Sustainable Futures. "Reducing New Mining for Electric Vehicle Battery Metals: Responsible Sourcing through Demand Reduction Strategies and Recycling." https://www.uts.edu.au/sites/default/files/2021-04/20210423_EW%20report%20final.pdf.

Jenkinson, Stephen. *Come of Age: The Case for Elderhood in a Time of Trouble*. Berkeley, CA: North Atlantic Books, 2018.

Kaza, Stephanie. *Conversations with Trees: An Intimate Ecology*. New York: Shambhala, 2019.

Keel, Lukas. "Frenemies: John Muir and Gifford Pinchot." National Endowment for the Humanities. https://www.neh.gov/article/frenemies-john-muir-and-gifford-pinchot.

Kesebir, Selin, and Pelin Kesebir. "How Modern Life Became Disconnected from Nature." *Greater Good Magazine*, Sep 20, 2017. https://greatergood.berkeley.edu/article/item/how_modern_life_became_disconnected_from_nature.

Kimmerer, Robin Wall. *Braiding Sweetgrass*. Minneapolis: Milkweed, 2019.

Kohak, Erazim. *The Green Halo: A Bird's Eye View of Ecological Ethics*. Chicago: Open Court, 2000.

Lane, C. Belden. *The Solace of Fierce Landscapes: Exploring Desert and Mountain Spirituality*. New York: Oxford University Press, 1998.

Leonard, Annie. *The Story of Stuff: How Our Obsession with Stuff is Trashing the Planet, Our Communities and Our health—and a Vision for Change*. New York: Free Press, 2010.

Leopold, Aldo. *A Sand County Almanac*. New York: Oxford University Press, 1949.

Lloyd, W. F. "Two Lectures on the Checks to Population." In *Population, Evolution, and Birth Control*, edited by Garrett Hardin. San Francisco: Freeman, 1964.

Louv, Richard. *Last Child in the Woods: Saving Our Children from Nature-Deficit Disorder*. New York: Workman, 2008.

Lukaš, Mirko, and Emerik Munjiza. "Education System of John Amos Comenius and Its Implications in Modern Didactics." *Život i škola br.* 31 (2014) god. 60, str. 32–44.

Luntley, Michael. "On Education and Initiation." In *Reading R. S. Peters Today: Analysis, Ethics and the Aims of Education*, edited by Stefaan Cuypers and Christopher Martin. West Sussex, UK: Wiley-Blackwell, 2011.

McNeeley, Shannon, and Heather Lazrus. "The Cultural Theory of Risk for Climate Change Adaptation." *Weather, Climate, and Society* 6 (2014) 506–19.

Mills, Mark. "The 'New Energy Economy': An Exercise in Magical Thinking." https://media4.manhattan-institute.org/sites/default/files/R-0319-MM.pdf.

Morse, J. W., et al. "COVID-19 and Human-Nature Relationships: Vermonters' Activities in Nature and Associated Nonmaterial Values during the Pandemic." *PLoS ONE* 15 (2020) e0243697. https://doi.org/10.1371/journal.pone.0243697.

Morton, Timothy. *Ecology without Nature: Rethinking Environmental Aesthetics*. Cambridge: Harvard University Press, 2007.

Murray, Robin L., and Joseph K. Heumann. *Monstrous Nature: Environment and Horror on the Big Screen*. Lincoln, NE: University of Nebraska Press, 2016.

Norton, B. G. "Environmental Ethics and Weak Anthropocentrism." *Environmental Ethics* 6 (1984) 131–48.

"Proportion of Population in Cities Worldwide from 1985 to 2050." Statista. https://www.statista.com/statistics/264651/proportion-of-population-in-cities-worldwide/.

Richardson, M., et al. "A Measure of Nature Connectedness for Children and Adults: Validation, Performance, and Insights." *Sustainability* 11 (2019) 3250. https://doi.org/10.3390/su11123250.

Rolston, Holmes, III. "Value in Nature and the Nature of Value." *Royal Institute of Philosophy Supplements* 36 (1994) 13–30. https://doi.org/10.1017/S1358246100006421.

Sepie, Amba Jessida. "Tracing the Motherline: Earth Elders, Decolonising Worldview, and Planetary Futurity. A Thesis Submitted in Fulfilment of the Requirements for the Degree of Doctor of Philosophy in Geography." PhD diss., University of Canterbury, 2018. https://ir.canterbury.ac.nz/handle/10092/15916.

Sokolowski, Robert. *Introduction to Phenomenology*. New York: Cambridge University Press, 2000.

Sokolowski, Robert. *Phenomenology of the Human Person*. New York: Cambridge University Press, 2008.

Steil, C. A., and I. C. M. Carvalho. "Epistemologias Ecológicas: Delimitando um Conceito." *Mana* 20 (2014) 163–83.

Styres, Sandra, et al. "Towards a Pedagogy of Land: The Urban Context." *Canadian Journal of Education* 36 (2013) 34–67.

Taylor, Affrica, and Veronica Pacini-Ketchabaw. "Learning with Children, Ants, and Worms in the Anthropocene: Towards a Common World Pedagogy of Multispecies Vulnerability." *Pedagogy, Culture & Society* 23 (2015) 507–29.

Thoreau, Henry David. *Henry David Thoreau Reflects on Nature*. New York: N.p., 1910.
Thompson, Michael, et al. *Cultural Theory*. Boulder, CO: Westview, 1990.
"What Are Some Major Environmental Worldviews?" https://docslib.org/doc/647731/environmental-worldviews-ethics-and-sustainability-25.
White, G. "Cultures in Collusion: Traditional Knowledge and Euro-Canadian Governance Processes in Northern Land-Claim Boards." *Artic* 59 (2006) 401–14.
Williams, Jerry, and Shaun Parkman. "On Humans and Environment: The Role of Consciousness in Environmental Problems." *Human Studies* 26 (2003) 449–60.
Zylstra, M., et al. "Connectedness as a Core Conservation Concern: An Interdisciplinary Review of Theory and a Call for Practice." *Springer Science Reviews* 2 (2014) 119–43.

2

A Test of Character and an Enticement to Love

Comenius on Educating for Human Responsibility toward Other Creatures

David I. Smith

INTRODUCTION

In sketches of the history of environmental education it is not too hard to find dutiful nods to the 17th century Moravian educator and reformer John Amos Comenius. His interest in the study of nature and his focus on experiential learning, we are told, helped lay the groundwork for environmental education.[1] Those impulses are indeed relevant contributions, yet such passing gestures are also vulnerable to a recurring complaint in recent scholarship on Comenius. As various scholars have noted, when Comenius is mentioned merely as a forerunner of some general good that we currently value, the mention can function as self-congratulation under the guise of

1. E.g., Carter and Simmons, "History and Philosophy of Environmental Education"; Higgins and Nicol, *Outdoor Education*; Knapp, "Outdoor and Environmental Education"; Maurer and Bogner, "How Freshmen Perceive Environmental Education."

history.[2] When we imagine the past mainly as a less developed version of our own interests and conclusions, we risk missing ways in which it might surprise us or challenge our priorities. Comenius was a complex and subtle thinker who authored a wide-ranging and varied body of work. As the very few writings addressing his potential for actively informing present-day environmental education have noted, if we pay closer attention, we may find more food for thought than the summaries suggest.[3]

In this brief chapter, I will focus on some key facets of Comenius's account of the interconnections among human nature, the goals of education, and the flourishing of non-human creatures.[4] It would be anachronistic to seek modern conceptions of "the environment" or "environmental education" directly in his writing.[5] It is, however, striking how intimately he connects the question of human responsibilities toward non-human creatures with the core purposes of education. He does not approach these responsibilities as a discrete topic within the curriculum, but rather as a basic structural part of what a general education is for and what both human and non-human flourishing require. The natural world, power, service, love, delight, and learning turn out to be deeply interconnected. This clustering of concepts grounds a vision of the philosophical basis for "environmental education" that ties it more closely to love than to mastery or expediency.

Fully exploring Comenius's treatment of these matters would far exceed the bounds of this essay. For now, I propose to focus on suggestive passages from three works. The *Didactica Magna* (*Great Didactic*) has been the most widely circulated of Comenius's several overviews of his educational thought, especially in English, and it provides an articulate account of the relevance of human power over other creatures to the basic concerns of education.[6] The *Pampaedia* (*Universal Education*) is a further summation drawn from a more mature phase of his work. It articulates the stake that non-human creatures have in our educational practices. Our third passage

2. E.g., Hábl, *Lessons in Humanity*; Schifferová, "Bemerkungen zur Idee."

3. Janáková, "Pedagogický a Filozofický Koncept"; Heidebrecht, "Learning from Nature."

4. I would like to thank Candace Vogler and David Warners for helpful comments on a draft of this essay and Jan Hábl for bibliographic assistance.

5. This is why I refer to "non-human creatures," which include the animal, vegetable, and mineral realms, rather than to "nature" or "the natural world," since Comenius's understanding of that world differs from modern conceptions. Cf. Čížek, "Pansophia of Jan Amos Comenius."

6. Translations in this article from the *Didactica Magna* are my own, drawn from the Latin edition in Comenius, *Opera Didactica Omnia*. There is an English translation, Keatinge, *The Great Didactic of John Amos Comenius*, though it is dated and sometimes unreliable.

is from the *Panorthosia* (*Universal Reform*).[7] Together with the *Pampaedia* it forms part of the seven-volume *De Rerum Humanorum Emendatione Consultatio Catholica* (*General Deliberation Concerning the Reform of Human Affairs*) that was the culmination of his prolific literary activity. In the *Panorthosia* Comenius presents human contemplation of non-human creatures as a specific kind of moral test. Considered together, these passages provide a suggestive sketch of Comenius's conception of the kind of relationship to the environment that education should foster.

WHY EDUCATE HUMANS?

Comenius is famous as an early advocate of education for all. All human beings, young and old, male and female, rich and poor, of differing gifts stood, according to Comenius, in need of an education that would form them in wisdom. Why is this so? What is it about human beings that makes education for all of them necessary and fitting? Comenius's answers to these questions are grounded in a holistic account of how humans fit into the world.[8]

Mundus (The World). From John Amos Comenius, *Orbis Sensualium Pictus* (1658)

7. Translations in this article from the *Pampaedia* and *Panorthosia* are my own, drawn from the Latin edition in Comenius, *De Rerum Humanorum Emendatione*. Both works exist in English translation. See Dobbie, *Comenius's Pampaedia*, and Comenius, *Panorthosia or Universal Reform*.

8. Čížek, *Conception of Man*; Habl, *On Being Human(e)*; Pelcová, "Das Vermächtnis von Comenius."

In the fourth chapter of the *Didactica Magna*, Comenius describes the need for education as arising from a threefold human vocation. Human beings are "placed among visible creatures in order to be: I. a rational creature. II. a creature that is lord of creatures. III. a creature that is the image and delight of its creator."[9] These three vocational emphases imply three basic human needs if humans are to grow fully into their humanity. As creatures with this threefold calling, "humans have a genuine need to I. have knowledge of all things, II. have power over things and themselves, III. return themselves and all things to God, the source of everything."[10] These needs are in turn summarized as three basic educational goals: learning, virtue, and piety.

If we unpack these triads a little, following Comenius's argument in the surrounding chapters, we find him painting broadly the following picture. Humans, more than any other creature, have an open-ended capacity to understand all kinds of things and to reflect on their significance. No matter how many things we think about, there is room in our minds and appetites for more. Try to keep us from thinking about something, and it will be like telling the tide to stop. We are creatures that by nature are driven to keep track of other creatures, not just for immediate practical purposes, but through a wider process of perceiving, naming, comprehending, classifying, remembering. If our powers of thought are not developed as well as our capacity allows, our human potential is frustrated and a miraculous facet of our constitution is undervalued.

Yet humans do not just contemplate the world as detached observers or isolated thinkers. Humans are full participants in the game. We exert an active influence over other creatures (including other humans), putting them to use and exerting power over their well-being. This influence has a moral as well as a practical character. Human behavior is more consequential than the behavior of other creatures; a human mistake can do significantly more damage in the world that that of, say, a squirrel. Moreover, humans are prone to corruption and abuse. A landslide may cause simple destruction; humans damage the world and each other not merely through physical causation, but through error and ill will, by doing what should not be done. The reality of human power, magnified by human rationality and guided by human will, thus calls for an education that is fundamentally and pervasively moral in character, an education in virtue. An education approached as simply a survey of or inquiry into the facts, without a close integration with moral

9. Comenius, *Didactica Magna*, 4.2.

10. Comenius, *Didactica Magna*, 4.6.

formation, would fail to take responsibility for human agency and fall short of being genuine education.

The way we use our intellectual grasp of and practical power over things, as well as the degree to which we are able to discipline ourselves, has consequences for the wellbeing of the world. These moral questions are further rooted in our beliefs and commitments, our objects of reverence and sources of joy. What we do with our power is rooted in what we do with our heart. Questions about power must be answered in connection with the further question of where we find our center, our source of purpose and delight. If this center becomes located within our own appetites and self-centered agendas, or within some facet of the material world, our trajectory will become eccentric, like a wheel with an off-center hub.[11] Learning to relate knowledge of all things and action in the world to God, the non-utilitarian source of fundamental delight and value, is therefore basic to keeping other relationships in proper harmony.

To summarize, our capacity for knowledge increases our power, proper use of knowledge and power depends on our self-giving to the proper source of meaning and delight, and education is meant to help all of this turn out well. Learning, virtue, and piety are not goals that can be approached one by one (for instance by a science education that ignores faith and ethics, or a moral or religious education divorced from study of the natural world). They are "so intimately joined that no separation among them can be admitted."[12] This stands in some tension with the modern tendency to think of moral and religious education as enterprises quite distinct from the pursuit of scientific understanding of the material environment. It is also quite important for grasping how Comenius thinks about our relationship to other creatures.

WHAT ARE OTHER CREATURES FOR?

The wider picture of reality within which this argument is articulated can at times seem quite human-centered. Human beings, as rational creatures in God's image, have been given authority over other creatures (a category that includes the animal, vegetable, and mineral realms) and license to use them. Humanity is "intended to govern the lower creatures, themselves, and their neighbor."[13] Ultimate human destiny lies beyond the present material world in the perfected age to come, and the natural world serves as a temporary

11. Comenius, *Pampaedia*, 2.23; Habl, *On Being Human(e)*.

12. Comenius, *Didactica Magna*, 4.2.

13. Comenius, *Pampaedia*, 2.29.

nurturing environment to school humans for their present responsibility and eternal future. Comenius states that "everything is therefore for the sake of humankind."[14]

Taken out of context, such statements can sound as if other creatures stand in a purely instrumental relationship to humans, there to be exploited before we head for heaven. If we read carefully, however, we find a different picture. If humanity is "intended to govern the lower creatures, themselves, and their neighbor," then what Comenius means by "govern" must be something that he is comfortable applying not just to the natural world but also to the neighbor who is to be loved and the self that is to be shaped into the virtues of humility and charity.[15] As we saw earlier, Comenius sees human power over the environment as leading directly to the necessity of moral formation; this connects in turn to the idea of governing oneself. Comenius distinguishes conflicting accounts of virtue, highlighting the push for self-confidence, self-love, pride, and ambition found in classical texts and contrasting these with a theologically grounded focus on love and humility.[16] When Comenius speaks of governing, the focus is on proper use of one's power to affect self, other, and world *in a beneficent and virtuous manner*, not on successful exploitation of disposable resources.

With regard to non-human creatures, this helps generate a degree of symmetry: other creatures are there for the sake of humans, and the human calling is to serve the good of other creatures. Humans are called not just to be "kings" over the world, but also to serve as "priests" before God for the sake of other creatures.[17] The chance to grow in this calling and be formed in its virtues is a significant part of what it is that other creatures provide for the sake of humans. Other creatures provide humans with opportunities to become human.[18]

A striking passage from the *Pampaedia* seems worth quoting at length here:

> Finally, that all humans be developed toward a rational life is also a matter of concern to things themselves, so that they too might be better under the wise direction of wise people. Just as a garden is better under a good gardener, a craft under a skillful craftsman, a family under a wise head of household, a kingdom

14. Comenius, *Didactica Magna*, 3.4.

15. Comenius, *Pampaedia*, 2.29.

16. Comenius, *Didactica Magna*, 25.17–18, 26.7.

17. Comenius, *Pampaedia*, 2.29.

18. For Comenius, human nature is both a given, grounding human dignity, and something to be lived into, framing a vocation.

> under a wise king, and an army under a tested leader, rather than under the unskilled; in the same way things too are better under humans who justly possess and use them if they know how to use them fittingly. It is notable what Solomon says: the just man also cares for the life of his beast of burden; but the wicked man is cruel (Proverbs 12:10).[19] Oh how great is the cruelty that all things everywhere experience through the wickedness or ignorance of humans who use them illicitly! The apostle pointed to this, testifying that all creatures are subjected to vanity and sigh, desire, and hope to be liberated from such wicked servitude. It is certainly to be desired that what creatures long and hope for should be pushed forward, and everything everywhere should proceed more justly, and all creatures should have cause to praise God with us (Psalm 148). Therefore, it is also to be desired that all people be taught to know and understand things rightly and to use and enjoy things rightly; for without the cultivation of dispositions this has never been brought into existence, nor will it ever be.[20]

In this passage, Comenius foregrounds human impact on non-human creatures, recognizes that the latter have their own lives, longings, and need for flourishing, frames the goal in terms of care, advocacy, and shared delight, and points to an education focused on dispositions as well as understanding as being necessary to moving in that direction. These points, as I will briefly show, elaborate the argument about educational goals outlined above in a way that makes non-human creatures vital stakeholders in the educational process.

Present abuse of non-human creatures, Comenius says, makes the need for universal education of the kind outlined earlier obvious "if we attend to how God, humans, and things themselves have a stake in it."[21] If human beings could learn to use things "rightly" (that is, in a way that honors their proper end and intended flourishing), then it will not only be human creatures that experience delight. Rather, "the world in its entirety will become a garden of delight for God, for us, and for things."[22] The destination is not human triumph over a disposable environment but a harmony in which every kind of creature can find fulfillment in being what God created it to be.

19. Comenius's text has Proverbs 12:9; modern Bible translations number the verse as 12:10.

20. Comenius, *Pampaedia,* 2.13.

21. Comenius, *Pampaedia,* 2.3.

22. Comenius, *Pampaedia,* 2.25.

While this state of being will not be accomplished in the present age, it may begin to take shape now, with God's help, through an education redesigned in "imitation of the School of Paradise, where God revealed the whole choir of His creatures for man to behold."[23] Such an education is meant to serve the basic purposes of human existence, which are "to serve God, creatures, and ourselves, and to enjoy the delight that God, creatures, and we ourselves disclose."[24] If we are to serve other creatures well as we intrude upon their environments, we will need to work towards an understanding of what is fitting for them, what helps them to flourish, and this will involve direct study of nature so that we can learn the order in the lives of non-human creatures. But more is involved than gaining relevant empirical information. The ethical (what counts as a licit use of other creatures) and the spiritual (where do we root our joy) are directly involved. As education seeks to give form to the human capacity for thought, power, and commitment, the goal is service and delight, with other creatures' delight as well as our own in view. As we serve and delight in other creatures, we grow into our proper humanity. As other creatures make this possible, they are there for our sake. To the degree that we succeed, we are also there for their sake. A world in which some creatures are unable to praise their creator because of harm inflicted is one that falls short of a proper relationship to God, and an education that divorces information and skill from delight and mutual service falls short of a proper education. Moving in a better direction involves not just understanding but a cultivation of our basic dispositions through an education in which learning, virtue, and piety are closely intertwined.

A few sentences before his comment about the visible world being for the sake of humanity, Comenius lists three ways in which it is meant to engage us. The visible world is provided so that we might be "seized by admiration, pushed onward in knowledge, and enticed to love of the creator."[25] These three facets of the world's address to us echo the threefold focus on learning, virtue, and piety. The non-human world fuels the growth of delight in its creator as it makes the "dependability, beauty, and sweetness" of divine reality accessible to sight, touch, and taste (piety).[26] It awakens and fuels our thirst for knowledge of God as it impinges on our senses (learning). The third phrase thus evokes the remaining element, the power/virtue theme, which is here framed as the idea that the world is there to entice us to love

23. Comenius, *Pampaedia*, 2.23.

24. Comenius, *Didactica Magna*, 10.8.

25. Comenius, *Didactica Magna*, 3:3.

26. Comenius, *Didactica Magna*, 3:2.

of God, which along with the other two elements implies the admirability, order, and worth of creatures themselves. The capacity to love is the human good that the world is there to serve, the virtue that is to be fostered, and the form in which human power is to be exercised. This is the standard to which we are to be held accountable.

WHAT SHOULD WE LEARN FROM OUR ENVIRONMENT?

In the *Panorthosia*, a volume focused on the reform of societal institutions rather than education, Comenius suggests that every town should have a *Paradisum deliciarium*, a garden or paradise of delight.[27] This parallels his recommendation elsewhere that each school should have a garden. His description of what this would entail sounds like a botanical garden with features of a museum or zoo. He suggests that:

> It would also be good to have a paradise of delight in every kingdom, republic, and market town, that is: 1. All kinds of plant. 2. Minerals and materials dug from the ground. 3. Animals of the land, water, and air. 4. All kinds of artifacts.

The rationale is:

1. This would be one powerful restorative for cultivation among all nations,
2. And also an outward symbol that the new Adam has opened up for us not only a heavenly paradise, but also an earthly one, Isaiah 11: 6–9.
3. It would be a source of pleasure to the devout, as they rejoice in the reform of our affairs.
4. And it would be a beneficial medicine for the body, and for the human mind a noteworthy test of character [δοκιμασία], so as to be a spur to each person to plant such a garden of delight in themselves.[28]

This passage resonates with the picture that we have seen emerging thus far. The point of assembling representative samples of the vegetable, mineral, and animal kingdoms is not just to amass information or to amuse. Comenius aims for a more holistic formation of the self and its community. Even this short description pulls together pleasure, delight, bodily health,

27. Comenius, *Panorthosia*, 24.2; Comenius, *Panorthosia or Universal Reform*, 117. I have discussed this passage in more detail in Smith, "It Would Be Good to have a Paradise: Comenius on Learners Past and Present," and draw here from that account.

28. Comenius, *Panorthosia*, 24.2.

spiritual discipline, theological hope, virtuous character, national culture, and social reform. Learning, virtue, and piety are here again not to be separated, whether from one another or from our agency in the world.

The choice of the term "paradise of delight" for the proposed community gardens is rooted in Genesis. What we know as the "Garden of Eden" has long been rendered in Latin as *paradiso voluptatis*, "garden of delight," the environment in which the first humans were to find beauty, virtue, meaningful labor, and communion with God (Gen 2:15). There are also echoes of the Hebrew wisdom literature, in which exhortations to growth in wisdom invite us to picture ourselves as flourishing trees (e.g., Job 15:32–34; Ps 1; Prov 13:12). In the Hebrew prophets, the image of the garden of delight became an image of societal *shalom*, of peaceful, just community flourishing (Isa 5:1–8; 58:5–12). In his account of the community "paradise of delight," Comenius here cites Isa 11, which focuses on the removal of violence and destruction in a harmonious, renewed creation, the lion lying with the lamb and the earth filled with the kind of knowledge of God that yields peace. These allusions make it clear that time spent in the community garden is not only supposed to lead to individual inner refreshment or respite from stress. The garden is to serve as a reminder of our place in the larger story of things as those who are supposed to understand, to take delight, and to be enticed to love so that we might treat one another and other creatures justly.

Can a botanical garden really function this way? Comenius here directs this question back to us as a test of our formation and our fitness to govern self and world. If walking among the assembled choir of creatures fails to awaken in us a sense of the tug toward understanding, the aptness of delight, and the call to love and justice, something in us has failed a crucial test. When referring directly to this "test of character," Comenius retains the Greek word *δοκιμασία* in his Latin text, apparently wishing to draw attention to its particular force. A *δοκιμασία*, in ancient Athens, was a specific kind of test. The term denoted a public process for ascertaining the suitability of citizens for public rights and duties based on their lineage, life, and character.[29] The question at stake was whether the person under consideration was the right kind of person for taking up public responsibilities. In suggesting that the garden itself is a *δοκιμασία*, Comenius pictures the non-human environment as more than a backdrop for human action. It is here pictured as addressing and evaluating us. If we look at the non-human world gathered before us and fail to connect it to care, hope, justice, and delight, then something is revealed about us, about our lack of readiness for taking our place responsibly among other creatures and using our power appropriately.

29. Adeleye, "Purpose of the Dokimasia."

The gardens that Comenius proposes are not simply convenient visual aids, restful diversions, or recreational places to play frisbee; they are also tests of character. As well as being an enticement to love, non-human creatures are a test of our ability to respond appropriately.

Like most tests, this is one for which we are supposed to study. The study process, as we have seen, cannot be simply the accumulation of knowledge. The ability to respond rightly will depend on cultivating the appropriate dispositions. Testing our progress is a significant part of why it would be "good" to place a garden like this at the heart of each community and each school. The point is not just that such environments would be pleasant, but that they bring into focus a network of connections crucial for the proper flourishing of human communities and non-human creatures before the face of God. Schools will educate appropriately about the environment if they help students to see it in this light and develop the corresponding dispositions.

CONCLUSION

I have outlined some of the key connections that Comenius draws between human nature, the goals and processes of education, and the flourishing of non-human creatures. I hope it is clear that we have moved some distance beyond naming experiential education and interest in nature as the essence of his contribution to thinking about environmental education. Indeed, there are versions of experiential learning and the study of nature that Comenius might have struggled to see as educational, let alone as adequate accounts of education about and for our environment. Without intentionally cultivating dispositions of care and a willingness to confront questions of belief and commitment, the collection of knowledge and experiences would for him miss the point and misread the environment in which we find ourselves. It matters not just that we learn about the environment but that we attend to what it is we see when we encounter the environment and to how our delight and that of other creatures relate to our power, our formation, and our learning. Such an account resists an easy collocation of environmental education with the natural sciences. It becomes a matter for the whole curriculum, tied to basic questions about what kind of people we will be.[30] Perhaps our capacity as educators to avoid compartmentalizing study of the environment as a matter separate from literature, history, ethics, politics, and faith will serve as our own test of character, our own *δοκιμασία*.

30. For a specific example of implications for the wider curriculum, with further reference to Comenius's curricular practices, see Smith, "For the Birds."

QUESTIONS FOR DISCUSSION AND DEBATE

1. Where should learning about "nature" fit in the school curriculum? Is it a science subject? Why/why not?
2. Does Comenius's view of nature as addressing ethical and spiritual questions to us have any advantages over a mechanistic view?
3. In your experience, how is human power to change the world related to the goals and methods of schooling? How should it be? Why?
4. What might Comenius have affirmed or resisted in our modern conception of "the environment"?
5. How well do you fare in Comenius's *δοκιμασία*?

BIBLIOGRAPHY

Carter, R. L., and B. Simmons. "The History and Philosophy of Environmental Education." In *The Inclusion of Environmental Education in Science Teacher Education*, edited by A. Bodzin et al. 3–16. Dordrecht, Germany: Springer, 2016. doi: 10.1007/978-90-481-9222-9_1.

Čížek, J. *The Conception of Man in the Works of John Amos Comenius*. Frankfurt: Lang, 2016.

———. "The Pansophia of Jan Amos Comenius with Regard to his Concept of Nature." *Acta Comeniana* 28 (2014) 51–93.

Comenius, J. A. *Opera Didactica Omnia*. Prague: Academia Scientiarum Bohemoslovenica, 1957.

———. *De Rerum Humanorum Emendatione Consultatio Catholica*. Prague: Academia Scientiarum Bohemoslovenica, 1966.

———. *Panorthosia, or Universal Reform, Chapters 19–26*. Translated by A. M. O. Dobbie. Sheffield, UK: Sheffield Academic Press, 1993.

Dobbie, A. M. O., trans. *Comenius's Pampaedia*. Dover, UK: Buckland, 1986.

Hábl, J. *Lessons in Humanity from the Life and Work of John Amos Comenius*. Bonn: Verlag für Kultur und Wissenschaft, 2011.

———. *On Being Human(e): Comenius' Pedagogical Humanization as an Anthropological Problem*. Eugene, OR: Pickwick, 2017.

Heidebrecht, P. "Learning from Nature: The Educational Legacy of Jan Amos Comenius." *Christian History* 13 (1987). https://www.christianitytoday.com/history/issues/issue-13/learning-from-nature.html.

Higgins, P., and R. Nicol. *Outdoor Education: Authentic Learning in the Context of Landscapes* Volume 2. Kisa, Sweden: Kinda Education Centre, 2002. http://www.docs.hss.ed.ac.uk/education/outdoored/oe_authentic_learning.pdf.

Janáková, M. "Pedagogický a filozofický koncept J. A. Komenského prizmatem teorie environmentální výchovy." In *Fórum mladých výzkumníků VI*, by Barbora Petrů Puhrová et al., 97–108. Zlín, Czech Republic: Univerzita Tomáše Bati ve Zlíně, Fakulta humanitních studií, 2018.

Keatinge, M. W. *The Great Didactic of John Amos Comenius*. London: Black, 1907.

Knapp, C. E. "Outdoor and Environmental Education: Defining Terms, Objectives and Purposes, Instructional Methods, History and Status in the United States and Abroad." https://education.stateuniversity.com/pages/2305/Outdoor-Environmental-Education.html.

Maurer, M., and F. X. Bogner. "How Freshmen Perceive Environmental Education (EE) and Education for Sustainable Development (ESD)." *PLoS ONE* 14 (2019) e0208910. https://doi.org/10.1371/journal.pone.0208910.

Schifferová, V. "Bemerkungen zur Idee der Ganzheitlichkeit bei Comenius." In *Gewalt sei ferne den Dingen! Contemporary perspectives on the works of John Amos Comenius*, edited by W. Goris et al., 189–98. Wiesbaden: Springer, 2016.

Schifferová, V. "Bemerkungen zur Idee der Ganzheitlichkeit bei Comenius." In *Gewalt sei ferne den Dingen! Contemporary perspectives on the works of John Amos Comenius*, edited by W. Goris et al., 189–98. Wiesbaden, Germany: Springer, 2016.

Smith, D. I. "For the Birds: Absence and Vision in Teaching Texts." *International Journal of Christianity & Education* 25 (2021) 259–64. doi:10.1177/20569971211031437.

———. "It Would Be Good to have a Paradise: Comenius on Learners Past and Present." In *The Restoration of Human Affairs: Utopianism or Realism?*, edited by Jan Hábl, 29–44. Eugene, OR: Wipf & Stock, 2022.

3

"A Reflection of My Soul"

Understanding How Children Conceptualize Humans and/as Nature

Kirsty Jackson a, Peter Renshaw a,
Melanie Burgess c, Ron Tooth a,b
and Harriet Mortlock b[1]

INTRODUCTION

In this chapter we consider how children conceptualize their relationship to/with the more-than-human. We use the term "more-than-human" rather than "nature" to problematize the divide between humans and nature that arose in part from the dualist philosophy of Descartes and the ideology of colonialism that justified the exploitation of nature for human interests.[2] In the dualist framework, humans are positioned as distinct from, and superior to nature, with rights to unlimited access to natural resources in order to

1. a School of Education, University of Queensland, Australia
b Pullenvale Environmental Education Centre, Pullenvale, Queensland, Australia
c Year 7 Student, Brisbane, Australia

2. Abram, *Spell of the Sensuous*; Moore, "Capitalocene, Part I"; Moore, "Capitalocene, Part II."

meet human needs and indeed human whims.[3] In recent decades the dualist notion of human-nature relations has been critiqued by feminist scholars[4] and post-humanist scholars.[5] Insights from these scholars have been taken up by educators to advocate for the transformation of educational practices so that children learn to understand themselves, not as distinct and superior but as kin with more-than-human others,[6] enmeshed in the systems and assemblages that sustain life.[7]

How might children shift towards a sense of kinship and equality with other living beings? Current social conditions are not conducive. Research indicates that children are spending less time outdoors due to digital technologies and parental concerns for children's safety.[8] Much attention has been given to the "extinction of experience,"[9] or as popularized by Louv,[10] "nature deficit disorder." Researchers have sought to understand "this growing divide"[11] by investigating how time in nature can positively influence children's development and emotional well-being.[12] Such research tends to reinforce the dualist framework by representing nature as something "out there" and useful to humans for their well-being. Tillmann et al.,[13] for example, investigated how children in rural Canada perceived and defined nature. Three key themes were identified: children conceptualized nature as a "whole community" separate from humans; they experienced nature through "doing" fun activities; and they made use of nature to regulate their emotional states. Similarly, Aaron and Witt[14] found that urban fifth-grade students conceptualized nature as something that is "outside," fun, needs protecting, and is a place to be active. Other studies have found similar

3. Malone, "Reconsidering Children's Encounters with Nature."

4. Merchant, "Ecofeminism and Feminist Theory"; Shiva, *Staying Alive*; Plumwood, "Gender Eco-Feminism."

5. Barad, "Posthumanist Performativity"; Haraway, "Anthropocene, Capitalocene, Plantationocene, Chthulucene"; Haraway, *Staying with the Trouble.*

6. Haraway, "Anthropocene."

7. Cutter-Mackenzie et al., "Childhoodnature: An Assemblage Adventure"; Tooth and Renshaw, "Pedagogy as Advocacy"; Somerville and Powell, "Thinking Posthuman with Mud."

8. Rixon et al., "Childhoods Past and Present."

9. Soga and Gaston, "Extinction of Experience."

10. Louv, *Last Child in the Woods.*

11. Braus and Milligan-Toffler, "Children and Nature Connection."

12. Linzmayer and Halpenny, "'I Might Know'"; Tillmann et al., "'Nature Makes People Happy.'"

13. Tillmann et al., "'Nature Makes People Happy.'"

14. Aaron and Witt, "Urban Students' Definitions and Perceptions."

results, where children draw from their place-based experiences, family orientations, and habitual activities to conceptualize nature.[15] Whilst these studies promote research on children's perspectives regarding "nature," they are problematic in the way that they perpetuate the Cartesian nature-human dualism.

Our work aligns instead with scholars such as Malone[16] and Taylor,[17] whose research focuses on opening up space for environmental learning that decenters the human and supports children's non-binary relations with the more-than-human world. Like Malone[18] and Taylor,[19] we are interested in what kinds of pedagogies might challenge the dualist framework and evoke for children an enmeshed understanding of human-nature relations. This paper focusses on Melanie Burgess' understanding of this relationship. Melanie, a Year 6 school student in 2021, participated as a co-researcher in a project[20] that investigated how a narrative-based environmental education program (Storythread) influenced children's sense of themselves in relation to the more-than-human. Below we introduce the research team to foreground our distinctive perspective as environmental educators and applied researchers rather than philosophers or psychologists. We describe briefly the key features of Storythread pedagogy, especially *dadirri*, that offers children the opportunity to experience themselves as enmeshed with, rather than separate from the more-than-human. We also highlight the importance of *perezhivanie*, that is, emotionally charged experiences, in shifting children from their established views to new ways of conceiving themselves and their relationships with others (human and more-than-human others).

THE RESEARCH TEAM

We approach this topic as environmental educators and applied researchers. Ron Tooth, Principal of Pullenvale Environmental Education Centre (PEEC), has conducted environmental education programs since the 1980s deploying a narrative-based pedagogy called *Storythread.*[21] This pedagogy engages children in firsthand experiences of the more-than-human (forest,

15. Burgess and Mayer-Smith, "Listening to Children"; Cheng and Monroe, "Connection to Nature."

16. Malone, "Children in the Anthropocene."

17. Taylor, "Beyond Stewardship."

18. Malone, "Children."

19. Taylor, "Beyond."

20. Renshaw et al., *Digital Mediation of Children's Interactions.*

21. Tooth, "Pedagogy as Story in Landscape."

creek, bug-garden) combined with dramatic roleplay that threads together historical and contemporary stories embedded in a particular place. The children are active participants in the unfolding drama, role playing identities such as a "bush kid" or "entomologist-in-training" or "environmental advocate." Their learning arises both from their firsthand experiences of the more-than-human and through their emotional experiences associated with the unfolding drama.

Harriet Mortlock worked as an environmental educator at PEEC during the time we collected research data. She was the PEEC teacher on the excursions we observed, and she participated in the research process by interviewing children and contributing to the analysis of their ideas. Kirsty Jackson is a current doctoral student whose research centers on children's emotional experiences during environmental excursions. Along with the research team, she theorizes emotional experience deploying the Vygotskian concept of *perezhivanie* (as explained further below). Peter Renshaw is a researcher who has collaborated with Ron Tooth for more than a decade on the investigation of place-responsive pedagogy, and recently he and Ron began to research emotional experience (*perezhivanie*) as a key aspect of children's learning during environmental excursions.[22]

Melanie Burgess joins the team as a co-author for this paper. In November 2021, Melanie participated in a children's conference where she and other children in the research project presented their personal projects on a local environmental issue. Melanie describes her project below (see Figure 1). It reveals her view of human-nature relations as one based on equality between living beings. In conducting the research project with Melanie (and other children from four state primary schools in Queensland, Australia), we adopted a co-researcher methodology,[23] which entailed full disclosure of the purposes of the research and opportunities for children to be decision-makers and leaders in aspects of the project. For example, the children's conference was introduced and chaired by children. They provided background information about the conference, explained how the day would unfold, and clarified what was expected of the adult audience (teachers and parents). The children's leadership at the conference and Melanie's co-authorship of this paper are indicative of our commitment to extend the co-researcher role beyond the data collection phase to include communication

22. Renshaw and Tooth, "Diverse Place-Responsive Pedagogies"; Tooth and Renshaw, "Pedagogy as Advocacy."

23. Barratt Hacking et al., "Children as Active Researchers"; Fielding, "Beyond 'Voice'"; Glithero, "Educating for Student Agency"; Groundwater-Smith and Mockler, "From Data Source to Co-Researcher?"

and dissemination of the research outcomes. We agree with Murris[24] that children's insights and contributions to knowledge-making need to be more explicitly acknowledged and valued.

THE PEDAGOGY: DADIRRI

As a team of educators and researchers, we hope that children learn to see themselves as enmeshed in multiple ways with the more-than-human and learn to act according to an ethic of care towards the living systems of our planet. To make this ontological and ethical shift possible for children, we deploy different strategies in the pedagogy of Storythread. A key strategy is *dadirri*, an inner and outer deep listening practice that was gifted to us by Miriam-Rose Ungunmerr Baumann, a Ngangikurungkurr elder from the Nauiyu community, Northern Territory, Australia. Miriam-Rose describes *dadirri* as a special gift:

> What I want to talk about is another special quality of my people. I believe it is the most important. It is our most unique gift. It is perhaps the greatest gift we can give to our fellow Australians. In our language this quality is called dadirri. It is inner, deep listening and quiet, still awareness.[25]

It isn't something that can be taught formally. Rather, it is a practice that is learnt by doing, by slowing down, by sitting quietly, by listening to the more-than-human, by becoming aware of country. This is the outer listening, the "quiet, still awareness" mentioned above by Miriam-Rose. But there is also the "inner deep listening" that is equally important in the practice of *dadirri*. Miriam-Rose suggests there is a "deep spring inside us"[26] that can be drawn upon through *dadirri*. She likens it to contemplation, especially during difficult times. She writes,

> It is something like what you call "contemplation." When I experience dadirri, I am made whole again. I can sit on the riverbank or walk through the trees; even if someone close to me has passed away, I can find my peace in this silent awareness. There is no need of words.[27]

24. Murris, "Posthuman Child and the Diffractive Teacher."
25. Ungunmerr-Baumann, "Dadirri," 1.
26. Ungunmerr-Baumann, "Dadirri," 1.
27. Ungunmerr-Baumann, "Dadirri," 1.

In prior research where we ask children to reflect on what they've learned from *Storythread* excursions, we see evidence of this inner deep listening. As reported by Renshaw,[28] after practicing *dadirri* during an excursion, a Year 7 student reflected on her inner self in the following way:

> Well, this is a bit weird but . . . inside of my body used to be dark and focused on one thing at a time. . . . but now inside where it used to be all dark and nothing special about it, it's sort of got these green leaves and it's just twirling around and I think that if people keep on doing this (dadirri) that's what will happen to them. And so, I think that I've grown more exciting and passionate and not so dull and blank that I was before[29] .

It is not uncommon during *Storythread* excursions for children to reflect on their inner selves after experiencing *dadirri*. To practice *dadirri* they are invited to find a place apart from their classmates, sit in silence for about fifteen minutes, and at the end of the time, report to the group something they noticed or experienced. Most students share moments of outer awareness regarding the more-than-human, such as becoming aware of fungi growing on branches, or ants and other insects going about their daily activities, or noticing the sunlight and breeze interacting with trees and leaves in interesting ways. Some students focus on their inner selves and report sensing themselves as "new persons" or embarking on a "new journey" or "bonding with nature."[30] *Dadirri* seems to provide memorable experiences for children that enable them to reconsider who they are becoming and how they relate to the more-than-human. It doesn't impose a particular view. It raises their awareness and attentiveness inwardly and outwardly and from this practice emerge new insights and understandings.

HOLISTIC LEARNING: PEREZHIVANIE

Storythread pedagogy is designed to arouse children's emotions by engaging them in role-playing different characters such as a "bush kid" or "entomologist-in-training" or "environmental advocate." Within their roles, children are confronted by different dilemmas that unfold during the excursion, for example, the need to protect the habitat of endangered frogs, or prevent the extermination of insects, or protect endangered birds in a local creek. Shifting back and forth between their collective role in the drama and their

28. Renshaw, "Feeling for the Anthropocene."
29. Renshaw, "Feeling for the Anthropocene," 18.
30. Tooth and Renshaw, "Pedagogy as Advocacy," 40.

everyday selves, creates tensions for children and arouses their emotions, especially when they have to improvise how to counter threats to the more-than-human. These moments in the roleplay often instigate reflection and reliving of the whole experience, and for some children these moments become memorable events in their lives. We theorize these moments as *perezhivaniya* as conceptualized by Vygotsky.[31] *Perezhivanie* entails "living through" an emotional experience that can be significant enough to alter one's actions, thoughts and identity in some way.[32] Similar to the dual focus of *dadirri* on outer experience and inner contemplation, *perezhivanie* directs attention to the emotional experience per se (the actual significant "event") and the "working over" of the experience in hindsight.[33] *Perezhivanie* is not a specific practice like *dadirri*. It is an analytical tool that assists in understanding moments where deep learning can occur about oneself and one's relationship to/with the more-than-human. Beyond its analytical value, the concept of perezhivanie is also influencing debate about worthwhile learning (see Roth and Jornet[34]). It is shifting the focus from learning as a cognitive and information-processing activity, to learning as a holistic process that entails a combination of emotions, thinking and reflection. *Perezhivanie* provided us, therefore, with both an analytical tool and a way of rethinking the features of worthwhile learning.

THE CHILDREN'S CONFERENCE

The research project on *Storythread* and *perezhivanie* began in 2019. Students were drawn from four different state primary schools near Brisbane, Australia (eight students per school). At the beginning of the project, they were in Year 4 and at the conclusion of the project in 2021 they were in Year 6. Each year they participated in a *Storythread* excursion conducted by PEEC and we collected data on their experiences through participant observation, interviews, and collection of artifacts such as digital photos and videos. Melanie attended one the four schools, participated in all the excursions, and in November 2021 was involved in the children's conference which was the culminating event for the research project. In preparation for the conference, we asked children to focus on a topic related to the more-than-human that was of particular interest and relevance to them. We conducted three workshops with the children prior to the conference to

31. Vygotsky, "Problem of the Environment."
32. Blunden, "Translating Perezhivanie into English."
33. Blunden, "Translating Perezhivanie into English," 277.
34. Roth and Jornet, *Understanding Educational Psychology.*

assist their preparation. Most children chose topics arising from their experiences in their local neighborhoods. For example, topics included how to recognize frog spawn as distinct from cane-toad spawn in a local waterway, how to attract sugar-gliders back to the local bushland by building nesting boxes, how to map the relationships between species in a forest reserve, and how to educate the public about the rate of deforestation locally and globally. Melanie was initially unsure what she wanted to present, but we assured her that an art piece was entirely appropriate, so she decided to focus on communicating her ideas through the art piece.

MELANIE'S ONTOLOGICAL STANCE

My project, "A Reflection of My Soul," consisted of designing an art piece that depicts the equality of humans, plants, and animals. I created a drawing of a young woman standing in front of a mirror, but her reflection is a tree. I chose a fig tree for the center of my artwork because they are strong and sturdy, like how strong our opinions should be about the equality of nature. My artwork is about bridging the gap between humans and the other creatures of the Earth. I did this project [artwork] because I hate to think of people who think they are above all others. I don't want to criticize them, but I do want to show them a better way of thinking. I learned that I can use my drawings to do more than just look pretty. I can show a different perspective and change opinions of the better. I want to help end Earth inequality.

"A Reflection of my Soul"

I've walked to a lot of places. I've done a lot of hiking with my family, and one thing I've always hated is the fact that in places where it's a national park or the trees are very treasured and then people have carved their names into the trees, and it just makes me feel so disappointed in whoever did that. So, I'm going to make sure that it doesn't happen. My project is about making sure that people understand that all beings are equal, no matter whether they have legs or roots or paws. I think that so many more people would care about flora and fauna equality if they were just taught the same way I have been.

Reflecting on Melanie's Ontological Stance

The title of Melanie's project, "A Reflection of My Soul" resonates with Miriam-Rose's description of *dadirri* as focusing on inner deep listening that tunes into "the deep spring inside."[35] Miriam-Rose connects this inner deep listening to recognition of the "great Life-Giving Spirit."[36] By using "my soul" in the title, Melanie alludes to this spiritual dimension, and indicates that her commitment to the equality of living things is an inherent feature of her being, something that is fundamental to her as a person. Based on her inner conviction, Melanie is now looking beyond herself to the goal of educating others and helping them understand "that all beings are equal."

Melanie's account of her artwork reveals also how a lived through emotional experience (perezhivanie) influenced her longer-term thinking. She remembered a specific moment on the hike with her family where she noticed damage to trees caused by humans and the emotion of disappointment that accompanied the experience. This concrete event spurred Melanie to reflect on the equality of living beings ("whether they have legs or roots or paws") and later to communicate creatively in the artwork her understanding of human relationships with the more-than-human. This is an exemplary illustration of the dual aspects of *perezhivanie* (the event per se and the reliving/reflection), and it suggests that deeper learning and understanding can emerge when experiences are emotionally engaging and authentic rather than routine and repetitive.

NON-DUALIST ONTOLOGIES ARTICULATED BY OTHER CHILDREN

Melanie articulated clearly through her art piece and commentary her ontological stance regarding the equality of all living beings on Earth. Her stance contrasts markedly with the findings we reviewed above that found children typically framed their relationship to nature in dualist terms, considering nature as distinct and separate from humans but useful in meeting human needs and desires. In our previous research, however, we have encountered children who hold similar views to Melanie. As Tooth and Renshaw[37] explained, when children participate in the *Storythread* excursion to Karawatha Forest Reserve, many express a new understanding of their relationship to the more-than-human. As they experience the forest firsthand, the children learn about Bernice Volz, a local resident who led a campaign in the 1990s to preserve Karawatha Forest from real estate developers. At the end of the excursion, they talk to Bernice via mobile phone and conclude by writing her a letter, giving an account of what they learned during the

35. Ungunmerr-Baumann, "Dadirri," 1.

36. Ungunmerr-Baumann, "Dadirri," 2.

37. Tooth and Renshaw, "Pedagogy as Advocacy."

excursion. In analyzing these accounts, we found that children experienced Karawatha as an active, relational, and emotional partner. They had begun to see themselves as related to the forest in significant ways: (i) some children reported a sense of kinship with Karawatha and becoming part of it ("I feel as if I'm a part of the environment"); (ii) others began to assign agency to the more-than-human ("Nature talks to me and it has so many stories to tell"); (iii) for some children there was a sense of solidarity with the more-than-human ("I learnt that a group of people can save a whole forest and it is truly stunning"); (iv) and for some there was the realization that they shared life with other beings ("I think the most important discovery I made today was we're not the only living things that live on the earth.").[38] Like Melanie, these children had engaged in the practice of *dadirri* and had the opportunity to become attuned inwardly and outwardly to new experiences and ways of thinking and feeling about the more-than-human. So, while Melanie stands out as particularly articulate and passionate about her ontological stance, it is clear that other children who have experienced the *Storythread* pedagogy and the practice of *dadirri* are also capable of reimaging their relationship to the more-than-human.

CONCLUDING COMMENTS

Our research is distinct from other studies of human-nature relations which typically focus on how children "perceive" nature and how time in nature can positively influence their development and mental and emotional well-being.[39] Such research is problematic because it reinforces the Cartesian dualist ontology. Although we use the term "nature" when interviewing children in our research, thereby implying a boundary between them and nature, we've found that they aren't limited in their responses by this implied boundary. They work against it. Using pedagogies such as *Storythread* and by honoring Indigenous epistemologies and ontologies through practices such as *dadirri*, children are able to consider themselves as part of nature, equal to other living beings and embedded in living systems. As Morton[40] asserted in his provocative book, *Ecology without Nature*, "we cannot grieve the loss of the human-nature connection because we are so deeply attached to it—we suggest that *dadirri* is one practice that can evoke and sustain this sense of "being nature."

38. Renshaw, "Feeling for the Anthropocene," 11

39. Linzmayer and Halpenny, "'I Might Know'"; Tillmann et al., "'Nature Makes People Happy.'"

40. Morton, *Ecology without Nature*, 186.

Melanie's art piece is "profoundly pedagogical."[41] It was designed to offer a different perspective, to invite her audience to reimagine who they are, to challenge them to reconsider the value inherent in trees and other living beings, to promote the ontological stance of equality. Melanie provides some insight into her journey towards this stance—involving her family, their hikes in the bush, and the quality of pedagogy that she experienced. Melanie took these opportunities to "play" with a different ontology and create an aesthetic way to communicate it to her peers. Melanie's art piece is similar to the arts-based practice proposed by Somerville[42] as "becoming other" through playful embodiment, for example, Somerville describes young children dancing as frogs after visiting a wetland. The mirror in Melanie's art transforms the young woman into a strong tree—she has "become other" in this artifact. Somerville suggests that "becoming other" can and should be part of every child's education. Taylor and Pacini-Ketchabaw[43] likewise suggest that encounters with other species, however short, can heighten our awareness of shared vulnerability and entanglement. It is our hope that pedagogies like these, based on deep listening, acute awareness and playful encounters with the more-than-human, will interrupt the Cartesian worldview and enable "people to understand that all beings are equal, no matter whether they have legs or roots or paws." (Melanie)

QUESTIONS FOR DISCUSSION AND DEBATE

1. How important is it to involve children in educational research, especially in relation to the climate crisis?
2. How can educational researchers work with children as co-researchers as an important part of their mainstream schooling?
3. How do we meaningfully accept the gift of *dadirri* offered to us my Miriam Rose Ungunmerr-Baumann in a way that doesn't treat it like another educational commodity or technique?
4. In what ways do Storythread and *dadirri* pedagogies invite children to consider an ontology based on equality?
5. How else can educators make space for children to access their own "deep spring" that Miriam Rose Ungunmerr-Baumann speaks about?

41. Gruenewald, "Foundations of Place."
42. Somerville, "Place Pedagogy for 'Global Contemporaneity,'" 342.
43. Taylor and Pacini-Ketchabaw. "Learning with Children."

BIBLIOGRAPHY

Aaron, Rachel F., and Peter A. Witt. "Urban Students' Definitions and Perceptions of Nature." *Children, Youth and Environments* 21 (2011) 145–67.

Abram, David. *The Spell of the Sensuous: Perception and Language in a More-Than-Human World*. New York: Vintage, 1997.

Barad, Karen. "Posthumanist Performativity: Toward an Understanding of How Matter Comes to Matter." *Signs: Journal of Women in Culture and Society* 28 (2003) 801–31.

Barratt Hacking, Elisabeth, et al. "Children as Active Researchers: The Potential of Environmental Education." In *International Handbook of Research on Environmental Education*, edited by Robert B. Stevenson et al., 438–58. New York: Routledge, 2012.

Blunden, Andy. "Translating Perezhivanie into English." *Mind, Culture and Activity* 23 (2016) 274–83.

Braus, Judy, and Sarah Milligan-Toffler. "The Children and Nature Connection: Why It Matters." *Ecopsychology* 10 (2018) 193–94. https://doi.org/10.1089/eco.2018.0072.

Burgess, Donald J., and Jolie Mayer-Smith. "Listening to Children: Perceptions of Nature." *Journal of Natural History Education and Experience* 5 (2011) 27–43.

Cheng, Judith Chen-Hsuan, and Martha C. Monroe. "Connection to Nature." *Environment and Behavior* 44 (2012) 31–49. https://doi.org/10.1177/0013916510385082.

Cutter-Mackenzie-Knowles A., et al. "Childhoodnature: An Assemblage Adventure." In *Research Handbook on Childhoodnature*, edited by Amy Cutter-Mackenzie-Knowles et al., 1–15. Cham, Switzerland: Springer, 2019. https://doi-org.ezproxy.library.uq.edu.au/10.1007/978-3-319-67286-1_2.

Fielding, Michael. "Beyond 'Voice': New Roles, Relations, and Contexts in Researching with Young People." *Discourse* 28 (2007) 301–10. https://doi.org/10.1080/01596300701458780.

Glithero, Lisa. "Educating for Student Agency: Perspectives from Young Eco-Civic Leaders in Canada." In *International Perspectives on the Theory and Practice of Environmental Education: A Reader*, edited by Guiliano Reis and Jeff Scott, 71–83. Cham, Switzerland: Springer, 2018.

Groundwater-Smith, Susan, and Nicole Mockler. "From Data Source to Co-Researchers? Tracing the Shift from 'Student Voice' to Student-Teacher Partnerships in Educational Action Research." *Educational Action Research* 24 (2016) 159–76. doi :10.1080/09650792.2015.1053507.

Gruenewald, David A. "Foundations of Place: A Multidisciplinary Framework for Place-Conscious Education." *American Educational Research Journal* 40 (2003) 619–54.

Haraway, Donna J. "Anthropocene, Capitalocene, Plantationocene, Chthulucene: Making Kin." *Environmental Humanities* 6 (2015) 159–65.

———. *Staying with the Trouble: Making Kin in the Chthulucene*. Durham, NC: Duke University Press, 2016.

Linzmayer, Cara D., and Elizabeth A. Halpenny. "'I Might Know When I'm an Adult': Making Sense of Children's Relationships with Nature." *Children's Geographies* 12 (2014) 412–28. DOI: 10.1080/14733285.2013.821262.

Louv, Richard. *Last Child in the Woods: Saving Our Children from Nature-Deficit Disorder*. Chapel Hill, NC: Algonquin Books of Chapel Hill, 2005.

Malone, Karen. "Reconsidering Children's Encounters with Nature and Place Using Posthumanism." *Australian Journal of Environmental Education* 32 (2016) 42–56. https://doi.org/10.1017/aee.2015.48.

———. "Children in the Anthropocene: How Are They Implicated?" In *A Research Handbook on Childhoodnature*, edited by Amy Cutter-Mackenzie-Knowles et al., 507–33. Cham, Switzerland: Springer, 2020.

Merchant, Carolyn. "Ecofeminism and Feminist Theory." In *Reweaving the World: The Emergence of Ecofeminism*, edited by Irene Diamond and Gloria Ornstein, 100–105. San Francisco: Sierra Club, 1990.

Moore, Jason W. "The Capitalocene, Part I: On the Nature and Origins of Our Ecological Crisis." *The Journal of Peasant Studies* 44 (2017) 594–630. https://doi.org/10.1080/03066150.2016.1235036.

———. "The Capitalocene Part II: Accumulation by Appropriation and the Centrality of Unpaid Work/Energy." *The Journal of Peasant Studies* 45 (2018) 237–79.

Morton, Timothy. *Ecology without Nature*. London: Harvard University Press, 2007.

Murris, Karin. "Posthuman Child and the Diffractive Teacher: Decolonizing the Nature/Culture Binary." In *Research Handbook on Childhoodnature*, edited by Amy Cutter-Mackenzie, Karen Malone, and Elisabeth Barratt-Hacking, 31–55. Cham, Switzerland: Springer, 2020. https://doi.org/10.1007/978-3-319-67286-1_7.

Plumwood, Val. "Gender Eco-Feminism and the Environment." In *Controversies in Environmental Sociology*, edited by Rob White, 43–60. Cambridge: Cambridge University Press, 2004.

Renshaw, Peter, and Ron Tooth. "Perezhivanie Mediated through Narrative Place-Responsive Pedagogy." In *Open Spaces for Interaction and Learning Diversities*, edited by Alessio Surian, 13–23. Rotterdam: Sense, 2016.

———. "Diverse Place-Responsive Pedagogies: Historical, Professional and Theoretical Threads." In *Diverse Pedagogies of Place: Educating Students in and for Local and Global Environments*, edited by Peter Renshaw and Ron Tooth, 1–21. London: Routledge, 2018.

Renshaw, Peter, et al. 2019. *Digital Mediation of Children's Interactions with the More-Than-Human World: Perezhivanie and Literate Practices*. Canberra: Australian Research Council Discovery Grant, 2019.

Renshaw, Peter. "Feeling for the Anthropocene: Placestories of Living Justice." *The Australian Educational Researcher* 48 (2021) 1–21.

Rixon, Andy, et al. "Childhoods Past and Present: Anxiety and Idyll in Reminiscences of Childhood Outdoor Play and Contemporary Parenting Practices." *Children's Geographies* 17 (2019) 618–29.

Roth, Wolff-Michael, and Alfredo Jornet. *Understanding Educational Psychology: A Late Vygotskian Spinozist Approach*. Cham, Switzerland: Springer, 2017.

Shiva, Vandana. *Staying Alive: Women, Ecology and Development*. London: Zed, 1989.

Soga, Masashi, and Kevin J. Gaston. "Extinction of Experience: The Loss of Human-Nature Interactions." *Frontiers in Ecology and the Environment* 14 (2016) 94–101. https://doi.org/10.1002/fee.1225.

Somerville, M. J. "A Place Pedagogy for 'Global Contemporaneity.'" *Educational Philosophy and Theory* 42 (2010) 326–44.

Somerville, Margaret, and Sarah J. Powell. "Thinking Posthuman with Mud: And Children of the Anthropocene." *Educational Philosophy and Theory* 51 (2019) 829–40.

Taylor, Affrica. "Beyond Stewardship: Common World Pedagogies for the Anthropocene." *Environmental Education Research* 23 (2017) 1448–61. DOI: 10.1080/13504622.2017.1325452.

Taylor, Affrica, and Veronica Pacini-Ketchabaw. "Learning with Children, Ants, and Worms in the Anthropocene: Towards a Common World Pedagogy of Multispecies Vulnerability." *Pedagogy Culture and Society* 23 (2015) 1–21.

Tillmann, Suzanne, et al. "'Nature Makes People Happy, That's What It Sort of Means': Children's Definitions and Perceptions of Nature in Rural North-Western Ontario." *Children's Geographies* 17 (2019) 705–18. DOI:10.1080/14733285.2018.1550572.

Tooth, Ron. "Pedagogy as Story in Landscape." In *Diverse Pedagogies of Place: Educating Students in and for Local and Global Environments*, edited by Peter Renshaw and Ron Tooth, 45–69. London: Routledge, 2017.

Tooth, Ron, and Renshaw, P. "Pedagogy as Advocacy in and for Place." In *Diverse Pedagogies of Place: Educating Students in and for Local and Global Environments*, edited by Peter Renshaw and Ron Tooth, 22–44. London: Routledge, 2018.

Ungunmerr Baumann, Miriam-Rose. "Dadirri: Inner Deep Listening and Quiet Still Awareness." https://www.miriamrosefoundation.org.au/wp-content/uploads/2021/03/Dadirri_Handout.pdf.

Vygotsky, Lev S. "The Problem of the Environment." In *The Vygotsky Reader*, edited by René van der Veer and Jan Valsiner, 338–54. 1934. Reprint, Oxford: Blackwell, 1994.

4

The Philosophy of Nature throughout History

Grant Havers

INTRODUCTION

This chapter provides a historical survey of famous philosophical attempts to understand what "nature" is. We begin with the ancient Greeks, who were the first philosophers to look to nature in order to answer the question: Why do human beings exist? Plato and Aristotle's answer was that nature assigns a purpose to everything, including humanity, within the universe or cosmos. Next, we turn to the medieval philosophy of nature, which reached its summit in the thought of Saint Thomas Aquinas. Although Aquinas agreed with Aristotle that there is a purpose-driven order to the universe, he also believed that the providence of the biblical God transcended the purposes of nature. Finally, the modern philosophy of nature rejected the premodern (ancient and medieval) idea of a purpose unfolding within nature, although moderns agreed that there is an order to the universe. While modern philosophers dismissed the premodern philosophy of nature as unscientific, they failed to answer the question with which philosophy originally began: why do human beings exist?

THE ANCIENT PHILOSOPHY OF NATURE

Ancient Greek philosophy, the oldest tradition of Western philosophy, began with the question: "What is Nature?" The ultimate answer to this question, which was most famously provided by Plato and Aristotle,[1] is that nature (*physis*) is an unchanging reality, which human beings must seek to understand and live by. Greek philosophers "discovered" nature in this sense when they first began to seek out the beginnings (or "first things") of reality itself. Humanity cannot be the "first thing" because the universe did not begin with human existence. Something must have preceded humanity. This reality must have brought into being all other things, including humanity, which existed in the universe. Greek philosophers reasoned that this first reality that preceded humanity was not subject to human action or control. The only things that humanity controlled were generally objects and customs (*nomoi*) that, according to Leo Strauss, "owe their being to human contrivance."[2] Yet humanity could not control nature because it did not create nature. The most that mortals could do with nature is to comprehend how it shapes human destiny.

This inquiry into the reality of nature also inspired Greek (and later Roman) philosophers to seek an answer to the questions: Why do human beings exist? What makes human beings unique? Does nature provide any answer? Aristotle begins with the common sense observation that everything has a material cause in the universe. As he explains, "it would be impossible for anything to come to be if nothing were present previously."[3] Aristotle further reasoned that everything in the universe depends upon nature for its existence. Everything has a "final cause" or purpose (*telos*) that explains why something is what it is. It logically follows that there is an order to the

1. Plato (429?-347 BC.) was a student of Socrates (470–399 BC) as well as the most famous philosopher of Greek antiquity. His works, which he usually wrote in dialogue form, include deep inquiries into ethics, political philosophy, metaphysics, and epistemology. His student Aristotle (384–322 BC) also made famous and influential contributions to these branches of philosophy.

2. Strauss, *Natural Right and History*, 88. The German-Jewish philosopher Leo Strauss (1899–1973) was one of the most influential interpreters of the philosophy of nature from antiquity to modernity.

3. Aristotle, *Metaphysics*, 144. This passage is at 1032b30. The word "metaphysics" refers to the oldest branch of philosophy, which studies the foundations of reality.

universe. As Aristotle puts it, "nature makes nothing purposeless or in vain."[4] What, then, is the purpose that nature assigns to human beings?

To answer this question, one must understand what Aristotle calls "a thing's essential characteristic," or what distinguishes one thing from another.[5] In the case of humanity, the faculty of reason (*nous*) makes us unique or distinct from animals.[6] It was evident to Plato and Aristotle that the purpose of humanity is to cultivate that capacity which defines our nature or "essence." As Strauss explains, "All human beings have a natural end, a natural destiny, which determines what kind of operation is good for them. In the case of man, reason is required for discerning these operations: reason determines what is by nature right with ultimate regard to man's natural end."[7] This purpose is both natural and good. What is naturally good applies to all human beings. It is good, indeed the highest good, for human beings to employ their faculty of reason to understand the universe and their place within it.

Why did Greek philosophy understand nature better than Greek religion did? The problem was that religion taught that the cosmos was full of gods, whose actions were supposed to explain the workings of nature.[8] Yet Greek religion did not demonstrate anything with certainty about the universe because the gods constantly conflicted with each other. As Plato shows in his dialogue *The Euthyphro*, the gods are "at variance with each other" because they disagree as to what is right and wrong.[9] Because the gods disagreed, it was unclear to mortals what their purpose was. It was up to philosophy to set things right. Although it was not the intent of the Greek philosophers to discredit belief in the gods altogether, the most intellectually acute Hellenes sought a reality—namely, nature—which transcended or surpassed the shaky authority of the gods. Post-Aristotelian schools of ancient philosophy were even more skeptical about the importance and authority of the gods. In the first century BC, the Roman Epicurean poet and philosopher Lucretius (99–55 BC) observed in his work *On the Nature of the Universe* (*De Rerum Natura*) that nature "runs the universe by herself without the aid of gods."[10] The Stoic tradition of philosophy, which emerged

4. Aristotle, *Politics*, 21. This passage is in book one, 1256b12.

5. Aristotle, *Metaphysics*, 9. This passage is at 983a.

6. Aristotle, *Politics*, 314. This passage is in book seven, 1332b12. The abilities to use language and to possess "a perception of good and evil" are also unique to humanity. See *Politics*, 6. This passage is in book one, 1253a11–12.

7. Strauss, *Natural Right and History*, 7.

8. Voegelin, "What is Nature?" 75.

9. Plato, *Euthyphro*, 175. This passage is at 7e of the dialogue.

10. Lucretius, *On the Nature of the Universe*, 64. This passage is in Book Two,

after the age of Plato and Aristotle, ultimately concluded that both gods and mortals fit "into the vast divine plan (*logos*) of the cosmos."[11]

What else did Greek philosophers learn with certainty about nature and its purposes? Two lessons stand out. First, they learned that nature constantly moves the universe through endless cycles of fortune and misfortune. Mere mortals can do little to control or defy these cycles. The purposes of human beings cannot help but be carried along by these cycles. The ancient Greek historian Polybius described how these cycles fatally shape the lives of mortals, including the rise and fall of ancient city-states.[12] It is inevitable that a good regime (e.g., monarchy) will degenerate into a bad one (e.g., tyranny). "For he alone who has seen how each form naturally arises and develops, will be able to see when, how, and where the growth, perfection, change, and end of each are likely to occur again."[13] Moreover, this cycle is "appointed by nature."[14] Polybius attributed this theory of "natural transformations" of good regimes into bad regimes to "Plato and certain other philosophers."[15]

Second, Greek philosophers also learned that nature, despite the constant cyclical movements that it generates, provides a universal ethical standard of right and wrong. Aristotle called this standard "natural right."[16] It is the purpose of all human beings to adhere to this standard in order to live a happy and virtuous life. Philosophy also demonstrates that there is universal agreement on certain principles. This agreement points "to the workings of nature."[17] According to Strauss, the agreement between Greek philosophy and the Bible on matters of right and wrong demonstrates that this standard of natural right exists. He writes, "It is as obvious to Aristotle as it is to Moses that murder, theft, adultery, etc., are unqualifiedly bad."[18]

1091–93. The philosophy of Epicureanism, which was inspired by the teachings of the Greek philosopher Epicurus (341–270 BC.), taught that the universe consists of matter and that the pursuit of pleasure and avoidance of pain (hedonism) is the best way to live.

11. Finnis, *Natural Law and Natural Rights*, 376. Stoic philosophy, which originated in the teachings of the Greek philosopher Zeno of Citium (334–262 BC.) taught that the cultivation of reason and control of one's emotions was the best life, one that is lived in accord with nature.

12. Polybius (200–118 BC) is most famous for writing *The Histories*, a comprehensive account of the Punic Wars between ancient Rome and Carthage.

13. Polybius, *Histories*, 275–77. These passages are fragments from Book Six.

14. Polybius, *Histories*, 289.

15. Polybius, *Histories*, 277. See also Löwith, *Meaning in History*, 7–8.

16. Strauss, "On Natural Law," 140.

17. Strauss, *Natural Right and History*, 101.

18. Strauss, "Progress or Return?" 105.

No universal agreement on right and wrong would be possible unless nature revealed a standard that is intelligible to all rational human beings. This teaching had tremendous influence on the philosophy of nature that arose during the Middle Ages.

THE MEDIEVAL PHILOSOPHY OF NATURE

With the rise of Christianity as the dominant religion in western civilization following the collapse of the Roman Empire in the West, the philosophy of nature underwent a major change during the Middle Ages. Living in the late Roman imperium, Saint Augustine squarely rejected the ancient Greek idea of cyclical time on the grounds that it was incompatible with God's benevolence. "God forbid that what the (Greek and Roman) philosophers threaten should be true, that our genuine misery is never to have an end, but is only to be interpreted time and time again, throughout eternity, by intervals of false happiness."[19]

Other medieval philosophers built on the *teleological* (purpose-driven) conception of nature that Aristotle famously advanced. In fact, the Christian faith of these "scholastic" thinkers inspired them to attempt a synthesis of his philosophy with biblical revelation. The most famous of these attempts is found in the philosophy of Saint Thomas Aquinas.[20] He agreed with Aristotle (whom he called "The Philosopher") that there is a natural order to the universe, which a first cause (God) brought into being. This fact is generally intelligible to rational human beings. As he writes in his *Summa Contra Gentiles*, "For seeing that natural things run their course according to a fixed order, and since there cannot be order without a cause of order, men, for the most part, perceive that there is one who orders the things that we see."[21] Aquinas also defended Aristotle's position that human beings can use their "natural reason" to understand what their purposes are and how

19. Saint Augustine, *City of God*, 499. Augustine (354–430) was the first Christian theologian of the late Roman Empire to articulate a systematic interpretation of the relation between Greek philosophy (especially Platonism) and biblical revelation.

20. Saint Thomas Aquinas (1225–1274) was a very influential philosopher and theologian of the late Middle Ages. His most famous works are the *Summa Theologica* ("Summary of Theology") and the *Summa Contra Gentiles* ("On the Truth of the Catholic Faith against the Errors of the Unbelievers").

21. Aquinas, *Introduction to St. Thomas Aquinas*, 454. This passage is from *Summa Contra Gentiles*, book three, chapter thirty-eight. All quotes from the *Summa Contra Gentiles* are from this text.

their virtuous acts help them live in accordance with this order, although some obey reason more "instantaneously" than others.[22]

Most importantly, Aquinas derived his theory of *natural law* from Aristotle's philosophy. As he explains in his *Summa Theologica*, natural law teaches that certain practices are right and just according to nature, a universal standard that is demonstrable according to reason and intelligible to most human beings, who understand through their "natural reason" that they ought to seek good and avoid evil. God Himself instils knowledge of the natural law in the human mind.[23] Of course, this assertion presupposes that there is a common human nature. Aquinas cautioned that there is no guarantee that people always choose good over evil. Sinful "sensual impulses" tend to interfere with the rational judgment of human beings.[24] Nevertheless, human beings have knowledge of the natural law. Aquinas also insisted that there is universal agreement as to the most basic precepts of natural law, some of which are listed below:[25]

1. Life ought to be preserved.
2. Man ought to propagate his kind.
3. Children ought to be educated.
4. Man ought to know the truth about God.
5. Man ought to live in society.
6. Ignorance ought to be avoided.
7. Offense ought not to be given unnecessarily.

Human or man-made laws are just and ethical as long as they adhere to these universal precepts. Most importantly, just laws must serve the common good, not the interests of only a few.[26]

Despite this common ground that Aquinas and Aristotle share, there is a considerable difference between their philosophies. For example, they disagreed profoundly on the authority of nature. Aristotle never subordinates nature to a higher divine authority, even though he asserts that there

22. Aquinas, *Introduction to St. Thomas Aquinas*, 581. See *Summa Theologica*, I-II, question 58 (article 2). All quotes from the *Summa Theologica* are from this text.

23. Aquinas, *Introduction to St. Thomas Aquinas*, 615, 618. See *Summa Theologica*, I-II, questions 90 (article 4) and 91 (article 2).

24. Aquinas, *Introduction to St. Thomas Aquinas*, 626. See *Summa Theologica*, I-II, question 91 (article 6).

25. Nielsen, "Examination of the Thomistic Theory," 51.

26. Aquinas, *Introduction to St. Thomas Aquinas*, 612–14, 620–21. See *Summa Theologica*, I-II, questions 90 (articles 2 and 3) and 91 (article 3).

is a first cause ("unmoved mover") of the universe. In contrast, Aquinas, as a Christian, subordinated nature to the providence (the "Eternal Law") of the biblical God: there is no idea of providence in Aristotle's philosophy.[27] Because the God of the Bible is omnipotent, not only can He disobey the natural law that He created, He can also command human beings to disobey it. Aquinas went so far as to admit that if God commanded human beings to commit theft, a crime which violates natural law, then they are required to obey His command. "For whatever is taken by the command of God, to Whom all things belong, is not taken against the will of its owner, whereas it is in this that theft consists."[28] In short, human beings are allowed to violate natural law if God commands them to do so.

Although Aquinas's philosophy of nature had its critics in the Middle Ages, it gradually came to dominate the universities of the late medieval period and early modernity. This success may not have surprised him, given his assumption that the principles of natural law were "self-evident" or obviously true to rational human beings.[29]

27. Jaffa, *Thomism and Aristotelianism*, 187.

28. Aquinas, *Introduction to St. Thomas Aquinas*, 644. See *Summa Theologica*, I-II, question 94 (article 6).

29. Aquinas, *Introduction to St. Thomas Aquinas*, 636. See *Summa Theologica*, I-II, question 94 (article 2).

MODERN PHILOSOPHY OF NATURE

From the standpoint of modern philosophy, the existence of natural law as well as a teleological design within the universe were far from "self-evident." With the rise of the modern scientific revolution in the sixteenth century, scholars agreed that there is an order to the universe. Yet they did not agree that this order is evidence of a grand and benevolent purpose. During the Age of the Enlightenment in the seventeenth century, philosophers such as René Descartes, Thomas Hobbes, and Benedict Spinoza repudiated this teleology altogether. Although they acknowledged that laws govern nature, these laws did not count as evidence of an overall purpose in the Thomistic-Aristotelian sense. Rather, these laws (e.g., the law of gravity) simply reflect the structure of the universe, without revealing any good intent in the process.

Although Hobbes, as a philosophical materialist, argued that human beings should make sense of this natural order through the means of science, they should not base their politics or morality on nature. If they did so, they would live in a "state of nature," in which no laws or government existed.[30] In short, modern philosophers understood nature as an amoral force that provides no guidance as to how human beings ought to live with each other, even though it exerted great power over all creatures in the universe. Although Hobbes believes that we have the "natural right" to preserve our existence (which the state alone enforces), this right reflects the survival instinct, not a grand purposive design. Most tellingly, if nature is simply matter in motion, without any moral authority over humanity, then the human mastery of nature becomes an actuality. As Strauss explains, modern man "is then subject to nature and necessity in such a way that by virtue of nature's gift of "brain" and through knowledge of nature and necessity he is enabled to use necessity and to transform matter."[31]

The fact that human beings adapt to nature does not count as evidence for a divinely sanctioned order in which everything has a purpose or natural end. As Kai Nielsen has argued, the modern scientific method, which stresses the empirical verification of all statements about the universe, poses the following challenge to the premodern focus on an ultimate purpose or supreme good (*summum bonum*). "How could we test whether the human eye, the solar system, or ants were so designed?"[32] It is one thing to observe

30. Hobbes, *Leviathan*, chapter 13. The English philosopher Thomas Hobbes (1588–1679) is most famous for being the first modern defender of the "social contract," a political order that is beyond the state of nature.

31. Strauss, *Thoughts on Machiavelli*, 253.

32. Nielsen, "Examination of the Thomistic Theory," 57. Kai Nielsen (1926–2021) was a famous defender of philosophical atheism. He wrote extensively on ethics, the

that natural things have functions, which explain how these objects operate. It is quite another thing to claim that a function is the same as a purpose, which assumes that a designer imposed this purpose. To answer "What is the liver for?" requires only a scientific explanation based on its function, not a theology of divine purpose.[33]

Modern philosophers have also generally faulted Aquinas's philosophy for engaging in the "naturalistic fallacy." This fallacy occurs when we falsely conflate what is "natural" with what is "good." The point of this fallacy is to warn of the temptation to confuse nature with human desires and interests. This temptation is based on an illusion because we are falsely projecting onto nature what already exists within ourselves. Looking into nature as if it were a "mirror," human beings end up ignorantly obeying nature as if it were an authority independent of human existence and desire.[34] Put differently, talk of "purpose" in nature reveals more about human interests than it does about nature.

There is another reason to avoid the naturalistic fallacy. Modern philosophers such as David Hume and others insisted that the bare facts of the universe do not reveal a good purpose. For this reason, they developed the "is-ought" distinction. What "is" is not identical to what "ought" to be. The fact that something naturally happens in the universe does not make it good.[35] By the late eighteenth century, the is-ought distinction had become so influential that some modern philosophers were openly wondering whether human nature ought to be transformed altogether. Just because human beings behave in certain ways that appear *natural* does not mean that they *ought* to act in these ways. As Jean-Jacques Rousseau contended, the fact that human nature exists should not discourage a political leader (a "legislator") from feeling "himself capable, so to speak, of changing human nature" in order to create a more humane society.[36]

The "is-ought distinction" also directly challenges Aquinas's identification of the natural order with a good order. Aquinas and Aristotle's assertion that nature is purposive leads to a false conflation of fact and value. The problem with this conflation is that it rests on the assumption that nature's "purposes" are always good.

philosophy of religion, and political philosophy.

33. Nielsen, "Examination of the Thomistic Theory," 64.

34. Polka, *Truth and Interpretation*, 83, 111.

35. Nielsen, "Examination of the Thomistic Theory," 55, 59.

36. Rousseau, *Social Contract*, 194. Jean-Jacques Rousseau (1712–78) was a radical philosophical opponent of any appeal to nature and human nature as the basis of political authority. In his view, human nature is so malleable that a humane politics can unlock and encourage the goodness within human beings.

NATURE AND DESTRUCTION

This premise is hard to reconcile with the disorder and suffering caused by nature. Aquinas contended that the natural order of things is good precisely because its creator has a benevolent intent that undergirds this order. The problem with this assumption is that it needs to demonstrate that everything in nature operates in the service of some good. Yet there are plenty of examples of nature causing terrible pain and suffering to human beings and other creatures. The eighteenth-century German philosopher Immanuel Kant[37] opposed this equation of order with a good purpose because, in his judgment, it could not explain natural disasters. In a series of articles published in 1756, Kant argued that the great Lisbon earthquake of 1755, which caused extensive damage and loss of life, was completely explicable from a scientific (non-teleological) standpoint. The only discipline that could adequately explain this natural event was the science of geology. Although he acknowledged that human beings must adapt to destructive natural phenomena and that some examples of the latter even benefit human interest (e.g., volcanoes can create hot springs), none of this is evidence of a purposeful design.[38] At the very least, the burden of proof was on Aquinas, who argued that "corruption and defects in natural things" serve God's providence.[39]

HUMAN NATURE AND SURVIVAL

Some modern philosophers have also concluded that the fact that human beings engage in purposive behavior does not prove that there is an *ultimate* purpose to what they do. Nielsen writes, "That there are purposes *in* life does not at all show or even suggest that there is a purpose *to* life or that man was made *for* a certain purpose. But it is this last sort of purpose that we need in order to show that there are natural moral laws."[40] For example, most human beings wish to survive and live a long life. It is entirely probable that this desire is based on an instinct to survive. Most societies enact and enforce laws that perpetuate the survival of its members. Yet none of these facts demonstrates that human beings were *made* for survival. Put

37. Immanuel Kant (1724–1804) wrote extensively on ethics, political philosophy, metaphysics, and epistemology. His most famous work, *The Critique of Pure Reason* (1781/1787), is a systematic critique of the teleological philosophy of nature.

38. Kant, "On the Causes of Earthquakes," 253–59.

39. Aquinas, *Introduction to St. Thomas Aquinas*, 219. See *Summa Theologica*, I, question 22 (article 2).

40. Nielsen, "Myth of Natural Law," 77. (Emphasis in the original)

differently, there is no evidence that a designer intended survival to be the ultimate purpose of life. The "common-sense core" that these facts about survival reveal are easily explicable according to the modern scientific account of nature, without resorting to a metaphysics of teleology.[41]

Charles Darwin's theory of evolution in the nineteenth-century represents one of the most famous modern attempts to emphasize survival as the only "purpose" that human beings have. According to evolutionary theory, all species evolve and survive by adapting to nature. As the evolutionist philosopher Larry Arnhart explains, although "Darwinian theory surely does away with any cosmic teleology by which the universe as a whole would be seen as ordered to an end," goals do not disappear altogether. Instead, "Darwin's biology does not deny—rather, it reaffirms—the immanent teleology displayed in the striving of each living being to fulfill its specific ends.[42] In short, if "each living being" successfully adapts to nature, it achieves the goal of survival. Still, there is no purpose to life apart from survival.

Modern science, which has deeply influenced modern philosophy, leaves little room for an empirically verifiable account of premodern teleology. In the process, science has also eliminated the "why?" question with which philosophy began.[43] Why do human beings exist at all? To focus on survival as an answer to this question is unsatisfactory. At best, the bare fact of survival tells us *how* human beings tend to function, not *why* they do. Is there any room for an ultimate purpose in the modern age, in the wake of the scientific revolution? An answer to this question is particularly pressing today, in the face of modernist ideas that reject any attempt to emphasize the distinctive "essence" or "nature" that defines human beings. The focus on survival does not explain what is unique about human nature, given the fact that all animal species share a common instinct to survive.

THE FUTURE OF THE PHILOSOPHY OF NATURE

In the eighteenth and nineteenth centuries, the philosophy of nature gradually gave way to the philosophy of *history*. In the wake of the modern repudiation of teleological metaphysics, history replaced nature as the new standard to which human beings must adhere. It was now up to history to answer the "why?" question about humanity's purpose. History became the secularized version of God's providence, which enabled human beings to act as if they

41. Nielsen, "Myth of Natural Law," 80.

42. Arnhart, *Darwinian Natural Right*, 245.

43. Arendt, *Human Condition*, 269–70; Polka, *Truth and Interpretation*, 109.

freely push history in a "progressive" direction.[44] The belief that history is the story of freedom and moral progress appealed to modern philosophers who opposed premodern teleology. Still, the violent conflicts of the twentieth century have hardly proved that human beings are "progressing" in an ethical sense. Moreover, current attempts to reinvent human nature through biogenetics, often justified in the name of "progress," have encouraged some philosophers to rediscover a more traditional approach to nature which resists this reinvention.[45] Perhaps it is time, once again, to address the question with which philosophy began: Why do human beings exist?

QUESTIONS FOR DISCUSSION AND DEBATE

1. Why did ancient Greek philosophers contend that philosophy, not religion, best explains the workings of nature?
2. How did premodern philosophers attempt to prove that there is such a thing as natural right and natural law?
3. How did Aquinas's philosophy of nature differ from that of Aristotle's philosophy?
4. Why do modern philosophers generally reject the idea of natural law?
5. Why is the is-ought distinction useful for helping us understand nature or the universe?

BIBLIOGRAPHY

Aquinas, Saint Thomas. *Introduction to St. Thomas Aquinas*. Edited with an introduction by Anton C. Pegis. New York: Modern Library, 1948.

Arendt, Hannah. *The Human Condition*. Garden City, NY: Doubleday Anchor Books, 1959.

Aristotle, *Metaphysics*. Translated by Richard Hope. Ann Arbor: University of Michigan Press, 1985.

———. *The Politics of Aristotle*. Edited and translated by Ernest Barker. Oxford: Oxford University Press, 1958.

Arnhart, Larry. *Darwinian Natural Right: The Biological Ethics of Human Nature*. Albany: SUNY Press, 1998.

Augustine, Saint. *The City of God*. Translated by Henry Bettenson with an introduction by John O'Meara. London: Penguin Books, 1986.

Finnis, John. *Natural Law and Natural Rights*. Oxford: Clarendon Press, 1996.

44. Strauss, *Natural Right and History*, 317.

45. Havers, "Natural Rightism and the Biogenetic Debate," 93–105.

Havers, Grant. “Natural Rightism and the Biogenetic Debate.” In *Values And Technology: Religion & Public Life*, vol. 37, edited by Gabriel R. Ricci, 93–105. New Brunswick, NJ: Transaction Publishers, 2011.

Hobbes, Thomas. *Leviathan*. Edited by Michael Oakeshott. New York: Collier Books, 1962.

Jaffa, Harry V. *Thomism and Aristotelianism*. Chicago: University of Chicago Press, 1952.

Kant, Immanuel. *Critique of Pure Reason*. Translated by Paul Guyer and Allen W. Wood. Cambridge: Cambridge University Press, 1999.

———. “On the Causes of Earthquakes on the Occasion of the Calamity which Befell the Western Countries of Europe Towards the End of Last Year.” *Annals of Science* 40 (1983 [1756]) 253–59.

Löwith, Karl. *Meaning in History*. Chicago: University of Chicago Press, 1949.

Lucretius. *On the Nature of the Universe*. Translated by R. E. Latham. London: Penguin Books, 1994.

Nielsen, Kai. “An Examination of the Thomistic Theory of Natural Moral Law.” In *God and the Grounding of Morality*, 41–68. Ottawa: University of Ottawa Press, 1991.

———. “The Myth of Natural Law.” In *God and the Grounding of Morality*, 69–84. Ottawa: University of Ottawa Press, 1991.

Plato. *Euthyphro*. In *The Collected Dialogues*, edited by Edith Hamilton and Huntington Cairns, 169–85. Princeton: Princeton University Press, 1982.

Polka, Brayton. *Truth and Interpretation: An Essay in Thinking*. New York: St. Martin’s Press, 1990.

Polybius. *The Histories*, vol. 3. With an English translation by W. R. Paton. London: Loeb Classical Library, 1979.

Rousseau, Jean-Jacques. *The Social Contract*. In *The Social Contract and Discourses*, translation and introduction by G. D. H. Cole, 165–277. London: Everyman’s Library, 1983.

Strauss, Leo. *Natural Right and History*. Chicago: University of Chicago Press, 1953.

———. “On Natural Law.” In *Studies in Platonic Political Philosophy*, with an introduction by Thomas L. Pangle, 137–46. Chicago: University of Chicago Press, 1983.

———. “Progress or Return? The Contemporary Crisis in Western Civilization.” In *Jewish Philosophy and the Crisis of Modernity: Essays and Lectures in Modern Jewish Thought*, edited with an introduction by Kenneth Hart Green, 87–136. Albany, NY: SUNY Press, 1997.

———. *Thoughts on Machiavelli*. Chicago: University of Chicago Press, 1958.

Voegelin, Eric. “What Is Nature?” In *Anamnesis*, translated and edited by Gerhart Niemeyer, 71–88. Columbia, MO: University of Missouri Press, 1978.

5

Philosophical Perspectives

Stories from a Practitioner: A Process of Building Environmental Literacy

Matti Erpestad

INTRODUCTION

Picture this: as a teacher you are immersed in a lecture that greatly interests you, yet upon assessment of your class, you realize that they did not learn what you intended. An important realization to make as educators is that we do not teach our students, but rather they learn. What we try to teach and what they actually learn do not always align. Instead, we should aim to create environments conducive to learning and act as facilitators of their learning experience.

In this chapter, I will outline three philosophical approaches I have used in engaging students in their learning in environmental education. I will start with context for my claim in the introductory paragraph, then situate learning experiences in the context in environmental education (EE) goals, and finally share two stories from my experience as an educator. I will conclude with a few closing thoughts.

LEARNING VERSUS TEACHING

Carl Rogers "argued that people can't really teach anything to anyone, they can only facilitate the learning of others."[1] Along with Rogers, countless others have advocated for philosophies of education, which posit that people, especially children, learn best through direct, authentic experiences with the natural world.[2] As educators, we facilitate educational experiences for children, and it is critical to create student-centered experiences if we want to achieve our educational goals. Smith clarifies Rogers's use of the term "facilitating" instead of "teaching": "Teaching involves passing on purported wisdom from the outside of the students, while facilitation involves releasing the wisdom of the students from within themselves."[3] So, if we involve the students in an experience that guides them to the content we want to teach, then they can more effectively learn.

Lev Vygotsky's concept of the Zone of Proximal Development (ZPD) also supports the active role in facilitation. Vygotsky defined ZPD as "the distance between the actual development as determined through problem solving under adult guidance or in collaboration with more capable peers."[4] As Seaman and Gingo clarify, "In the ZPD, children, aided by more expert partners, appropriate the skills needed for a participation in activity that is slightly beyond their competence."[5] To clarify, educators need to structure learning experiences that meet students where they are at and then challenge and push them further. One recognized method of doing this is scaffolding as conceived by Bruner, in which a peer or educator "provides temporary support for the learner as skills develop," so that they can use the practiced skill or knowledge later on.[6] David Kolb's model of the experiential learning cycle, which is one of the best-known standards for learning by experience, "emphasizes structured setting, time-frames, and instructional techniques for experiential learning to occur. These should be contrasted with a Vygotskyan framework, which would see experiential learning as the natural way we learn through collaborative participation in everyday

1. Smith, "Carl Rogers," 188. Carl Rogers was a well-known American psychologist who also wrote about educational experiences.

2. McCrea, "Roots of Environmental Education," 2–3 outlines many contributors, notably Jean-Jacques Rousseau, Anna Botsford Comstock, and John Dewey.

3. Smith, "Carl Rogers," 189.

4. Vygotsky, *Mind in Society*, 86.

5. Seaman and Gingo, "Lev Vygotsky," 162.

6. Bruner, "Ontogenesis."

community practices."[7] Both of these approaches could be useful depending on the context of the school where it is taught.

ENVIRONMENTAL LITERACY THROUGH ENVIRONMENTAL EDUCATION

According to the Belgrade Charter of 1975–76, the goal of environmental education is to develop a global population that is aware of and concerned about total environment and its associated problems. Furthermore, people have the knowledge, attitudes, skills, motivation, and commitment to work individually and "collectively toward solutions of current problems and the prevention of new ones."[8] A second foundational document, the Tbilisi Declaration of 1977, defines environmental education as

> a learning process that increases people's knowledge and awareness about the environment and its associated challenges, develops the necessary skills and expertise to address the challenges, and fosters attitudes, motivations, and commitments to make informed decisions and take responsible action.[9]

Then, as educators we should not just teaching students about the environment, but rather we should help them develop the motivation and skills to become involved in their communities through intentionally crafted experiences, classes, and programs that sequentially lead to the ultimate goal of EE: environmental literacy. Environmental literacy is defined as "an individual's understanding, skills and motivation to make responsible decisions that considers his or her relationships to natural systems, communities and future generations."[10] Three goals for environmental education arose from the Tblisi Declaration, and I contend that these can be used as a route towards environmental literacy. The goals of environmental education can be understood in five categories: awareness, knowledge, attitudes, skills, and participation: as cultivating an awareness and sensitivity to the environment, developing basic knowledge of the environment and its problems,

7. Seaman and Gingo, "Lev Vygotsky," 158, referencing David Kolb's model of the experiential learning cycle, which involves four stages: Concrete Experience; Reflection upon the Experience; Formation of Abstracts, Concepts, and Generalizations from the Experience; and Active Experimentation or Testing Implication of Concepts in New Situations. After the fourth stage, the cycle leads to concrete experience again. For more information, see Kolb, *Experiential Learning*, 21.

8. UNESCO-UNEP, "Belgrade Charter."

9. UNESCO-UNEP, "Tbilisi Declaration."

10. "Oregon Environmental Literacy Program."

acquiring a set of values and feelings of concern for the environment and motivation for participating in improving and protecting it, acquiring skills for identifying and solving environmental problems, and encouraging active involvement in resolving and preventing environmental problems.[11] Through EE we strive to develop engaged, responsible citizens, yet it is crucial for us as educators to remember that we should teach students *how* to think, not *what* to think.[12] We should facilitate experiences through which they develop critical thinking and problem-solving skills so that they can make the decisions from their own perspectives and worldview, remembering that we can guide students using the concept of the zone of proximal development as they move towards environmental literacy.

I will briefly share an example from a rural kindergarten to sixth grade school where I taught as the environmental educator. For context, environmental education can take place in a myriad of ways in formal schools, if it even takes place at all. Jacobson et al. outline approaches to incorporating EE in the school curriculum, and in this school, EE was both inserted and infused into the curriculum depending on the teacher.[13] As the environmental educator I had each class of students every other week in an hour of environmental education. As such, this is an example of insertion, which "involves creating a separate conservation education course of specific them focused on conservation topics."[14] This was the basis of many teachers' expectations of environmental education in their curriculum. That is, their students would attend my EE course every other week. Other teachers, however, infused EE into their curriculum, "incorporat[ing] conservation education content or process into established courses."[15] These students wove EE into their curriculum, and I would build off the lessons and units to continue to deepen their experiences in EE. I started with the youngest students with awareness and knowledge components listed above and progressively worked toward the participation or action components.

11. UNESCO-UNEP, "Tbilisi Declaration," 26–27.

12. After environmental education was introduced in the context of environmental movements there was a strong backlash to the field in the 1980s and more in the 1990s contending that it advocated environmentalist values, provided flawed information and forced information on students. EE's response to this backlash was to focus on critical thinking and problem-solving skills. See Cushman, "Critics Rise Up," and Disinger, "K-12 Education and Environment" for more information.

13. Jacobson et al., *Conservation Education*, 106.

14. Jacobson et al., *Conservation Education*, 106. Although this book uses the terminology "conservation education," these same concepts can be applied to environmental education.

15. Monroe and Cappaert, *EE Toolbox*, as cited in Jacobson et al., *Conservation Education*.

As sixth graders in an infused classroom, the students were tasked with investigating environmental issues based on their interest. One group of students explored emissions from vehicles and their effect on creating greenhouse gases. As they continued they came to the realization that they could actually do something about this at their school. The school was already very energy-efficient and used food waste for off-site compost, so the students chose to reduce emissions from the school buses that idled in front of the building as they waited to transport students home from school. The sixth graders drafted a petition, which they eventually presented to the principal. They laid out their rationale to stop buses from idling based on their research, and in the end their proposal was accepted. The reduction of emissions from these buses was a quantifiable amount of carbon that the sixth graders tracked as they studied math.

These students were in the seventh year of the environmental literacy progression from awareness to action and were well poised to participate in solving an environmental problem that they identified. Recognizing not all students are at this point, for purposes of this chapter, I will share two stories that serve as example of a possible venue for cultivating awareness and knowledge of the natural world, which is a foundational starting point for the youngest students to the oldest students.

PHILOSOPHICAL APPROACHES

To provide context for these stories I will explain some methods that stem from various philosophical approaches that can be used in EE. One philosophical approach that pairs well with environmental is constructivism. According to constructivist theory, "students come to learning situations with a variety of knowledge, feeling, and skills, and this is where the learning should begin."[16] As such, it is crucial to assess students' prior knowledge and experiences about a topic to know where to begin. If this does not happen, it could lead to a situation like one that I witnessed at the school I mentioned before. The school often had environmental education students come in as guest teachers to present a lesson. This both contributed to the EE curriculum of the school as well as met expectations from the university courses that guest teachers were enrolled in. One guest teacher came in to teach about how to identify common songbirds in the winter. As the teacher dove into her lesson, a student raised their hand and said, "we already know this." At this point, the guest teacher's lesson became irrelevant, and they floundered for what to do next. This is an example of

16. Schulte, "Definition of Constructivism," 25.

not recognizing the knowledge base of the students, for that is where the learning should begin."[17]

Story 1: Pileated Woodpecker

Another philosophical approach I take incorporates what's called the "three Hs"—"Heart, Hand, Head," coined by Sir Patrick Geddes in 1919.[18] This approach combines affective learning—what students feel—with sensory learning—what they physically experience—and intellectual learning. As Higgins and Nicol state, "This concept of the integration of affective and intellectual learning with a physical dimension resonates with experiential education, the progressive education movement, and both environmental and outdoor education."[19] The Heart Hand Head method engages students with the way they feel about the outdoors, based on feeling, sensory engagement that leads to intellectual learning. One example is a lesson I taught to fifth graders at a residential environmental learning center.

According to my lesson plan, I had three outcomes, one of which was to create an authentic, hands-on experience in the outdoors that sparked feeling of wonder, excitement, and curiosity. I met this objective through a guided hike in a mixed hardwood and coniferous forest (oak, maple, aspen, birch, fir). The students felt that they were going on an adventure because of the unfamiliar, novel setting (they had not been in this part of the forest, and some had not been in a forest like this before) and the outcome of the hiking experience was uncertain. I prompted them with one possible objective: "there is a big foot and a half tall woodpecker with a big red mohawk with a beak larger than my hand . . . and we're going to go outside and see it!"[20] This sparked curiosity and focused their attention as we walked. So, as we approached a large stand of aspens, we heard a bird call. Options at this point would be to hear it and move on, thus ignoring the learning opportunity. Hear it and I identify it, thus closing off their observation and critical thinking. Or hear it. Pause. Listen. And investigate, which activated their curiosity and attention. First, I said that if it flies away, watch. "It's going to jump out, it's going to droop, flap, flap, come back up, droop, flap, flap." So, it has an undulating wave pattern. The students repeat the motion

17. Schulte, "Definition of Constructivism," 25.

18. Geddes, "Final Lecture" as cited in Geddes, *Cities in Evolution*.

19. Higgins and Nicol, "Sir Patrick Geddes," 36.

20. The Pileated Woodpecker, *Dryocopus Pileatus*, is the largest woodpecker native to North America at 40–49 cm (16–19 in) tall with a wingspan of 66–75 cm (26–30 in). Winkler et al., *Woodpeckers*.

I make with their arm. Then I slowly shift to a spot where we see the bird and I have them describe it—a large black and white bird with a large red crest on its head. I ask the students to bring out their binoculars, which I made sure previously that they knew how to use. As they were focusing in on the bird, it takes off and flies deeper into the forest uses the undulating pattern I described. We observed it making a hole in the aspen tree, so we creep up to the tree and investigate the hole. I ask what they think made the hole. "Uh, that woodpecker." "Exactly! What was the name of that woodpecker?" I assess their knowledge as they respond "pileated woodpecker." "If we hadn't seen the bird, why would we think this is a pileated woodpecker hole?" Response: "it is a big hole." "Right! I can fit my fist in that hole, I can stick my whole hand in the hole, and this is how long its beak is, this how massive this thing is . . . and we just saw it!" I could see on their faces that this experience hit them—they felt the wonder and excitement of seeing the woodpecker and the holes it made. After we check this out, we're going to walk down this other path, which is the habitat it lives in, and we're going to see it again. I was following the objective I had, and that was the experience. Based on the lesson I just planned, I reflect own my own experience (my past experience and how I felt in it) to plan a positive, memorable learning experience for my students. As they are in it, I try to gauge how they are feeling. Do they feel safe? Included? Was the lesson oriented towards them? What were the barriers to learning? How can I mitigate any barriers so the lesson is as inclusive as possible? I try to meet them where they are at, to create the most positive, effective outdoor education lesson so they want to do it again. I hope that as we facilitate outdoor experiences, we build the students' motivation to do that again—to venture out and explore the natural world around us.

Afterwards, we reflect on what we experienced.[21] What did we see? What was the bird doing? Why was it pecking at the tree? What was inside the hole? After we reflect, we try to make sense of it, to generalize what we experienced. The woodpecker was searching for food; we could see the insect tunnels in the hole it made. That is how it survives in the forest, by finding the holes of carpenter ants and slurping them up as they're too cold to move. So next time we're out, what kind of path should we follow to find them again? Here we link their feeling of excitement with the act of hearing the bird, seeing it through the binoculars and feeling the inside of the hole with the knowledge of its ecological relationship with aspen trees and carpenter ants as well as how other animals, such as pine martens, owls,

21. This paragraph uses the four stages of David Kolb's experiential learning cycle: 1) experience, 2) reflection, 3) abstract conceptualization (aka generalization), and 4) active experimentation. See Kolb, *Experiential Learning*, 21.

bats, and ducks, use the nesting cavities they create. Then bring the concept further to potential threats that birds in general face due to climate change working to the action component of environmental education. Ask the students to generate ideas of what they can do and then plan it, implement and evaluate it.[22]

Story 2: Scavenger Hunt

Throughout the school year I would take students out each season for a scavenger hunt, which I used as both a way to track what was to be found in their school forest and how things changed from season to season.[23] Each year I would make the objects to be found progressively harder. In this process I used guided discovery, which is a common method in outdoor and environmental education,[24] but in this example it also exemplifies Lev Vygotsky's zone of proximal development.

I started each class period inside and ask students what interesting things they had been seeing or hearing outside. I would take a range of responses so the students could share their observations with enthusiasm and begin to spark interest in their peers. As we transitioned outside, I provided each small group of two to three students with a scavenger hunt sheet, which included written directions that I explained orally as well and sixteen boxes listing different objects to observe while they were out exploring. Before they set out, I gather them close: "explore this part of the forest, and *carefully observe* what is going on here. It's fall, and we will see some changes going. I want you to think of what these changes mean. Once you observe something cool or interesting, call out 'look what I found' so that those nearby can gather to see the observation." As they spread out in the area, the boundaries of which I identified (within earshot of a callback signal that I established and a specified time limit), they were set free to discover what they could find. Soon I heard "Look what I found!" I met the student and nearby peers and heard their observations about a blue-green mushroom

22. Jacobson et al., *Conservation Education and Outreach Techniques* is an excellent source for guidance through this process.

23. This example occurred at the rural K-6 environmental charter school that I referenced previously.

24. Gilbertson et al., *Outdoor Education Methods and Strategies*, 129 explain guided discovery: "With this method the instructor also provides general parameters to guide the students, and from that point on the students work on their own to complete the task." One key point is that "in guided discovery the instructor steps in occasionally to help the students so they are successful. Without guidance, students are at risk of learning incorrect information or skills."

growing from the crack in a down log. I encouraged students to propose hypotheses of what it was doing, what role it was playing in the forest, and how their observations could connect to a bigger story of the changes that were going on in the forest.[25] I like to create experiences for small group sharing. Many students are much more comfortable sharing what they see in a small group or one-on-one instead of large group sharing. Because, as I prompted before they set off, "after your exploration, we will gather as a group and you will be asked to share your observations."

After about five minutes a student wandered up and asked, "what is a cradle knoll?"[26] This was one of the words I included on the sheet that I guessed not many students would know. I include this purposefully so they can learn what the object is by asking me and then by sharing the information with others if asked. For each season and each grade level that I led a scavenger hunt for, I would progressively push the students' level of understanding so they could grow in their knowledge of the forest and engage them in learning through using the concept of the zone of proximal development. That is, I assisted students in defining terms they didn't know, and I encouraged them to teach their peers what they learned, knowing that not all the students would come up to me to ask.

Once I signaled students back with a hoot of barred owl, which I demonstrated before they left, I gathered them up in a circle to share their observations and reflections on their experience and the meaning of what they saw, heard, etc. Many students were eager to relate cool things they observed. I guided them bit by bit to a greater understanding on how what they observed was part of the story of the transitions the forest was going through in this season. I hold this to be an example of how through guided discovery and the zone of proximal development students immerse themselves in their learning with gentle prompting from the educator. As we walked back to the classroom, I heard students using words like "cradle knoll" as part of their new active vocabulary. They built upon their previous knowledge as well as gained more awareness and knowledge in their school forest. This is how I planted seeds earlier in the year to started them in a process towards environmental literacy.

25. In this forest, it was very common to see a lot of mushroom growth in the fall, so it was a common theme to explore the role of mushrooms as decomposers as well as share what other species would be present because of the abundance of mushrooms.

26. A cradle knoll is the area of mounded dirt next to the unearthed roots of a fallen tree.

CONCLUSION

To end, I will leave you with three thoughts. First, "In the end, all who use camping, outdoor education, or adventure education are united by one simple framework: the belief that people learn best through direct personal experience."[27] I encourage you to focus classroom learning environments on students' hand-on experiences of the subject matter whenever possible. Second, Carl Rogers recognized that there is risk in creating student-centered classroom. "Who knows whether students can be trusted and whether a process can be trusted? One can only take the risk; and the risk is frightening.[28] From my past experiences and the ones that I have shared here, I have made mistakes, but through making mistakes we learn to become better. I invite you to take that risk in your teaching because, the third point, is that as educators we are role models that can ignite the passion for the environment in our students.[29] Don't underestimate the positive impact you can make.

QUESTIONS FOR DISCUSSION AND DEBATE

1. Why should the role of an educator not focus on teaching? What should it focus on instead?
2. What are the goals of environmental education, and how do they relate to environmental literacy?
3. How could you link the concept of the zone of proximal development with building environmental literacy?
4. Besides the examples mentioned in this chapter, what is an example of an activity that you can lead using the method of guided discovery?
5. How can you apply concepts of this chapter in your professional career as an educator?

27. Ewert and Garvey, "Philosophy and Theory," 23.

28. Rogers, *Carl Rogers*, 4.

29. Many sources support the assertion that adult role models and mentors play a key role in leading students to be interested and inspired to pursue environmental education. One example is Erpestad, *Motivations and Values*.

BIBLIOGRAPHY

Bruner, Jerome Seymour. "The Ontogenesis of Speech Acts." *Journal of Child Language* 2 (1975) 1–40.

Cushman, John H., Jr. "Critics Rise Up Against Environmental Education." *New York Times*, April 22, 1997. https://www.nytimes.com/1997/04/22/us/critics-rise-up-against-environmental-education.html.

Disinger, John F. "K-12 Education and the Environment: Perspectives, Expectations, and Practice." *The Journal of Environmental Education* 33 (2001) 4–11. https://www.tandfonline.com/doi/pdf/10.1080/00958960109600795.

Erpestad, Matti. "Motivations and Values of Outdoor Education Students: Perspectives from North Karelia, Finland and Minnesota." Master's thesis, University of Minnesota Duluth, 2013.

Ewert, Alan, and Dan Garvey. "Philosophy and Theory of Adventure Education." In *Adventure Education Theory and Applications*, edited by Dick Prouty et al., 19–32. Champaign, IL: Human Kinetics, 2007.

Geddes, Patrick. "Final Lecture at the University of Dundee." In *Cities in Evolution*. London: Williams and Norgate, 1919.

———. *Cities in Evolution*. Rev. ed. London: Williams and Norgate, 1949.

Gilbertson, Ken, et al. *Outdoor Education Methods and Strategies*. Champaign, IL: Human Kinetics, 2006

Higgins, Peter, and Robbie Nicol. "Sir Patrick Geddes: Vivendo Discimus—by Living We Learn." In *Sourcebook of Experiential Education: Key Thinkers and their Contributions*, edited by Thomas E. Smith and Clifford E. Knapp, 32–40. New York: Routledge, 2011.

Jacobson, Susan K., et al. *Conservation Education and Outreach Techniques*. Oxford: Oxford University Press, 2015.

Kolb, David A. *Experiential Learning: Experience as the Source of Learning and Development*. Englewood Cliffs, NJ: Prentice-Hall, 1984.

McCrea, E. J. "Roots of Environmental Education: How the Past Supports the Future." *Environmental Education and Training Partnership (EETAP)* (2006) 1–12. https://files.eric.ed.gov/fulltext/ED491084.pdf.

Monroe, Martha C., and David Cappaert. *EE Toolbox—Workshop Resource Manual. Integrating Environmental Education into the School Curriculum*. Dubuque, IA: Kendall Hunt, 1994.

Oregon State University. "Oregon Environmental Literacy Program: What Is Environmental Literacy?" https://oelp.oregonstate.edu/oelp-plan/what environmental-literacy.

Rogers, Carl. *Carl Rogers on Personal Power: Inner Strength and Its Revolutionary Impact*. New York: Delacorte, 1977.

Seaman, Jayson, and Mathew Gingo. "Lev Vyvotsky: Experiential Education—A View from the Future." In *Sourcebook of Experiential Education: Key Thinkers and their Contributions*, edited by Thomas E. Smith and Clifford E. Knapp, 157–65. New York: Routledge, 2011.

Schulte, Paige L. "A Definition of Constructivism." *Science Scope* 20 (1996) 25–27.

Smith, Thomas E. "Carl Rogers: A Way of Being an Experiential Educator." In *Sourcebook of Experiential Education: Key Thinkers and their Contributions*, edited by Thomas E. Smith and Clifford E. Knapp, 185–92. New York: Routledge, 2011.

United Nations Environmental, Scientific and Cultural Organization (UNESCO) and United Nations Environment Programme (UNEP). "The Belgrade Charter." *Connect: UNESCO-UNEP Environmental Education Newsletter* 1, no. 1 (January 1976): 1–2.

———. "The Tbilisi Declaration." *Connect: UNESCO-UNEP Environmental Education Newsletter* 3 (1978) 1–8.

Vygotsky, Lev S. *Mind in Society*. Cambridge, MA: Harvard University, 1978.

Winkler, Hans, et al. *Woodpeckers: An Identification Guide to the Woodpeckers of the World*. Boston: Houghton Mifflin, 1995.

6

Turtles All the Way Down

Ecosystems, Markets, and Human Preferences

BRUCE PARDY[1]

Who trusted God was love indeed
And love Creation's final law
Tho' Nature, red in tooth and claw
With ravine, shriek'd against his creed

—ALFRED LORD TENNYSON, *IN MEMORIAM A. H. H.*, 1850

INTRODUCTION—TURTLES ALL THE WAY DOWN

In the US Supreme Court decision in *Rapanos v. United States*, Justice Antonin Scalia offered a version of the traditional tale of how the Earth is carried on the backs of animals. In this version of the story,

1. Executive Director, Rights Probe (https://www.rightsprobe.org/), professor of law, Queen's University. This chapter is adopted and adapted from chapters 2 and 3 of *Ecolawgic: The Logic of Ecosystems and the Rule of Law* (Fifth Forum Press, 2015), "The Logic of Ecosystems: Capitalism, Rights and the Law of 'Ecosystem Services,'" *Journal of Human Rights and the Environment* 5 (2014) 136 and "The Only Legitimate Rule: A Reply to MacLean's Critique of *Ecolawgic*" *Dalhousie Law Journal* (2017) 393.

> An Eastern guru affirms that the earth is supported on the back of a tiger. When asked what supports the tiger, he says it stands upon an elephant; and when asked what supports the elephant he says it is a giant turtle. When asked, finally, what supports the giant turtle, he is briefly taken aback, but quickly replies "Ah, after that it is turtles all the way down."[2]

Arguments about ethical and legal norms are arguments about what is true, right, fair, and just. In ecosystems, where everybody eats somebody else, there are no such norms. In evolutionary terms, success means surviving to reproduce. No other rules govern behaviour. The law of the jungle is not based on philosophy. In ecosystems, red in tooth and claw, anything goes, and might is right.

In human society, does might make right? Legal philosophers typically say that it does not. They say that laws are inherently right not because they are enacted and enforced by the powerful but because they reflect some other value that has inherent validity. For some, legitimacy derives from the law's consistency with moral standards. For others, legitimacy depends upon the law's effectiveness at achieving desirable social outcomes, such as aggregate economic welfare, equality, environmental protection, or other objectives.

But these values are merely competing preferences. They are turtles all the way down. The proposition that the law should reflect that which is good, moral, just, or desirable is a fiction. People disagree, and no opinion can be proven to be correct.

One need not be a moral relativist to make this case. It is one thing to believe in a moral code, and quite another to impose that code on other people who do not agree. Moral reasoning is harmless if it is personal, theoretical, and unenforced. People can decide for themselves if they agree, and if not, no sanctions follow. In contrast, what is at stake in legal theories of moral justification is not truth but power. The search is for standards with which to coerce. If those standards cannot be proven to be objectively valid, they are mere preferences and opinions, and have no legitimacy as a basis for coercive legal norms.

This claim, of course, is not new or novel.[3] For example, Richard Posner dismisses the work of legal philosophers when he writes:

2. *Rapanos*, 2233.

3. "Even if one concedes that there are objective answers to the questions about the identification of the law, one could still maintain that objectivity about the content of the law is highly suspect. We may know for sure what the law is on a given issue, but whether it is right or wrong is something that we cannot objectively determine. Now, is this just the age-old worry about the objectivity of moral values? Not necessarily. There

> It would be a disaster if moral theorists succeeded in their implied aim of imposing a uniform morality on society. Of course, these theorists, in our society anyway, do not agree on what that morality should be.[4] . . . [E]ven if I am wrong in thinking that there are no interesting moral universals, they would be unusable in moral argument if we could not determine what they are.[5]

It is easy to be blind to one's own preferences. While Posner dismisses legal theory as a source of universal morality, he has notoriously argued that legal rules and judgments should seek to achieve economic efficiency and maximize aggregate welfare.[6] However, economic efficiency and aggregate welfare are preferences too. In so doing, he assumes that his own normative preferences have inherent validity and ignores the value judgments embedded within them.

ECOSYSTEMS

You may think of your body as a thing. After all, it has a physical existence and identifiable boundaries. It is a solid object, with mass and substance, and you know where your body ends and the rest of the world begins. Atoms and molecules make up cells, which make up organs and tissue, which make your body the thing that it is.

Except that it is not a thing in the same way as a chair or a rock. Like chairs and rocks, at this moment your body is made up of a particular collection of atoms and molecules. But unlike these objects, every day some of your atoms and molecules are lost, and others replace them. You consist of different material today than yesterday, last year, and ten years ago. New atoms and molecules are laid down in a particular place and manner, so that they interact with the others just so. You are not a fixed object but a pattern—the product of a system of processes expressing a package of information.

Ecosystems are not things either. Unlike bodies, rocks, and chairs, they do not even have physical shapes or boundaries. Nor do they consist of a

is a jurisprudential issue that has to be settled first. The issue is whether legal norms' appraisals in terms of right or wrong necessarily reduce to moral worth. Can we simply avoid this question just by talking about the objectivity of values in general? After all, legal discourse, even if not reducible to moral values, is part of a larger frame of evaluative discourse in general; why not, then, simply discuss the objectivity of values?" Marmor, "Essay on the Objectivity of Law," 15 (reference omitted).

4. Posner, "Problematics of Moral and Legal Theory," 1642.
5. Posner, "Problematics of Moral and Legal Theory," 1645.
6. See, e.g., Posner, *Economic Analysis of Law.*

particular set of materials. Instead, they are intangible systems producing patterns and outcomes. An ecosystem is a model that explains the dynamics of interactions amongst living and non-living elements that function as a system.[7] These systems are not just collections of organisms—crickets and water lilies—but consist of relationships and interactions that together amount to something different from the sum of their parts. They operate according to their own immutable characteristics and rules. The way ecosystems work defines what they are.

In ecosystems, population growth makes resources scarce.[8] Because resources are scarce, competition for resources is inevitable.[9] Some organisms obtain the resources necessary to survive and reproduce, and others do not.[10] In this way, competition for scarce resources in ecosystems is the dynamic that drives natural selection.[11] When organisms succeed, their genes are passed to the next generation. When they fail, they become a genetic dead end.

Natural selection is the engine of evolution.[12] As the genetic makeup of populations changes through time by natural selection, new genetic variations emerge, and species evolve. Genetic variation that impedes survival is

7. An ecosystem is "a community of organisms and their physical environment interacting as an ecological unit." Lincoln et al., *Dictionary of Ecology*, 75.

8. "The key to natural selection is Malthusian economics. . . . Malthus described how basic environmental resources would ultimately limit populations, thus creating a struggle for existence. Competition is inevitable (because of population growth) and thus only some within a population ultimately survive, while others must perish." Kricher, *Balance of Nature*, 57–58; Ashworth, *Economy of Nature*, 98–99.

9. "[W]hen any essential resource becomes limited, there will inevitably be some form of competition, direct or indirect, within the population for access to that particular resource. Not all will obtain it, and, if it is vital to survival or reproduction, not all will survive or reproduce." Kricher, *Balance of Nature*, 58–59.

10. "Losers die and winners eat. The honey bird, skunklike mammal and hunter . . . are predators and the hive is prey. But that's not the whole cast of characters. The bees and their honey wouldn't exist without flowers, but the flowers wouldn't exist without bees, and so on. Put it this way: Competitions for feeding and breeding take place in an arena. The arena is a habitat. The fittest panther in the jungle is a goner if its habitat goes. And what is a habitat? It's an intricate, complicated web of interdependencies." Jacobs, *Nature of Economies*, 21–22.

11. Natural selection: "A complex process in which the total environment determines which members of a species survive to reproduce and so pass on their genes to the next generation." Allaby, *Dictionary of Ecology*.

12. "Natural selection will act on species leading to changes in genotype and, thus, phenotype. The mechanism is natural selection on heritable characteristics coupled with slight variability in the heritable characteristics. This theory is based on the Malthusian law of exponential growth in the absence of controls on growth, heritable characteristics that influence survival, and the selective process related to differential survival." Dodds, *Laws, Theories and Patterns*, 23–24.

weeded out. Variations can alternatively be beneficial if they provide a survival advantage.[13] When the organisms that hold advantageous genes reproduce, they pass the adaptation on to their offspring.[14] Natural selection produces a genetic makeup that determines anatomy, physiology, and behaviour.[15]

The logic of ecosystems is thus: competition for scarce resources leads to natural selection, where those organisms better adapted to ecosystem conditions survive and reproduce,[16] leading to evolutionary change.[17] All participants are equally subject to their forces; systems do not play favorites.[18]

13. "Stated formally, natural selection occurs whenever individuals with heritable variations differ in the number of surviving offspring they have compared to other individuals in the population (in other words, they differ in their *relative fitness*). Natural selection occurs most commonly and strongly when organisms inherit rare, harmful variations, like haemophilia (the inability to form blood clots), that impair an individual's ability to survive and reproduce. Such traits are less likely to be passed on to the next generation, thus reducing or eliminating them from the population. This sort of filter is called negative selection and often leads to a lack of change over time within a population, maintaining the status quo. Occasionally, however, positive selection occurs when an organism inherits by chance an *adaptation*, a new, heritable feature that helps it survive and reproduce better than its competitors. Adaptive features, by their very nature, tend to increase in frequency from generation to generation, causing change over time." Lieberman, *Story of the Human Body*, 9 (emphasis in original, footnotes omitted).

14. "Individuals vary genetically within populations. This variation will ultimately influence who survives when it is crunch time. Those variants most suited to whatever the environment imposes will tend to survive and reproduce better than those with different traits." Kricher, *Balance of Nature*, 57–58.

15. "Natural selection is the process responsible for adaptation. . . . Selection acts on anatomy, physiology, and, in animals, behavior. It is the force in nature that quite literally shapes all living things. It explains why African lions (Panthera leo) have such long canine teeth and powerful jaws; why certain wasps paralyze spiders and then lay their eggs on them; why red mangrove trees (Rhisophora mangle) have stilted roots; why some flowers are tubular in shape and red in colour; why some molds produce chemicals that inhibit bacterial growth." Kricher, *Balance of Nature*, 57. "Nothing in biology makes sense except in light of evolution." Lieberman, *Story of the Human Body*, 365.

16. "Natural selection is a purposeless process but an efficacious one. Impersonal, blind to the future, it has no goals, only results. Its sole standards of valuation are survival and reproductive success. From scattershot variations, culled and accreted, it produces pragmatic forms of order. Its driving factors are hyperfecundity and mortal competition; its products and by-products are adaptation, complexity, and diversity." Quammen, "Evolution and Intelligent Design," 6.

17. "Ecology is a branch of evolutionary biology." Kricher, *Balance of Nature*, x; "[E] volution provides the basis for ecology, or at least is a strong pattern driving it." Dodds, *Laws, Theories and Patterns*, 26.

18. "It is significant that one of the commonest objections to competition is that it is "blind." It is not irrelevant to recall that to the ancients blindness was an attribute of their deity of justice. Although competition and justice may have little else in common, it is as much a commendation of competition as of justice that it is no respecter of persons." Hayek, *Road to Serfdom*, 101.

To say that organisms compete for scarce resources is not to suggest that they are always engaged in direct physical struggle.[19] Conflict between organisms can indeed be direct, violent, and deadly, such as when predators consume prey. However, there are many ways to compete,[20] and competition in ecosystems encompasses a diverse array of adaptations and strategies. Survival does not necessarily depend on being the largest, fastest, or most ferocious, but on being effectively adapted to the requirements of the environment in which the organism lives.[21] Relationships between organisms cover the spectrum between conflict and coexistence: predation, parasitism, symbiosis, mutual dependence and cooperation.[22]

Ecosystems have no purposes, interests, or goals, only dynamics and consequences.[23] Organisms succeed in ecosystems by surviving to reproduce, but an ecosystem cannot succeed or fail. Evolution is always "correct" because it is dictated by and is a reflection of interactions and adaptations.

19. "Many are born, but not all survive to reproduce. Those that do are a select, non-random subset of the original cohort. Because individuals differ genetically, the population evolves as environments change in various ways. . . . Darwin recognized that fitness is largely a metaphorical term and need not literally mean 'nature red in tooth and claw.' Organisms may struggle against each other, against other species, or against the elements. But ultimately it will be the genetic endowment of the various individuals that will weigh most heavily in the struggle for existence and the ultimate survival of the fittest." Kricher, *Balance of Nature*, 59–60.

20. For example, competition may occur "between individuals of the same species (infraspecific competition), or between different species (interspecific competition) at the same trophic level, in which the growth and survival of one or all species or individuals is affected adversely. The competitive mechanisms may be direct (active) . . . or indirect, when a common resource is scarce." Allaby, "Competition," 100.

21. "Some people erroneously think that natural selection means 'survival of the fittest.' Darwin never used that phrase . . . nor would he have, because natural selection is better described as "survival of the fitter." Natural selection doesn't produce perfection; it only weeds out those unlucky enough to be less fit than others." Lieberman, *Story of the Human Body*, 365.

22. For example, some species of predators hunt in packs while others are solitary. Each is an adaptive behaviour. Zebras are one of many prey species that travel in herds, providing collective protection from predators. Cooperation occurs because of competition, not in spite of it. Cooperation in ecosystems is never universal; cooperation allows organisms to join forces against challenges to their survival. In no ecosystems do organisms cooperate for the mutual good of all.

23. "Natural selection is a purposeless process but an efficacious one. Impersonal, blind to the future, it has no goals, only results. From scattershot variations, culled and accreted, it produces pragmatic forms of order. Its driving factors are hyperfecundity and mortal competition; its products and by-products are adaptation, complexity, and diversity." Quammen, "Evolution and Intelligent Design," 6.

MARKETS

A hunter kills a deer. A woodworker makes a set of chairs. The hunter already has meat for the winter, and the woodworker already has chairs in her house. The result: a trade.[24]

Like ecosystems, markets do not really exist except as the aggregate results of a set of interactions. They are not collections of goods, or buyers or sellers, or places where things are bought and sold.[25] Like ecosystems, markets have dynamics but no goals. They do not exist to accomplish an objective. Both systems operate according to their own immutable characteristics and rules. Markets arise spontaneously whenever people think they will be better off by trading.

People trade when both parties perceive a benefit. Buyers trade $4 for a bag of apples if they want apples more than they want to keep their $4. Value is subjective. Perhaps they want the apples if they are fresh, or if they are a preferred variety, or if there are no comparable apples nearby for a better price. For whatever reason, they prefer the apples to the other goods or services they might be able to acquire for $4.

Laws and governments can make markets more stable and efficient, such as by enforcing contracts and creating a supply of money, but they create neither the activity of trading nor the market dynamics that the transactions create.[26] State initiatives make modern economies complex and no doubt laws and regulations facilitate and affect modern economies in many ways. However, a market is not a place or a legal structure but the dynamics of a collection of transactions. It does not exist before or independently of the transactions within it. The transactions make the market. Transactions are not created by governments but by the parties who enter into them.

24. "Give me that which I want, and you shall have this which you want, is the meaning of every such offer; and it is in this manner that we obtain from one another the far greater part of those good offices which we stand in need of. It is not from the benevolence of the butcher, the brewer, or the baker that we expect our dinner, but from their regard to their own interest. We address ourselves, not to their humanity but to their self-love, and never talk to them of our own necessities but of their advantages." Smith, *Wealth of Nations*, 7.

25. "The market system is not a place or a thing or even a collection of things. It is a set of activities of distinctive pattern." Lindblom, *Market System*, 52.

26. Ashworth, *Economy of Nature*, 116.

TURTLES ALL THE WAY DOWN: BENEFICIAL MARKETS AND DESIRABLE ENVIRONMENTAL OUTCOMES

People have preferences for particular kinds of economic and environmental results. Some are apt to condemn "free markets" because those markets do not achieve the outcomes that they want. Unencumbered markets, the argument goes, obscure government's ability to regulate to achieve desirable distributions and optimal results.

But markets do not have a purpose. They are merely the dynamics of a collection of voluntary transactions. Whatever results they produce is what you get. Those results may be advantageous or detrimental to the financial interests of certain players, but they are not incorrect. "Market failure" is a label for an outcome that you do not like. For example, over time in a tight market with limited supply, buyers may pay increasingly higher prices for homes and create a bubble that eventually bursts when prices fall precipitously. Homeowners then may hold property that is worth less than the mortgage debt they owe. That may be a bad outcome for many of the people, but it is not a market failure. It is the systemic result of many transactions for homes over time. Prices go up and down, sometimes gradually and sometimes suddenly. The supply of housing changes and so does demand, sometimes in lockstep and sometimes in opposite directions. Interest rates and inflation reflect economic conditions. The desire for markets that are stable, growing modestly and producing economic gains across a broad social spectrum is a subjective preference for a social order in which economic gains are distributed in accordance with a particular set of ideological sensibilities. Markets reflect aggregate results of multiple transactions, and each of those transactions expresses the individual choices of their participants. The aggregate results are what they are. A desire to fashion other results is just a preference.

Ecosystems do not exist to serve a purpose either. Yet governments manage ecosystems (or try to) to achieve outcomes that match the preferences of their constituencies. Sometimes that means aspiring to "natural" conditions, and sometimes it does not. Environmental management is a discretionary process in which regulators can make decisions one situation at a time by weighing political costs and benefits, thereby pursuing indeterminate and variable policy objectives. Such objectives reflect preferences. They are turtles all the way down. The preferences embedded in such decisions are rarely identified or acknowledged, much less justified.

VIOLENCE: WHAT DISTINGUISHES ECOSYSTEMS FROM MARKETS

Ecosystems and markets share many features, but they differ in one important respect. Violence plays an important role in ecosystems, but is not a part of voluntary market exchange. Ecosystems are arenas for mortal combat.[27] Lions eat antelopes if they can catch them. Nothing prevents taking a dead antelope from a lion except the lion's response. There are no restrictions on survival strategies, and organisms do not respect the interests, habitats, or lives of other organisms, who succeed or fail, live or die, as their genetically determined physiology and behavior allow. Every life feeds on the death of others, whether animal or plant, and those better adapted to their circumstances survive to reproduce. Ecosystems have rules, but they are not rules in the same sense as human laws or codes of political governance. Ecosystems exist in a state that political scientists would call "anarchy." No statutes restrict the actions of organisms. No legal or moral codes govern behavior. No police walk the trails and no courts enforce judgments. "The law of the jungle" prevails. If human actions diminish the habitat of bees, then according to the logic of ecosystems, the bees adapt or perish. In ecosystem terms, either result will do. The ecosystem does not benefit or suffer either way. Neither result is morally preferable since morality has no role in ecosystems. No right or wrong exists.

Markets, in contrast, proceed upon the judgment of the transacting parties that they are better off to trade than to fight. The hunter did not shoot the woodworker to get chairs, and the woodworker traded for meat instead of stealing it. They chose to trade because it made them better off than fighting. The reasons are their own. Perhaps they were friends, colleagues, or allies. Perhaps they believed that harming other people is wrong. Perhaps they hoped to have an ongoing trading relationship. Perhaps they

27. "The forest, as usual, is quiet apart from the muted sounds of rustling leaves, buzzing insects, and a few chirping birds. Suddenly, pandemonium breaks out as three chimpanzees tear through the trees high above the forest floor, leaping spectacularly from branch to branch, hair bristling, screaming wildly as they chase a group of colobus monkeys at breakneck speed. In less than a minute, an experienced older chimp makes a magnificent jump, catches a terrified monkey that was heading his way, and dashes its brains out against a tree. The hunt is over as suddenly as it started. As the victor rips his prey into pieces and starts to consume the flesh, other chimps hoot with excitement. Any humans watching, however, are likely to be shocked. Observing chimps can be disturbing, not just because of the violence, but also because we prefer to think of them as gentle, intelligent cousins. Sometimes they seem mirrors of our better selves, but when hunting, chimps reflect humanity's darker tendencies in their craving for flesh, their capacity for violence, and even their lethal use of teamwork and strategy." Lieberman, *Story of the Human Body*, 25–26.

feared injury or retribution from fighting. Perhaps trading was less work than fighting. For whatever reason, they chose to trade. This choice is not universal. People have traded throughout human history, but they have also fought. Trading is no more "natural" or inbred than fighting, but neither is it is less so. When people choose to fight, they are no longer part of a market. Contracts consist of voluntary bargains. Force is employed only by those enforcing the rules of the market and not by its participants. Thus, markets are like ecosystems with the violence removed.[28] Only persons are subject to the rule of no-force and only in relation to each other. Hawks are not prohibited from eating mice, nor people from eating chickens. But people may not kill each other, nor take each other's chickens. Two systems of competition carry on in parallel, one in which any form of action or adaptation is fair game (ecosystems) and the other in which physical coercion may not be employed (markets). Markets are like ecosystems with the violence removed. They are the kinder, gentler version of ecosystems.

ONLY TWO CHOICES, ONLY ONE LEGITIMATE RULE—AND THE OTHER RULES THAT FOLLOW

The choice is ecosystems or markets. In ecosystems, there are no rules. In free markets, there is only one: no force. Any other rule is merely a preference: turtles all the way down. The logic is as follows:

(a) In the wild, organisms compete for scarce resources. Those organisms better adapted to conditions survive and reproduce. Their interactions constitute ecosystems. No legal rules govern behavior and might is right.

(b) Human beings trade spontaneously. Parties transact when they perceive themselves as better off to trade than to fight. Their transactions constitute markets.

(c) Moral values and policy goals are preferences whose inherent validity cannot be established. They are turtles all the way down. Therefore, laws based upon those preferences lack legitimacy.

(d) When governments use might to impose laws and policies that are illegitimate, they unintentionally imitate ecosystems, where might is right. Political constituencies use whatever means necessary to impose their preferences, and their opponents use whatever means necessary

28. "Serious sport . . . is war minus the shooting." Orwell, "Sporting Spirit," 153. Markets are ecosystems minus the violence.

to resist. They are "autonomous" in the ecosystem sense: there are no inherently valid restrictions on behavior. The result is a social order of division and conflict.

(e) The alternative is to model human governance on the other system that exists independently of state preference: markets. If the model for human governance is markets, interactions between people are voluntary. People are "autonomous" in the market sense: they may pursue their own interests without the threat of violence. Instead of imposing illegitimate rules and policies, the state uses force only to prohibit people from imposing force on each other. A plethora of sub-rules follow as corollaries of the rule against coercion: property, consent, criminal offences that punish violence and so on.

(f) There is no third choice. Violence is not right or wrong depending upon the goals being pursued since those goals are merely preferences. Their advocates cannot establish that their goals have inherent validity to the satisfaction of those who disagree. Therefore, giving priority to those objectives is to assert that might is right. If might is right, we are back to ecosystems, where any and all actions are legitimate.

(g) If might is right, anything goes, and the model is ecosystems. If might is not right, force is prohibited, and the model is markets. Choose one and all else follows.

THE ONLY LEGITIMATE RULE AND THE OTHER RULES THAT FOLLOW

If force between people is prohibited, other substantive rules[29] follow as corollaries of that proposition.

(a) Property

A monkey has a banana. If he is lucky, he will eat the banana before a bigger monkey takes it away. The jungle has no prohibitions on the use of force, so the monkey with the banana holds it for only so long as he can resist the

29. When I claim that a prohibition on force is the only legitimate rule, I mean the only substantive rule to govern relations between competent adults. No doubt the administration of a legal system, even a minimalist one, would require other kinds of laws to function. Constitutional rules, court administration, the conduct of elections and procedures to bring legal proceedings are a few of the other categories that would be necessary to give effect to the general rule.

encroachments of other hungry beasts. The monkey has a banana, but he has no property. The story changes if the monkey is a person and coercion is prohibited. Taking the banana by force then constitutes a wrong. Therefore, the holder of the banana must have the right to exclude others from it. That right is called property.

When people trade, they recognize the property interest held by the other party. It is that interest that they wish to obtain. When the woodworker trades chairs for the hunter's meat, she trades "her" chairs for "his" meat. The trade would not occur without a mutual understanding of the possession that both hold over their respective stuff. Sometimes those interests are recognized and protected by laws. However, since markets arise even where no property is legally recognized, the notion of property must be prior to the law. Markets have arisen where no legal regime has protected property rights: prehistorical trade, alcohol sales during Prohibition, black markets in the Soviet Union, the modern-day drug trade, smuggling of illicit goods, and the internal markets of prisons. Since trading occurs even in the absence of an approving legal regime, the notion of property must exist independently as well.

There is nothing particularly distinctive about property as a right, except that it relates to things and land. The right to bodily integrity, or the right not to be touched, for example, operate much the same way as a property right, except that they apply to one's own body instead of to a thing. Both provide the ability to prevent others from imposing their will. Property rights do not depend on the argument that they are inherently good or morally righteous. They are not legitimate because they maximize economic welfare, create incentives for self-interested stewardship, or democratize wealth. These are preferences. The case is merely that property is a feature of market systems that arise independently of state design.

(b) Consent

Trades consist of exchange of consent: to trade chairs for meat, to sell labour for money, to be touched, to mate, to arm wrestle, and so on. Without the ability to consent, no trades can be made. Without trades, no markets exist.

(c) Other Corollaries

If force is prohibited, then corollaries are laws that protect people from having force imposed upon them. Laws apply the force of the state to prevent or punish the application of force. A criminal law that prohibits assault is an extension of the general rule. A tax to finance the police department is legitimate if its purpose is to investigate and prosecute violent crimes. Traffic laws prevent people from running each other over. Civil liability compensates for physical injuries caused by the force of others. It is no coincidence that a rule against the use of force is consistent with much of the common law: tort causes of action in battery, false imprisonment, trespass, nuisance, and negligence; the rules of contract; rights of due process in criminal law; and so on.

Illegitimate laws use state coercion to seek other ends such as enforcing moral standards, pursuing social goals or saving people from themselves. A criminal law that prohibits the use of drugs uses state force to prevent an activity in which there is no coercion. A tax to fund the armed forces to protect the peace may be legitimate, but one to take wealth from Peter to give to Paul is not. The legal regimes of modern administrative states consist largely of instrumentalist laws and policies that are inconsistent with the general rule, including tax laws, economic development programs, bankruptcy, patent regimes, mandatory government-run pension plans and environmental management regimes, in which each decision turns on a political determination of the values to be applied.

CONCLUSION: ECOSYSTEMS OR MARKETS ALL THE WAY DOWN

Markets are the peaceful version of ecosystems. They transform life and death into buy and sell. Unfettered markets are closer to a state of nature than is any other kind of political system. In ecosystems and markets, there is no notion of common good, equality of outcome, or distributive justice. There is no requirement to share, except when sharing is a self-interested adaptation borne of competition for scarce resources. No one expropriates a squirrel's nuts for redistribution. The squirrel loses his nuts only to larger squirrels who take them by force.

Critics who laud ecosystems while condemning markets are in error. If environmentalists really wanted to make markets more like ecosystems, or to make human society more compatible with the law of the jungle, they would not insist on ever-increasing regulation and expansion of the managerial state. Instead, they would propose to remove restrictions on the use of force in human affairs. To extol ecosystems but fault features of markets that most closely reproduce the dynamics of ecosystems reflects a misunderstanding of the nature of these systems. The use of state coercion to redistribute resources opposes system dynamics, since redistribution depends on the taking of property, and any transfer that is not voluntary is coercive. Therefore, any system based upon redistribution is based upon the coercive use of force by the state. State force exercises control over system outcomes, something that no single organism can do in ecosystems, and no single buyer or seller can do in markets.

Either might is right or it is not. If it is, then human society is subject to the law of the jungle where people are at liberty to fight like animals if they choose to do so. If it is not, then human society is a marketplace where people transact voluntarily, and the state may justifiably use force only to prevent or punish the application of force.

There is no third choice. Some might insist that coercion is not categorically wrong, but that it can be right or wrong depending upon the other goals to be pursued. Those goals are merely preferences. They are turtles all the way down. I do not maintain that other rules will not be passed and enforced using the established machinery of government but only that they have no claim to legitimacy, any more than other rules that might have been chosen instead. If force is used to pursue those preferences, why would others not use force to resist? Such a choice results in a free-for-all. If state force is right only because it cannot be resisted, that means that might is right. The administrative welfare state prevails not because it is justified morally or socially but because it has managed to secure a monopoly on violence.

QUESTIONS FOR DISCUSSION AND DEBATE

1. Is there any moral proposition that can be proven to be objectively true, using logic and/or evidence?
2. What does it mean to "harm" an ecosystem?
3. Are there any voluntary transactions that do not make both parties subjectively better off?
4. If markets are the kinder, gentler version of ecosystems, why do many environmentalists demand that governments exercise more control over them?
5. Does might make right?

BIBLIOGRAPHY

Allaby, Michael. *A Dictionary of Ecology*. 4th ed. Oxford: Oxford University Press, 2010.
———. *Basics of Environmental Science*. London: Routledge, 2000.

———. "Competition." In the *Oxford Dictionary of Ecology*, 3rd ed. Oxford: Oxford University Press, 2005.

Ashworth, William. *The Economy of Nature: Rethinking the Connections between Ecology and Economics.* Boston: Houghton Mifflin, 1995.

Boaz, David. *The Libertarian Reader: Classic and Contemporary Readings from Lao-tzu to Milton Friedman.* New York: Free Press, 1997.

Botkin, Daniel. "Adjusting Law to Nature's Discordant Harmonies" *Duke Environmental Law & Policy Forum* 7 (1996) 25–38.

Dodds, W. K. *Laws, Theories and Patterns in Ecology.* Berkeley, CA: University of California Press, 2009.

Hayek, Friedrich. *The Road to Serfdom.* Chicago: University of Chicago Press, 1944.

Holling, C. S. "Resilience and Stability of Ecological Systems." *Annual Review of Ecology and Systematics* 4 (1973) 1–23.

Jacobs, Jane. *The Nature of Economies.* New York: Vintage, 2000.

Kricher, John C. *The Balance of Nature: Ecology's Enduring Myth.* Princeton: Princeton University Press, 2009.

Lieberman, David. *The Story of the Human Body: Evolution, Health and Disease.* New York: Pantheon, 2013.

Lincoln, Roger J., et al. *A Dictionary of Ecology, Evolution, and Systematics.* Cambridge: Cambridge University Press, 1982.

Lindblom, Charles E. *The Market System: What It Is, How It Works, and What to Make of It.* New Haven: Yale University Press, 2001.

Marmor, Andrei. "An Essay on the Objectivity of Law." In *Analyzing Law: New Essays in Legal Theory*, edited by Brian Bix. Oxford: Clarendon Press, 1998.

Odum, Eugene P. *Ecology and Our Endangered Life-Support Systems.* Sunderland, MA: Sinauer, 1989.

———. "Great Ideas for Ecology for the 1990s." *Bioscience* 42 (1992) 542.

———. "The Strategy of Ecosystem Development." *Science* 164 (1969) 262–70.

Orwell, George. "The Sporting Spirit." In *Shooting an Elephant and Other Essays.* New York: Harcourt, Brace & World, 1945.

Posner, Richard. *Economic Analysis of Law.* 7th ed. New York: Wolters Kluwer, 2007.

Posner, Richard. "The Problematics of Moral and Legal Theory." *Harvard Law Review* 111 (1997) 1637–717.

Quammen, David. "Evolution and Intelligent Design: Mr. Darwin's Abominable Volume." *Virginia Quarterly Review* 82 (2006) 4–6.

Rapanos v United States, 126 S Ct 2208 (2006).

Rothchild, Michael. "Economy as Ecosystem." In *The Libertarian Reader: Classic and Contemporary Readings from Lao-tzu to Milton Friedman*, by David Boaz. New York: Free Press, 1997.

Smith, Adam. *An Inquiry into the Nature and Causes of the Wealth of Nations.* Chicago: Encyclopaedia Britannica, 1952.

7

Taking Delight in Science

The Central Role of Beauty

BENJAMIN J. MCFARLAND

INTRODUCTION: HOW CAN BIOCHEMISTRY BE BEAUTIFUL?

As a biochemistry educator, I try to make my courses beautiful. I realize this is not the first adjective most people associate with biochemistry and that aesthetics is not considered a branch of chemistry. Yet I maintain that my field of study is indeed beautiful, and students should be invited to see the world the same way.

Here, I will describe two particular course exercises that introduce my students to the beauty of two natural entities, a beauty that at first is difficult to discern. The first of these teaches protein structure, where the hidden beauty is brought out by an artistic visual language first developed by a philosopher-scientist. The second of these teaches chemical ecology, where a central, crucial, even beautiful role is played by that ungainliest of animals, the wildebeest.

The delight of finding beauty hidden in nature is experienced by philosophers of all sorts, whether natural philosophers (to use the original term for scientists) or by modern academic philosophers. In particular, the

German philosopher and ethicist Robert Spaemann (1927–2018) elaborated on the theme of how we relate to nature through both science and beauty. Three essays by Spaemann, from the early, middle, and late portions of his career, align with the educational exercises from my biochemistry courses.

In the first of these essays, "Nature" (1973), Spaemann writes of the beauty of the repeatability of nature that is at the heart of every scientific experiment and explanation: "In our action, we experience nature as an order of things, the fundamental laws of which our action cannot change; to the contrary, precisely because of their regularity, these laws offer a reliability that we need in order to realize any given aim."[1]

Scientists describe this regularity with stately synonyms for beautiful: elegant, engaging, or fitting. Our minds fit with nature according to structured, repeatable rules, and this fit is beautiful. It takes years of patient study to dig beneath the superficial and isolate the regular rules so one can see the hidden beauty of the world. The sooner this can be brought to students, the sooner they can feel the fit and see the elegant beauty for themselves, internalizing and learning the science. Not every part of every science course can do this for every student. The subjective and occasional nature of beauty means that these moments must be scattered among less beautiful tasks. But every science course should at least have moments where students are invited to open their textbook and perceive a glimmer of beauty.

The teaching of science through beauty is not an incidental activity but is aligned with the very practice of science and even the structure of reason. As Carlo Lancellotti, professor of mathematics at CUNY–College of Staten Island, writes:

> The scientist does not study nature because it is useful; he studies it because he delights in it, and he delights in it because it is beautiful. If nature were not beautiful, it would not be worth knowing, and if nature were not worth knowing, life would not be worth living. Of course I do not speak here of that beauty that strikes the senses, the beauty of quality and appearances; not that I undervalue such beauty, far from it, but it has nothing to do with science; I mean that deeper beauty coming from the harmonious order of the parts, and that a pure intelligence can grasp. . . . In fact, when science is no longer rooted in reason's original attitude, i.e. wonder in front of the harmonious forms of creation, science immediately suffers. It succumbs to technical formalism, sociological trends, external pressure for technological returns, etc. Conversely, the great scientific revolutions

1. Spaemann, "Nature," 35.

> were started by people whose imaginations were fired up, in one way or another, by beauty.[2]

The task of the educator is to help students become "fired up" by beauty in the same way. Reviewing my own decades of teaching in the classroom and the laboratory as a professor in a department of chemistry and biochemistry, two particular cases stand out in which the students were introduced to hidden beauty. Each of these two cases is illuminated by an essay by Robert Spaemann, showing how beauty, once located and illuminated, played a central role in connecting minds to nature through science.

THE PHILOSOPHER-SCIENTIST WHO REVEALED THE BEAUTY OF PROTEIN STRUCTURE

Our curriculum includes a three-course biochemistry sequence: two quarters of lecture with laboratory followed by a third quarter seminar. The first topic that belongs primarily to the subdiscipline of biochemistry is protein structure. A foundation in the three-dimensional determination of atomic coordinates in proteins prepares students to understand specific chemical reactions, including how those atoms catalyze reactions in enzymes and transport oxygen in the blood. One can argue that biochemistry truly began only when the structures of biological macromolecules (proteins and DNA) were first determined at atomic resolution in the 1950s and 1960s.

This topic is also important to me as a teacher. My PhD program was titled "Biomolecular Structure and Design," and I work in the field of protein chemistry. I determined the structure of a protein using X-ray crystallography as a post-doctoral fellow, and my research continues to use structural information to guide experiments. The laboratory sections I oversee include authentic research tasks in this area, including a protein preparation project adapted from my post-doctoral experience that culminates in protein crystallization trials.[3] Students therefore need a strong foundation in understanding protein structure because they will use these concepts both in the lecture and laboratory for the remainder of the course and beyond.

Spaemann's mid-career essay "Education as an Introduction to Reality" (1988) summarizes the educational goals of the biochemistry course well:

> To educate means to introduce a person into one's own world, to interpret the world, to train a person to make distinctions, whether it be the distinction between a blackbird and a robin,

2. Lancellotti, "Redemption of Scientific Reason."
3. Peterson et al., "Preparative Protein Production," 986–89.

> between a brook and a canal, and between a Mercedes and a Volkswagen, or on the other hand the distinction between the important and the trivial, between the beautiful and the ugly, and between good and evil."[4]

It is easy for me to find examples for how protein structure is important rather than trivial, given its immediate relevance to the biomedical and pharmaceutical industries that many students are seeking to enter. But it's harder for students to distinguish proteins as beautiful rather than ugly. The raw data of X-ray crystallography is an electron density map coming from the protein's long chain curled in on itself like a ball of yarn. The chain is made of hundreds of asymmetric amino acid residues linked by amide bonds, which all add up to make thousands of atoms in an asymmetric assembly. It is difficult to see the beauty in the raw data—it is difficult to see anything in that confusion of atoms and bonds.

The raw data of electron density is made beautiful by data interpretation and modeling. Protein chemists, like all scientists, process data into a simpler, comprehensible form. We calculate a model of atoms and bonds that we then fit into the experimental electron density, validating it through mathematical tests. We rarely show every atom in a structure, but we select which atoms to show and how to show them in order to make our points. The subdiscipline of molecular modeling can even apply physical parameters like spring constants to the bonds, add energy, shake up the model, and see how it moves.[5]

Because the model is a calculated construct, the scientist can choose how to represent its microscopic (indeed, nanoscopic) visual elements: What colors should the atoms be? Should the surface be opaque to show its shape or transparent to show the elements beneath it? Should the main chain of the protein be emphasized or the side chains branching off of it? Making these choices well can result in an elegant model that emphasizes the function of the molecule. The scientist has the freedom to select and color the model in the same way that an artist has that freedom with a sculpture based on real life, and the end result can be beautiful. Many protein scientists have accounts on Instagram to show off the beauty of their structural images.

Scientists have developed several visual innovations to help the human brain comprehend a protein structure. Early protein structure models were carved from wood or assembled from metal sticks by hand.[6] The three-dimensional models were represented on two-dimensional paper

4. Spaemann, "Education as an Introduction to Reality," 114.
5. This is discussed in another class I teach, Survey of Physical Chemistry.
6. De Chadarevian, "John Kendrew and Myoglobin," 1136–43.

with beautiful drawings made by artists like Irving Geis. Scientists drew stereograms where a left-eye model was printed next to a right-eye model, so that with a little practice one could focus each eye on a different picture. The images would appear to merge and then appear in three dimensions on the printed page as the brain reconstructed the extra dimension.[7]

The immense complexity of proteins has always required computers for calculating the structural models.[8] As computational power increased, it was employed for representing the structural models too. The use of computers for video games (as well as more practical uses) improved the technological representation of virtual objects, which applied easily to the set of atomic coordinates making up a protein structure model. The atoms could be selected, hidden, colored, or rotated easily in the laboratory, on widely available hardware and software.

From the time I began to teach biochemistry in 2003, I have been able to bring this practice from the research lab into my teaching labs. We set up laptops in the lab and students run the model visualization software PyMol for a multi-week project. The first few years, we ran general exercises visualizing the proteins from a common disease like tuberculosis. Then I developed computational "dry-lab" projects that related to my biochemical "wet-lab" research. Now students design protein fragments on their own laptops, which we compare using online calculations and prediction tools, using these to choose some fragments to make in the next course in the biochemistry sequence.

The students write reports from this exercise that are graded according to a rubric that, in a hidden way, includes beauty. The instructions state each picture of protein structure should be edited to "answer some kind of question about the structure clearly and simply. Remove extra information by zooming in, hiding, or covering up with a surface. Good pictures help start a good report." These pieces of advice are implicitly aesthetic. Students learn that an elegant image captures the imagination and communicates truth with beauty.

Delight is difficult to quantify, but I have observed it in class, as the students work and decide on colors and viewing angles. They remember this exercise much later, which I attribute to the freedom they have to explore relevant questions, but also to the beauty of the protein structures that they arrange, color, and render. In the later courses in the sequence they return to these concepts in order to make images for new proteins, and some have used it for other courses as well. This exercise gives the students space to

7. This is the same idea used in the Viewmaster toy and red-blue 3D glasses.

8. De Chadarevian, "John Kendrew and Myoglobin," 1136–43.

create through the artistic impulse in a scientific laboratory, giving them distinctive experiences that they retain for years to come.

The most common representational mode used by students for full-protein pictures is called the "cartoon" mode on the software we use. This mode removes side chain atoms and streamlines main chain atoms into blocky ribbons and arrows. The invisible arrows are the "bones" of the protein. This idealized backbone points to the protein's function better than the chaotic, superficial reality of showing everything. Subjectively, I believe this representation is the most beautiful of the possibilities, in part because it was deliberately and artistically designed to be so. This communicative visual innovation was made by a biochemist with a degree in philosophy.

Jane S. Richardson invented this ribbon diagram representation, first publishing it in a review article in 1981 as a hand-drawn diagram illustrating "a uniform set of graphical conventions" of "spiral ribbons" and "arrows" to represent the two basic kinds of secondary structures found in proteins.[9] Others soon picked up on the representation, shown by more than four thousand citations of the original article, and Richardson's own use of ribbon diagrams to represent most of the fifty-four "notable" crystal structures that she chose for an important 2014 review.[10]

Richardson's writing style shows a personal focus on beauty both in art and science. First is Richardson's prioritization of beauty for communication, shown in the vivid adjectives in her writing. In the 1981 paper introducing the ribbon diagrams, Richardson described the electron maps as fitting the following description:

> like intricate, branched coral, intertwined but never touching. β-sheets do not show a stiff repetitious regularity but flow in graceful, twisting curves, and even the α-helix is regular more in the manner of a flower stem, whose branching nodes show the influences of environment, developmental history, and the evolution of each separate part to match its own idiosyncratic function.[11]

Richardson uses beauty to communicate in delightful prose, while using abstract concepts to place this beauty into an interdisciplinary context of environment, history, and evolution. She notes, "The vast accumulation of information about protein structures provides a fresh opportunity to do descriptive natural history, as though we had been presented with the tropical jungles of a totally new planet." She situates her language and diagrams

9. Richardson, "Anatomy and Taxonomy of Protein Structure," 167–339.

10. Richardson and Richardson. "Biophysical Highlights," 510–25.

11. Richardson, "Anatomy and Taxonomy of Protein Structure," 167–339.

as a taxonomy of proteins that echoes the taxonomy of species. Richardson performs these acts of classification using words and pictures to group and distinguish elements of the natural world, so that beauty helps accomplish the philosophical and pedagogical task of understanding.

Richardson's educational background explains why so many elements of philosophy and beauty are found in her scientific publications. Her bachelor's degree from Swarthmore College was in philosophy, with a minor in physics, followed by a master's degree from Harvard University in philosophy. She then joined a laboratory at Massachusetts Institute of Technology to work alongside her husband, David, with whom she continues to work today.

Ricahrdson's interests in classical philosophy interleaved with her biochemical investigations when her early classification work on protein structure found a repeating pattern called the "Greek Key" motif, so named for its similarity to the decorative border frequently used in Hellenistic art.[12] Biochemists continue to discuss the structural characteristics of "Greek Key" motifs in proteins, using the term the Greeks invented for the sake of beauty.

Richardson's work shows that the act of using language to classify the natural world is enhanced by beautiful diagrams. Her original design inspired decades of scientific investigations of protein structure in a manner that, like the diagrams themselves, accomplishes its purpose beneath the surface of things. This coincides with the point in Spaemann's "Education as an Introduction to Reality" that the center of the act of education and therefore reality is beauty itself:

> But beauty is not just some ornament to life; it is the very meaning of life. There is nothing more serious, nothing that is more worth pursuing, than beauty. . . . Here reality appears wholly as it truly is, not as foreign, as begrudging, as frustrating, but as awe-inspiring, powerful, and at the same time as friendly and brightly lit. Whoever has not experienced it in this way will think that celebration is an escape from reality into an illusory world, that it is just another sort of discotheque. The only thing to do with such a person is to invite him to celebrate along with us and in this way to discover for himself what the difference is between illusion and reality.[13]

Spaemann's comment on the "brightly lit" nature of the beautiful reality given to the student reflects the fact that the ribbon diagrams made on

12. Richardson, "β-Sheet Topology," 495–500.

13. Spaemann, "Education as an Introduction to Reality," 118–19.

the computer by students are themselves brightly colored and lit by virtual spotlights (which can be rearranged to improve the beauty of the image). Richardson's ribbon diagrams bring aesthetics to the natural world in a way that goes beyond simply putting a bow on it, illuminating the very core of the proteins' structure and bringing out the nature of the real, physical interactions inside. This is a beauty that teaches, letting scientists and students understand and appreciate protein chemistry.

THE MEEK BEAST THAT HOLDS THE SERENGETI TOGETHER

The second example of beauty in biochemistry is not structural but dynamic and comes at the beginning of the first course in our biochemistry sequence. The only pre-requisite for this course is completion of a year of organic chemistry. As a result, students arrive with a wide variety of experiences in other biology and chemistry topics, and no two students bring the same experiences. Early exercises in biochemistry must allow for students to refresh their diverse prior knowledge and start to fit it into a biochemical context, before they know the specific structures of amino acids or nucleotides.

This can be accomplished through chemical biology as an introduction to biochemistry. We focus on the familiar chemical elements, in the context of familiar animals linked in an ecosystem. Each animal is a homeostatic chemical system that eats elements as food and excretes elements as waste. Tracing the paths of three primary elements (carbon, hydrogen, and oxygen) and a handful of secondary elements (nitrogen, sulfur, phosphorus, and various metals) through the ecosystem sets up patterns of dynamic thinking used throughout biochemistry. Later, students can apply these patterns of thinking for metabolic pathways, which are similar dynamic cycles with more complex structures as intermediates.

Another goal of this course is to introduce students to the primary literature, so that each test unit includes an original research paper from a peer-reviewed journal. For these topics, I first assign a 2017 *Proceedings of the National Academy of Science* paper titled "Annual mass drownings of the Serengeti wildebeest migration influence nutrient cycling and storage in the Mara River."[14] Students can read this paper (as introduced by various news articles published at the time) without specific biochemical knowledge, and can understand the graphs with general chemistry and biology concepts. This paper's final figure explicitly shows the elemental fluxes between different parts of the ecosystem, even scaling the arrows to show greater or lesser

14. Subalusky et al., "Annual Mass Drownings," 7647–52.

fluxes, measured in simple units of metric tons. Students learn not only the science, but also how to read a scientific paper, preparing them for later biochemistry papers assigned in the course.

In this paper, scientific concepts interrogate a complex ecosystem and reveal the dynamic interplay of a few elements within. This is itself another example of hidden biochemical elegance and beauty: instead of Richardson's cartoon arrows within proteins, students learn to see chemical fluxes of carbon, nitrogen, and phosphorus among biological and geological entities.

At the center of this elegant system is an animal that very few would consider beautiful and that most would overlook: the wildebeest, *Connochaetes taurinus*. But the wildebeest plays a hidden, central, and important role, showing that true biochemical beauty can be found within an unlikely biological species.

This central role of the wildebeest in the Serengeti Mara ecosystem has been recently described by *National Geographic*, a classic nature magazine known for its aesthetically pleasing photography. In the December 2021 issue, three articles and two photoessays focus on this system, including "The Wildebeest: An Unlikely King."

Although these five articles are the centerpiece of the issue, I could find no pictures from it on the magazine's Instagram feed. The beauty appears in other media. The issue is associated with a Disney+ series, and a reviewer of the series found the beauty to be important enough to put in the sub-headline of the review, that this series is about "experiencing Earth's beauty and oddness."[15]

One of the *National Geographic* photoessays juxtaposes beauty with tragedy. A two-page photo spread shows the wildebeest herd mixed with white cattle egrets.[16] This wide-angle image was cropped and used for the cover of the issue, showing it conveyed a certain beauty. The reader who turns the page is greeted with a two-page photo of a muddy river full of carcasses and dingy vultures.[17]

Flipping through these pages, the photos inform each other, hinting at a beauty hidden in this movement from life to death. The images are interconnected as nature itself is an interconnected system with the wildebeest providing a physical connection between the two. The same wildebeest that provides a perch for egrets in life provides a meal for vultures in death.

The medium body mass of the wildebeest plus its status as prey rather than predator means it is too big to be solitary but too small to stay resident

15. Fienberg, "Disney+'s 'Welcome to Earth.'"
16. James, "Guardians of the Land," 52–53.
17. James, "Guardians of the Land," 54–55.

in the same place: therefore, it must migrate in large herds, crossing the Mara River in search of food, sometimes dying in the effort.[18] The migrating wildebeest carries the elements needed for life in its body, which are released after it dies, feeding other parts of the ecosystem.

Subalusky et al., the reading assigned to the students, teaches the hidden chemical migrations underneath the obvious biological migrations. The mass drownings in the Mara River provide soft-tissue food for vultures and crocodiles that is gone in a matter of weeks. The main finding of Subalusky et al. is that even more is provided at a chemical level: the bones of the wildebeests pour out phosphorus to the system for years as the skeletons dissolve and release phosphate into the ecosystem. Even the lowly biofilm plays an important role in the cycles of feeding and dying.

This chemical cycle mirrors biological cycles that depend on the wildebeest. The *National Geographic* articles describe how wildebeests foster forests: the grazing herds keep grass short, causing fewer and shorter fires, allowing more trees to grow. Similar connections can be found for connections between wildebeests and elephants, butterflies, and dung beetles. Most keystone species are predators, but the wildebeest is special in that it is both a keystone species and prey. This keystone is hidden, even rejected and overlooked by previous generations of scientists, unassuming as a lamb.

The importance, both chemical and otherwise, of the wildebeest to the Serengeti ecosystem gives those who examine the system an expanded sense of what is beautiful. The tragedy and death in the life cycle of the wildebeest herd should not obscure the beauty of the intricate cycles present for those with eyes to see and experiments to investigate. As Kevin L. Hughes states, "Tragedy means more than "a story ending badly"; instead, it is a vision of life that holds together the beauty and the failure of all our "human, all too human" endeavor."[19] *National Geographic* provides this vision by juxtaposing beautiful images with tragic ones. Biochemistry education can provide this vision by assigning this beautiful science in a tragic context to be read and discussed by students.

Now that we know that the wildebeest is so ecologically important, we can use that knowledge to preserve the ecosystem. Before we knew this, the scientific instinct was to control wildebeest herds. In the 1960s, many scientists "believed wildlife populations needed to be manipulated to stay in balance."[20] Two ecologists, Tony Sinclair and Mike Norton-Griffiths, argued against this and first demonstrated many of the ecological connections

18. Gwin, "Wildebeest, An Unlikely King," 67.

19. Hughes, "Western Civ Doesn't Need."

20. Gwin, "Wildebeest, an Unlikely King," 66.

that make the wildebeest an animal "singularly crucial to the structure and health of an ecosystem."[21] These crucial links are mediated by chemistry.

Spaemann's famous early essay, titled simply "Nature" (1973), gives a philosophical basis for letting ecosystems be, so that hidden keystones like the wildebeest can play their biological and chemical roles. Spaemann writes:

> The fact that it is against nature to remain in nature is a paradox that can be resolved only if we understand the concept of "nature" in a teleological manner and understand man as a being that is ordered by nature to transcend nature. . . . We genuinely transcend nature only when we preserve it in action as its measure. . . . The fundamental act of freedom is that of refraining from dominating what we are able to dominate, the act of "letting be": Only by reciprocally acknowledging the other and letting the other be free does the natural being transcend nature.[22]

Spaemann wrote this essay at the same time that ecologists were first recognizing the hidden links of chemistry, which have only been reinforced with the passage of time by papers like Subalusky et al.

CONCLUSION: THE INVISIBLE REALITY OF NATURAL BEAUTY

A third, late essay by Spaemann, not about science but art, emphasizes the beauty and importance of the hidden parts of a system. In "Art Imitates Nature?" (2007), Spaemann writes of the same distinctions he discussed in his 1988 essay about education:

> What the art seeks to show remains invisible. . . . It is a sense of spatial and temporal dimensions and of the reality of distinctions that are present in what we see but without appearing. . . .. When images take the place of what exists in itself and pours itself out, i.e. the place of nature, then art is given the task of leaving behind meager signs as traces that lead the one who follows them to the place wherein seeing, hearing, and feeling first come to be. That is, to the original source of life. . . . To imitate nature means to imitate the invisible, which is the fundamental reality.[23]

21. Gwin, "Wildebeest, an Unlikely King." 67.
22. Spaemann, "Nature," 36.
23. Spaemann, "Art Imitates Nature," 210.

We can apply this thinking to science as well as art. Spaemann identifies "the place of nature" as living things existing in themselves and pouring themselves out. The place of the wildebeest is literally to pour out its chemical nutrients into the ecosystem. At the same time, Spaemann's focus on the ability of art to reveal the invisible fits with Richardson's protein chemistry representations. Richardson's artistic, visual language is artificial (emphasis on the "art"), while revealing a deeper natural reality about protein structure and function. Despite invisibility, the hidden keystone species and the hidden ribbon diagrams are both real and beautiful.

To use another example connected to Disney: Spaceship Earth, the huge geodesic sphere at the Epcot theme park looms 180 feet up but actually is deeper than it is tall, because the underground pylons that anchor it against Floridian hurricanes extend 185 feet down.[24] What is hidden is greater than what is seen. Spaemann writes of a similar artistic example:

> The point that we are trying to make here becomes even more evident in the one-kilometer-long rod of polished brass that, on the occasion of a documentary in Kassel, Walter de Maria sunk into a pre-drilled hole. What you see now is a disk of about 50 cm in the earth. The fact that this disk represents the end of this rod is something you have to know in order to develop a feeling for the depth of the earth under our feet. . . . it is the knowledge of what one does not see that is the point.[25]

The knowledge of what is unseen makes art, architecture, biochemistry, ecology, and education that much more beautiful. Science reveals the depth of the chemical cycles beneath our feet and their height above our heads. Beauty is revealed in the importance of these hidden structures, both static and dynamic, discerned by the philosopher-scientist-artist and the ecologist, then taught in the introductory biochemistry courses. Beauty therefore has a crucial role to play not only in the practice of science, but in its teaching as well. It is not merely in the eye of the beholder—it is the very shape of reality.

QUESTIONS FOR DISCUSSION AND DEBATE

1. The terms "elegance" and "delight" are often applied by scientists to their own area after years of study. How does an educator convey

24. Mumpower, "Fun Facts."
25. Spaemann, "Art Imitates Nature," 209–10.

delight in scientific or quantitative areas to students who are being introduced to that area?

2. What are the elements of a clear design, like Richardson's arrow diagrams, that helps students to understand the most important parts of a complex structure or network?
3. How can students be guided to implement their own designs, like with the PyMol program to render protein structure? What kind of protocol gives students a path forward while allowing them flexibility and room for their own creativity to influence the design?
4. How can the beauty of a complex network, like the Serengeti ecosystem, be conveyed to students? How is this different from the beauty of a complex structure, like Richardson's arrow diagrams?
5. How is teaching an art that makes invisible reality available and visible to students? How is a classroom exercise like the artistic installations described in the final section?

BIBLIOGRAPHY

de Chadarevian, Soraya. "John Kendrew and Myoglobin: Protein Structure Determination in the 1950s." *Protein Science* 27 (2018) 1136–43.

Fienberg, Daniel. "Disney+'s 'Welcome to Earth': TV Review." *Hollywood Reporter*, Dec 8, 2021. https://www.hollywoodreporter.com/tv/tv-reviews/welcome-to-earth-review-1235058503/.

Gwin, Peter. "The Wildebeest, an Unlikely King." *National Geographic* 240 (2021) 58–71.

Hughes, Kevin L. "Western Civ Doesn't Need Tenured Radicals to Ruin Itself." *Cosmon in the Lost*, May 3, 2017. http://www.patheos.com/blogs/cosmostheinlost/2017/05/03/western-civ-in-a-tragic-key/2/.

James, Charlie H. "Guardians of the Land." *National Geographic* 240 (2021) 52–55.

Lancellotti, Carlo. "The Redemption of Scientific Reason." *Church Life Journal*, Nov 18, 2019. https://churchlifejournal.nd.edu/articles/the-redemption-of-scientific-reason/.

Mumpower, David. "Fun Facts about Spaceship Earth That Will Surprise You." *Mickey Blog*, Aug 17, 2019. https://mickeyblog.com/2019/08/17/fun-facts-spaceship-earth-surprise/.

Peterson, Megan J., et al. "Preparative Protein Production from Inclusion Bodies and Crystallization: A Seven-Week Biochemistry Sequence." *Journal of Chemical Education* 88 (2011) 986–89.

Richardson, Jane S. "The Anatomy and Taxonomy of Protein Structure." *Advances in Protein Chemistry* 34 (1981) 167–339.

———. "β-Sheet Topology and the Relatedness of Proteins." *Nature* 268 (1977) 495–500.

Richardson, Jane S., and David C. Richardson. "Biophysical Highlights from 54 Years of Macromolecular Crystallography." *Biophysical Journal* 106 (2014) 510–25.

Spaemann, Robert. "Art Imitates Nature?" In *A Robert Spaemann Reader: Philosophical Essays on Nature, God, and the Human Person*, translated by D. C. and J. H. Schindler, 193–210. Oxford: Oxford University Press, 2015.

———. "Education as an Introduction to Reality." In *A Robert Spaemann Reader: Philosophical Essays on Nature, God, and the Human Person*, translated by D. C. and J. H. Schindler, 100–120. Oxford: Oxford University Press, 2015.

———. "Nature." In *A Robert Spaemann Reader: Philosophical Essays on Nature, God, and the Human Person*, translated by D. C. and J. H. Schindler, 25–36. Oxford: Oxford University Press, 2015.

Subalusky, Amanda L., et al. "Annual Mass Drownings of the Serengeti Wildebeest Migration Influence Nutrient Cycling and Storage in the Mara River." *Proceedings of the National Academy of Sciences* 114 (2017) 7647–52.

8

Nature, Wilderness, and Discovery of the Self

The Spirituality of Wild Places

KEN BADLEY

This unapologetically personal chapter begins on a hillside in the Qu'Appelle Valley near the village of Lumsden, Saskatchewan. On that hillside, I first slept in a tent. This chapter also begins in canoes on the Churchill River in northern Saskatchewan, the Athabasca River in northern Alberta, and the Teslin and Yukon Rivers in the Yukon where I have paddled with friends, spoken honestly, solved world problems, longed for ice cream, seen the northern lights, and felt completely at home in the world. It also begins on and around mountains, mainly in the Coast Ranges and Rocky Mountains of western Canada and the United States, where I have hiked, climbed and backpacked for decades. This chapter begins in these wild—and not-so-wild—places because it is in these places that I have found it easiest to nurture my interior life or, as some prefer to put it, to discover myself.

Two immediate problems arise with the language of self-discovery. First, to some, it sounds narcissistic, bringing to mind phrases such as *navel-gazing* and *self-absorption*. That is, the phrase *self-discovery* may connote the view that one ultimately must moor one's life in one's self rather than in any larger cause, purpose, belief system, or reality outside oneself. I return to these connections late in the chapter. The second problem with the idea that self-discovery naturally happens—that is—happens in natural settings is that, in a literal sense, I keep finding myself in cities. I live in cities, and not to be overly clever with the language of discovery, but day after day I wake up and there I am, in a city. At the time of writing, that city is Calgary, Alberta. By the time you read this, I will have moved to Edmonton, Alberta. Except for one summer when I worked at a sawmill and lived in the bush near the village of Carcross, Yukon, I have always lived in cities, eight of them so far, and I have embraced them all, from Whitehorse, Yukon with its twenty-five thousand residents, to the Toronto metro region, with its six million. My work as an academic requires that I live in cities, and I don't complain. After all, I love history, libraries, music, art, and trains.

But I find myself in cities in the psychological or spiritual sense as well. I feel at home among people. I get a buzz from the idea that they all have things to do and places to go, as much as that may sound like any number of children's books. The intricacy of the city's economy fascinates me, as do the challenges of constructing tall buildings, supplying food to a large population, and managing transport. When I stand in front of my favourite paintings in the National Gallery in London, I imagine that, with my vast wealth and out of my equally vast generosity, I have put my works by Monet, Manet, Van Gogh, and the other boys (and girls) in the band on permanent loan so that these many people could see them without cost. Big cities make it possible for me to lend my works of art this way so that groups of middle-school children from Italy and Canada can see them. I feel at home in the National Gallery, in the grand spaces of the Tate Modern in London and the Walt Disney Concert Hall in Los Angeles, or in the intimacy of the Van Gogh museum in Amsterdam.

In fact, one evening I sat alone for two hours in one small room in the Van Gogh in Amsterdam. Those two hours became a spiritual retreat for me as I tried to understand Vincent's vision for an artists' community in Arles (in southern France) and how that vision unfolded and ultimately unravelled. The curator's inscription next to one painting quoted from a letter Vincent had written to his brother Theo. He had asked Theo, "What will my postcard to the world be?" As it happens, I was returning to Canada from Kenya and was myself brimming with vocational questions after working with teacher colleagues there. I found myself asking (again) what my postcard to the world would be. That night, I met Vincent in a city, not in the wilderness. That night, I found myself in Amsterdam—in both senses—although Vincent had lost himself many decades before in Arles.

Why go on at length about cities in a chapter meant to be about the life of the spirit and self-discovery in wild places? For one reason. Some people feel adrift or lost in cities, even when they are not literally lost. Some people feel adrift or lost in the wild, even when they may not be literally lost. Some feel at home in both kinds of settings, and I am one of those. But there is more to my dwelling on cities than the fact that I have dwelt in them. Over centuries, the concept of wilderness has shifted. Mapmakers in earlier centuries would often draw illustrations of fierce sea and land creatures in unexplored, unmapped areas. They might inscribe something along the lines of "wild beasts be here" to remind armchair adventurers of the wisdom of staying home. That is, wild and unknown places contained threats.

Mapmakers were not alone in their portrayals of the natural world as inhospitable. Biblical writers found high places threatening, preferring the reassurance of low places (valleys).[1] Ancient Roman writers described mountains in largely negative terms as well, using words such as *dangerous, hostile, horrid*, and *desolate*.[2] Likewise, forests—the homes of wolves and trolls—were places to be avoided and feared, a tradition of thought that persisted in children's literature until the 1800s. The idea that one would go to wild or remote places either for recreation or for spiritual restoration began to spread only in the late 1700s and 1800s. The magnitude of the shift in attitudes toward nature that began then can be assessed by looking at any number of cultural trends and artifacts: the plethora of children's books about nature, the number of stores selling outdoor gear, and the popularity of what is commonly called adventure tourism. How things have changed since Isaiah, the biblical writer, foresaw the day when a highway would be built in the desert, when every mountain would be made low, and when the rough places would be made smooth (Isaiah 40:3–4).

The transformation in attitude was sufficiently complete that by the late 1920s, Carl G. Jung was able to write these words:

> Whenever we touch nature, we get clean. People who get dirty through too much civilization take a walk in the woods, or a bath in the sea. Entering the unconscious, entering yourself through dreams, is touching nature from the inside and this is the same thing, things are put right again.[3]

We might change Jung's wording slightly in our time, and we might not even take the unconscious as seriously as does Jung, but readers in our own century instantly recognize what he means when he talks about putting things right. Indeed, most of us know from experience that, from time to time, we need to get into the forest or the hills. We need to see a waterfall

1. Nicholson, *Dictionary of the History of Ideas*, 252.
2. Nicholson, *Dictionary of the History of Ideas*, 252.
3. Jung, *Dream Analysis*, Lecture 6.

or animals big enough to harm us. Because I happen to live on the side of Calgary that faces the Rocky Mountains, and because I live on the very edge of the city, I can drive to the mountains without stopping at even one traffic light. As much as I love this good city, I know it contaminates me in the sense Jung describes. And I regularly drive west for the cleansing of my self that Jung claims we all need.

Mountains and forests are not the only places people go to be in or with nature. James Cameron, producer and director of the blockbuster film *Titanic* has actually spent his adult life exploring a part of the natural world that most of us tend not to think about: the bottom of the oceans. Without doubt, Cameron experiences awe and wonder when exploring the world's lowest places. While thousands of meters below the surface in the New Britain Trench near Papua New Guinea, his language turned openly confessional; he exclaims (in *Aliens of the Deep*), "This is my church down here."[4] Such is the power of nature to move us beyond ourselves. But notice the title of Cameron's film. The word "aliens" echoes the sentiments of explorers and mapmakers in earlier centuries who had a kind of magnetic attraction to the idea of dangerous beasts. Not to put words in Cameron's mouth, but natural settings may induce us to discover ourselves, but they also have the power to induce wonder and to help us discover something outside ourselves, something far larger than ourselves. Thus, the language of self-discovery may be more short-sighted than inaccurate.

Moving from the deepest trenches on the earth's surface to its highest peaks, I turn to Reinhold Messner, one of the outstanding mountaineers of the last century and the first to climb all fourteen 8000-meter peaks. He lamented the transformation of big wall climbing from a sport characterized by artistry and what Csikszentmihalyi calls flow[5] into a series of technical tasks simply meant to put the technician at the top of a route. Messner writes as follows:

> Climbing is like ballet. Every second of the performance is different, as the structure of the rock determines how I compose and choreograph the moves. When I'm climbing well, I'm not thinking, not at all. It's all instinctive, and if I find the right flow, the climbing just happens of its own accord. It's as if gravity has been abolished.[6]

For Messner, climbing was not always ballet and flow. In his account of his solo ascent of Nanga Parbat in Pakistan, at 8126 meters, the world's

4. Cameron and Quale, *Aliens of the Deep*.
5. Csikszentmihalyi, *Flow*.
6. Messner, *My Life at the Limit*, 45.

ninth highest peak, Messner (1980) talks about what he calls the *black loneliness* that can set in when climbing big walls. Granted, on Nanga Parbat, Messner was still in lament over a recent divorce, but readers of his account of that climb cannot miss the spiritual isolation he felt while on that climb. I introduce these references to Messner to make clear that the spirituality of remote places, while it can be about joy and self-discovery, is not all flow and ballet. Well into the twentieth century, the young Maasai male in Kenya and Tanzania was expected to go into the wild and come back only when he had killed a lion. For some, the wild place is intentionally a place of testing and challenge or even danger. To use a metaphor for a moment, in these settings, nature can become a hostile place or force; both Messner and the Masai boy come face to face with themselves—and with the objective, external threats to their continued existence—in some places.

Although compared to Messner, I never exceeded the climbing standard of dabbler, I have had moments when I wondered what I had been thinking to have put myself in life-threatening situations. I think of a descent from my Grassi Ridge climb on the west tower of Wiwaxy Peak in Yoho National Park in British Columbia. At one point my climbing partner and I stopped to assess the risk of traversing a cliff without placing protection (which would have entailed taking the time to dig the rope and some hardware out of a backpack) and protect each other for the short crossing. We decided to take the risk and save the time. I will never forget my fear as I inched my way around a corner on a narrow ledge, with no good hand holds. I thought about my marriage and the potential of my wife's becoming a widow because of my lack of skill or my sheer stupidity. I thought about (at that time) my one child becoming fatherless. I thought about my vocation, my friends, my goals in life. "What on earth am I doing here?" I wondered, perhaps a variant form of the question "What am I doing on earth?" To the point of this chapter, being exposed to danger in that way led to my reflecting deeply about my own love of life and the importance of being a good steward of my life. Despite the elevated levels of cortisol in my brain, I found myself in a spiritual moment. The fear and vulnerability I felt on that cliff on Wiwaxy Peak led to growth. I discovered a part of myself—my deep love of life itself—that I perhaps had neglected, a kind of neglect that cities, with their lack of existential threats, have the capacity to foster.

In his book *The Solace of Fierce Landscapes*, Beldon Lane discusses cliffs as well.

> The truth of the desert fathers and mothers has to be transferable, able also to be lived out in the canyons of our great cities, where steel and glass cliffs of mirrored indifference border the

> street corners of lonely anonymity at Madison and State, Fifth Avenue and 57th Steet. Where, in the modern landscape of our lives, do we find the moral equivalent of desert? What are the places in our experience desert abandonment is forced on us with the threatening insistence of fierce geographical terrain."[7]

In *Flow: The Psychology of Optimal Experience*, Csikszentmihalyi argues that for anyone to get into the flow zone they must be working near the limits of their abilities but experiencing success, finding what he calls the challenge-skills balance. On this account, no one will get into flow watching television because there is no challenge. And few of us would get into flow playing tennis against a world champion because we would lack the skill. Cities offer abundant opportunities for someone like me to get into a flow state, when preparing new material for teaching, for example, or when actually teaching. But I find myself in flow states more often when in the outdoors, possibly because the interruptions are fewer or because outdoor activity tends to involve rhythmic actions such as walking or paddling. In Csikszentmihalyi's terms, outdoor activities offer more opportunities to move toward or act in the challenge-skills balance; the person outdoors is constantly afforded opportunities to try this approach or see where that route leads, something one rarely does on the way to the grocery store or the library.

Nature has the power to lead one into self-discovery, even when it presents no danger. I recall a backpacking trip on the Skyline Trail near Jasper, Alberta with three boys, all of them twelve years old at the time. On the first day of the trip, fresh from their respective cities, they threw rocks at squirrels and talked endlessly, with great enthusiasm, and with many sound effects, about the latest action movies they had seen. Three days later, as we made our long, slow descent to our end point, I happened to be second or third in the party with one of the boys in the lead. He suddenly turned around, silently, held one finger to his lips to shush us, and then pointed to a ptarmigan attempting to hide in the undergrowth a few paces ahead. We all watched for a couple minutes then walked on. No one threw a rock. No one said anything. At the time, I thought, "This is what three days in the mountains does to a boy of twelve. He stops talking about action movies. He watches a bird but has no need to exercise power over the bird or to harm the bird." Forty years later, as I think about that trip, I understand what happened there. We lived in nature—with nature—for a few days and, in some sense, let nature be our teacher. We discovered ourselves, but we also discovered something bigger than ourselves.

7. Lane, *Solace of Fierce Landscapes*, 194.

Twenty-five years later, on another backpacking trip, I witnessed another member of the same species stop my three hiking partners and me in our tracks. The contrasts with the boys of twelve could not have been more marked. We were all doctors of one kind or another and had engaged in no discussion of action movies during our trip. Wanting always to save our energy to keep moving our legs, we had thrown no rocks. But when we came on a ptarmigan on the trail in front of us, we all stopped and watched it for a couple minutes, apparently the requisite time. I have written about this experience elsewhere, in a chapter about how educators need to plan curriculum and instruction that has the capacity to induce wonder.[8] But I repeat the story here because this simple bird had the power to move my partners and me into a moment of silence and reflection. Returning to my comments about cities momentarily, cities offer much—natural, architectural, interpersonal, and cultural—that could induce us to stop and reflect, but for reasons I will not explore here, we usually don't stop and wonder in the city. We do stop and wonder in the wild. For that reason alone, perhaps we should go there more often.

My memories of moments while climbing are not exclusively about reflection on the goodness of life and the possibilities of losing my own. The kind of satisfaction I experience on simply getting to the summit of a mountain is of a different quality from what I would experience were I to ride a gondola or helicopter to the same point. The risk and the exertion sweeten the reward immeasurably. A cliché I know, but the long views are of an order rarely experienced at a roadside viewpoint.

The Yukon Department of Tourism and Culture has long understood what the outdoors does to and for people like me. Many years ago, it published a poster with the words "Somewhere down there is your soul" printed on a band across the top of a photograph taken in the Ogilvie Mountains in the northern Yukon. This horizonal poster is a meter wide and only forty-six centimeters high, a format that increases the viewer's sense that one will indeed enjoy expansive views if one travels to Canada's north, in this case on the Dempster Highway. Having travelled through the region where photographer Richard Hartmier took the photograph used by the Yukon government, I have felt exactly what the poster's designers intended me to feel . . . that I need to go back there because my soul is there. That the poster—in one sense a mere piece of paper—has the power to induce that feeling in me speaks volumes about the power of its subject matter, the natural world, and that world's power to restore the soul.

8. Badley, *Faithful Teaching.*

CONCLUSION

Since reading Sam Keen's *Fire in the Belly: In Being a Man* three decades ago, and on his recommendation, I have regularly revised a list called "the ten best days of my life." My refusal to delist certain days meant that the list eventually grew to fifteen days. In its current form, that list includes great meals with friends, the births of my children, days of celebration and accomplishment, and many days out of doors. Some of those days outside also involved accomplishment since I completed an epic hike or climb (epic by my standards). But my memories of some of those days outdoors involved nothing more than simply paddling in the sun on smooth water while talking with a friend. Such is the outdoors, a world where one can discover and re-discover their inner self, but a place where that discovery happens because I am in a context much grander than my self.

QUESTIONS FOR DISCUSSION AND DEBATE

1. In light of spiritual traditions related to worship, Eucharist, and church feast days, what questions or objections might some raise against the view that the outdoors can be a place of spiritual renewal? What are some possible answers to such objections?
2. Recall times in the wild—or even simply outdoors—when you experienced deepened awareness of the spiritual dimension and of your own interior state. Besides the starting condition of being out of doors, what conditions are typically in place for you to have such deep experiences?
3. The two questions above both point to the fact that a cultural shift has taken place in the last several decades. In short, many people now go to the outdoors and into the wild in search of spiritual renewal and personal restoration . . . literally re-creation. Suggest possible implications of this shift for what has traditionally been called catechesis or Christian education.
4. Many have feelings of vulnerability and fear when in the wild, for example, the fear of getting injured or lost. To what degree to you think such vulnerability may contribute to (or diminish) one's likelihood of having a profound spiritual experience in the wild? Why?

BIBLIOGRAPHY

Badley, Ken. "Wonder." In *Faithful Teaching: Values and Themes for Teaching, Learning, and Leading Purposeful and Principled Education*, edited by Amy Dee and Gary Tiffin, 112–28. Eugene, OR: Wipf & Stock, 2012.

Cameron, James, and Steven Quale, dirs. *Aliens of the Deep*. Sydney: James Cameron and Australian National Maritime Museum, 2013.

Csikszentmihalyi, Mihaly. *Flow: The Psychology of Optimal Experience*. New York: Harper & Row, 1990.

Hartmier, Richard. *Colour of the Land*. Vancouver: Lost Moose, 1995.

Jung, Carl G. *Dream Analysis: Notes on a Lecture Given in 1928–1930*. New York: Routledge, 2013.

Keen, Sam. *Fire in the Belly: On Being a Man*. Toronto: Bantam, 1991.

Lane, Belden. *The Solace of Fierce Landscapes: Exploring Desert and Mountain Spirituality*. New York: Oxford University Press, 1998.

Messner, Reinhold. *My Life at the Limit*. Translated by T. Carruthers. Seattle, WA: Mountaineers, 2015.

———. *Solo Nanga Parbat*. Oxford: Oxford University Press, 1981.

Nicolson, Marjorie H. "Literary Attitudes Toward Mountains." In *Dictionary of the History of Ideas: Studies of Selected Pivotal Ideas*, edited by Philip P. Wiener, 3:253–60. New York: Scribners, 1973.

9

Intersections of Postcolonialism, Contemporary Icelandic Environmentalism, and Cultural Representations in Encounters with Ólafur Elíasson's Glacial Oeuvre

Brynjarr Þór Eyjólfsson

INTRODUCTION

In this chapter I will argue that Ólafur Elíasson's glacial oeuvre transposes Romantic notions of Icelandic nature in art and extends them towards postcolonial imagery, allowing for an environmentalist critique of capitalist conquests of nature that is uniquely Icelandic in character. I will explore the history of aesthetics in Iceland and examine its relationship with (de- and post-) colonial movements, having conceptions of Icelandic nature as a focal point. I will then mark the onset of the consequent re-conception of Icelandic nature as an aesthetic object as it appears in Elíasson's glacial works in the context of Icelandic cultural currents, underlining the importance of his artworks both in the promotion of Icelandic nature as well as its conservation.

In March of 2021, Iceland witnessed the eruption of the Fagradalsfjall volcano in the Reykjanes Peninsula, following an already year-long global battle against the COVID-19 pandemic.

Volcanic eruption on Iceland's Reykjanes Peninsula. People watch the lava flow field (image: @brianemfinger/twitter)

But this is not the first time that such a phenomenon has occurred in Icelandic history; one would need only to look at written works to see the relevance of such coincidentally correlated incidents in Icelandic cultural memory. As an example, two famous Icelandic works of literature depict similar "historical" events: Gunnar Gunnarsson's *Sælir eru einfaldir* (*Blessed are the Simple*)[1] and Sjón's *Mánasteinn: Drengurinn sem aldrei var til* (*Moonstone: The Boy Who Never Was*).[2] Both novels deal with volcanic eruptions and pandemics while serving to critique the society under whose cultural wing they were published. To this may be added another underlying element: both works, to a varying extent, address an aspect of Danish colonial rule within Iceland. Gunnarsson's novel was published in 1920 and was written, as with his other works, in Danish; the Iceland that he writes about remains under Danish rule. Sjón's novel, published in 2013, has the Iceland of 1918 as its setting and portrays moments of Danish colonial rule as a backdrop. In 2021, seventy-seven years after Iceland's independence

1. Originally published in Danish in 1920 under the title *Salige er de enfoldige* (Copenhagen: Gyldendal).

2. Sjón, *Mánasteinn*. The novel has been translated into English; see Sjón, *Moonstone*.

from Denmark in 1944, the country undergoes another volcanic eruption and pandemic outbreak, but references to colonialism do not seem to be as prominent as they are in the aforementioned novels, at least on the surface.

And yet, the experience of Icelandic nature as we have it today owes its status partly to the decolonisation efforts of Icelandic artists in Denmark in the nineteenth century as well as the postcolonial cultural core of modern Iceland. Many works by the Danish-Icelandic artist Ólafur Elíasson that deal with nature serve as an example of this historical-cultural undercurrent in Icelandic modernity.

POSTCOLONIALISM IN ICELAND AND ITS PRECEDENTS

The awakening of Romanticism amongst Icelandic thinkers in the nineteenth century brings with it questions on the relationship of Icelanders with beauty. The problem that Icelandic artists of that century were in constant battle with was what Birna Bjarnadóttir describes as their "compatriots' weak sensibility for beauty."[3] The Icelandic writer and aesthetic thinker Guðbergur Bergsson, in his contemplation of this mindset, refers to a well-known incident in the medieval Icelandic saga, *Brennu-Njáls saga*, wherein one of the chief characters, Gunnar of Hlíðarendi, reflects on the beauty of the land that lay before him and, in a moment of aesthetic regard that would later bring tragic consequences for him, chooses to stay in Iceland after having been outlawed, declaring: "Fögur eru hlíðin" ("Fair is the slope").[4] Bergsson remarks that Icelanders have rarely gotten past this aesthetic feeling for the landscape since then, neither in art nor in their outlook in life.[5] Sigurður Magnússon, however, adds that Gunnar's proclamation of the land's beauty "is not seen with the eyes of an esthete or an artist, but with the eyes of a practical farmer. It is neither rivers nor waterfalls, mountains nor glaciers that conjure up the winged words, but . . . the fat of the land."[6] This attitude, he explains, is what persists in Iceland until the nineteenth century.

The sentiment for the pragmatic beauty of the Icelandic landscape is overturned and reshaped by figures such as the Romantic natural historian

3. "Dauf fegurðartilfinning landans." See Bjarnadóttir, *Holdið hemur andann*, 59. Also *Recesses of the Mind*, 40.

4. See *Brennu-Njáls saga*, chapter 75.

5. "Yfir þetta höfum við sjaldan komist í listum og lífsmáta, hversu mikið sem þjóðfélagshættir okkar hafa breyst: fegurðarskynið tengist landslagi og tryggð." Bergsson, "Hugmyndir um fegurð," 111.

6. Magnússon, "Nature in Icelandic Poetry," 505.

and poet Jónas Hallgrímsson. He began to write poetry about landscapes that were of significance to Icelandic literature from the past, including the very setting of Gunnar's tragic decision, which becomes the subject of his poem *Gunnarshólmi* (Gunnar's holm).[7]

It was Hallgrímsson's poetry that first truly describes Icelandic nature as an artistic landscape.[8] Sveinn Yngvi Egilsson asserts, moreover, that the visual aesthetics of the nineteenth century Icelandic Romantics still play a significant role in Icelandic perceptions about the environment.[9] Indeed, the Icelandic Romanticist movement produced artists that turned their gaze back towards Icelandic nature as an aesthetic subject, and in the landscape paintings of artists such as Þórarinn B. Þorláksson, Ásgrímur Jónsson, and Jóhannes Kjarval—all of whom studied in Copenhagen—the visual imagery, a re-presentation of the essence of Icelandic nature, becomes more characteristic, and certain aspects of it are highlighted. In the works of these artists, the definition of what "Icelandic nature" is, in visual terms, begins to take shape: their subjects, as a principle, thus encompass mountains, fjords, rural farmlands, lava formations, and glaciers.

With the ardency of Icelandic Romanticism in Copenhagen and reawakened thoughts of national identity came fervent calls for the independence of Iceland from Denmark. The first demands came from students in Copenhagen, whose sense of Romantic nationalism urged them to look back at the Icelandic Golden Age that was depicted in the medieval sagas.[10] The nationalists in Denmark began making the Danish kingdom culpable for the devastating consequences of natural catastrophes that prevailed in Iceland during the eighteenth century, and the state of disarray in the homeland thereafter was blamed on the administrative failures of the Danish government.[11] Artists during that period such as Sigurður Guðmundsson also blamed Danish rule to an extent for the state of architecture in Iceland at that time.[12] Icelandic art was vital in this manner for the promotion of Icelandic self-identity, as with the rise of the notion of national identities during the Romantic period, the formation of what is characteristically "Icelandic" (oftentimes in opposition to what is "Danish") gave the nationalists

7. See, for example, Egilsson, *Náttúra ljóðsins*, 61.

8. Egilsson, *Náttúra ljóðsins*, 61.

9. "Það má því segja að sjónræn fagurfræði 19. aldar eigi sér framhaldslíf í umhverfismati okkar daga." *Náttúra ljóðsins*, 62.

10. See Hálfdanarson, "Iceland," 88, 90.

11. See Oslund, *Iceland Imagined*, 45–46.

12. See Hafsteinsson, "'Icelandic Putridity.'"

better ground at defining Iceland as its own nation.[13] Jónas Hallgrímsson himself, the aforementioned key figure in Icelandic Romantic aesthetics, promoted Icelandic patriotism through the journal *Fjölnir* alongside other countrymen writing at that time.[14] Thus, Denmark's colonial rule of Iceland may be seen as influential, directly or tangentially, in the constitution of Icelandic identity, since, in light of this, Icelandic art has been shaped partially as a reaction to that which was Danish.[15]

ICELANDIC ENVIRONMENTALISM AND ÓLAFUR ELÍASSON'S WORKS

Even during a time of a postcolonial Iceland, echoes of colonialism and decolonialism reverberate especially amongst perceptions of Iceland as a modern tourist destination. Conceptualisations of Iceland as such have their roots externally as they are to be found internally. With the nationalist reformation of self-identity in the nineteenth century in Iceland also came maps as well as travelogues from European travellers who have described Iceland as "exotic" or "uncivilised"—often in relation to Iceland's rough nature—that have thus led to the process of the country's "exoticisation."[16] Henk van der Liet, moreover, argues for the reconceptualisation of Iceland as a "postcolonial landscape . . . where people and political open wounds from the past are overwritten by the aesthetic gaze, which primarily focuses on the graphic qualities of the Icelandic countryside."[17] The narratives produced by these processes live on today, transposed into marketing strategies in a now more-capitalistic society. What is to be observed here is a movement away from internal, Icelandic self-conceptualisation as a nation, towards an emphasis on how the outside world perceives the country and its nature—"Iceland" as a cultural export.[18]

The Icelandic cultural and national identity thus underwent a form of rebranding wherein notions of its exotic and pristine nature—recalling earlier narratives of European travellers in Iceland in the eighteenth and

13. See also Listasafn Íslands. "First Steps in Promoting Icelandic Art in Copenhagen," https://www.listasafn.is/faldir-flokkar/udstilling-af-islandsk-kunst_/.

14. See Henning, "Saga for Dinner," 61.

15. See, for example, Loftsdóttir. "Exotic North," 248.

16. Cf. Oslund, *Iceland Imagined*, 31, 39. Loftsdóttir, "Dualistic Colonial Experiences," 47. Kristín Loftsdóttir, "The Exotic North," 249. Loftsdóttir, "'Danes Don't Get This,'" 38.

17. Van der Liet, "Iceland?," 469.

18. See also Gremaud, "Power and Purit," 78.

nineteenth centuries—played a crucial role in Icelandic tourism as we have it today.[19] This image of Iceland in global tourism was shaped largely by efforts by the government for a national "brand" that commenced in 2006 and reached new heights in 2010, particularly after the Eyjafjallajökull volcanic eruption, efforts that also became all the more significant especially after the economic crash in 2008.[20] Here, the *Inspired by Iceland* campaign[21] was a key movement especially in transforming perceptions of Iceland's rough nature into a safe experience of natural attractions.[22] The aesthetic emphasis on the beauty of Icelandic nature thus remains; but in postcolonial Iceland, the political effect of this artistic framework is geared towards a reconceptualisation of Iceland as a tourist destination for people who want to experience an exotic yet safe and pristine nature.

For the Danish-Icelandic artist Ólafur Elíasson, perceptions of Icelandic nature bear heavy significance in the phenomenological encounter of his works. He draws inspiration from the nature that he experienced as a child spending summers in his parents' home country[23] and begins to incorporate them into his work upon the realisation that "the Icelandic landscape is underrepresented in art history," beginning with photographs in the 90s.[24] Olivia Eriksson notes that Elíasson's work utilises "organic materials such as moss, ice, and rock in combination with innovative technology to reconfigure natural phenomena within the gallery walls."[25] These organic materials maintain a strong association with Iceland and its "hot pools, lava fields, volcanoes, waterfalls, caves and moss banks."[26] Elíasson's close relationship with the nature of Iceland allows him to also reflect on the cultural understandings that surround how nature itself is viewed, leaning towards an aesthetic appreciation of nature as one that is culturally influenced.[27]

In light of Elíasson's inspiration from Iceland, what proves to be a theme of special significance to Elíasson's artistic practice is what he calls "mediation," which he describes as "a degree of representation in the

19. Cf. Loftsdóttir, "Dualistic Colonial Experiences," 47. Loftsdóttir, "Exotic North," 252.

20. Cf. Loftsdóttir, "Exotic North," 253. Also, Loftsdóttir, "Dualistic Colonial Experiences," 48, and Benediktsson et al., "Inspired by Eruptions?," 80–81.

21. "Inspired by Iceland."

22. "Inspired by Iceland."

23. Skidmore, "Yes, But Why? Olafur Eliasson."

24. Gavin, "Ice and Emergency."

25. Eriksson, "Reaching Out!," 288.

26. Skidmore, "Yes, But Why? Olafur Eliasson."

27. Gestsdóttir, "It's More about the Principle."

experience of a situation."[28] This goes in accordance with the artist's phenomenological understanding of our relationship with nature in that we as viewers and experiencers of nature influence it—that is, our very experience and perception of nature as such—as much as it influences us.[29] Such an encounter tears down the binary division of nature and culture and places the viewer in the middle of this intersectionality as well as makes him/her the focal point in the aesthetic experience, the "perceiving subject" of the artistic space.[30]

GEOLOGICAL MATERIALS IN URBAN PUBLIC SPACES

However, what occurs when mediation takes place in the form of a physical importation of geological material into an urban public space, such as in Elíasson's *Ice Watch* series?

***Ice Watch*, 2014, Bankside, outside Tate Modern, London, 2018. Photo: Charlie Forgham-Bailey.**

As with his other works that deal with glaciers (the *glacier series*, *your waste of time*, and *the ice series* are a few examples), Ólafur Elíasson's *Ice*

28. May, *Olafur Eliasson*, 131.

29. "You could say I'm not really interested in the nature of the waterfall, I'm interested in how waterfalls influence me as a person." Gestsdóttir, "It's More about the Principle." See also Kanal, "In Conversation."

30. See also Eriksson, "Reaching Out!," 287 and Obrist, *Conversation Series*, 47.

Watch series utilises metonymical representations of Icelandic nature in the form of exported glacial chunks to raise awareness of a wider, more global climate crisis. For this project, twelve blocks of ice are imported from a fjord in Greenland and are, according to Elíasson's website, "presented in a clock formation in a prominent public space."[31] The first installation was in Copenhagen, the second in Paris, and the third in London. One may say that the first "trial" attempt for such a project started with *Your waste of time* in 2006 wherein Elíasson exported glacial ice from Vatnajökull in Iceland to the Berlin gallery neugerriemschneider in a closed, refrigerated space.[32]

Yet, long before these two projects, Elíasson had already been working with Icelandic glaciers through photography, taking note of the changes in nature through juxtapositions of photographs of glaciers (such as in the *ice series*, 1997). His most recent work along these lines is the *glacial melt series* wherein the artist juxtaposes photographs he took of several glaciers in Iceland in 1999 with ones he took in 2019. The differences are drastic. It is the critical conditions of the glaciers that are highlighted in these photographs that Elíasson draws attention to in his *Ice watch* series. As Louise Hornby explains, Elíasson's presentation of the glaciers in a public space is intended "to elicit a collective civic response to the increasingly acute crisis of global climate change."[33]

Mediation functions here to bring a sense of immediacy to the audiences where displaced geological objects are suddenly placed in centres of urban life in Copenhagen, Paris, and London. This creates what Hornby calls a "recursive fictive environment" that focalises on the spectator's experience and "undermines notions of nativity and the natural environment."[34]

I agree with Hornby to the extent that there is a focus on the individual's experience upon contact with the glacial ice, but it is also exactly from this point in which I will depart. The accentuation of the spectator's phenomenological experience of the environment is only made possible through the mediation of art—here, in the form of glacial chunks—between the subject (that is, the spectator) and the *real* object (not the glacial chunks themselves, which are but metonymical signifiers, but rather their signified, the critical conditions of climate change as they are manifested in Iceland). Without an object of contemplation, the spectator misses the opportunity for phenomenological experience. In her reflections on Elíasson's works, Joanne Baker writes that they "seem to transport you to another

31. See "Ice Watch."
32. See Hornby, "Appropriating the Weather," 61.
33. Hornby, "Appropriating the Weather," 61.
34. Hornby, "Appropriating the Weather," 62.

world—then remind you that it is this world."[35] Simone Hancox adds, in her deliberations on Elíasson's *your waste of time*, that "as soon [*sic*] the glacier is taken from its site and transplanted into the cultural institution, it begins to signify *more than glacial* ice. It might signify the growing contemporary concern with global climate change."[36] In light of this, the *Ice watch* series invites participation and engagement and gives environmental and political agency to the spectator, but in using the representational power of imported glacial ice, Elíasson brings that which is Icelandic to the forefront of environmental symbolism.[37]

CULTURAL REPRESENTATIONS

Indeed, since Icelanders began to look at their landscapes as objects of aesthetic contemplation since the nineteenth century, there has been an exponential increase in efforts to preserve its beauty. Literary and artistic works actively engage with various metaphors to tackle the problems that threaten Icelandic nature. For example, contemporary discussions on endeavors by foreign companies to exploit Iceland's natural resources have used decolonial rhetoric in their arguments. Most famous and influential of these is Andri Snær Magnason's book, *Draumalandið—Sjálfshjálparbók handa hræddri þjóð (Dreamland—a Self-Help Manual for a Frightened Nation)*,[38] wherein he engages with the issues of aluminium smelters—among other things—in Iceland, issues that have been in discussion since 1970.[39]

In the book, Magnason argues that Iceland's industrialisation is "a threat to the future and independence of Iceland and to the nation's self-perception"[40] and calls the construction of aluminium smelters a form of "neo-colonialism."[41] In support of his claims, Magnason cites research on the destructive effects of buildings reservoirs around the Vatnajökull glacier—the biggest glacier in Iceland.[42] Thus, in contemporary, postcolonial Iceland, the battle for independence from outside powers is no longer fought against the Danes, but rather against foreign, industrial companies that threaten to destroy Icelandic nature. "The beauty of Iceland," writes

35. Baker, "Big Bangs and Bronze Ice."
36. Hancox, "Performativity of Ice," 56.
37. See also Hornby, "Appropriating the Weather," 62.
38. Magnason, *Draumalandið*.
39. See Henning, 61. Loftsdóttir, "Iceland," 344.
40. Magnason, *Draumalandið*, 338; Henning, 68.
41. See Henning, 68.
42. Magnason, *Draumalandið*, 418.

Magnason, "lies at the heart of our image of the country and the way this nation perceives itself. In opinion polls it rates as more important to us than God or our language, and for many they are all part of the same thing. This beauty became the main enemy of the project."[43]

Additionally, in a chapter called "Að kveðja hvítan risa" ("Farewell to the white giants"), Andri Snær Magnason remarks in another book, *Um tímann og vatnið* (*On Time and Water*), that "in the future, glaciers will be an alien phenomenon, rare as a Bengal tiger; having lived in the time of the white giants, will become swaddled in a fairy-tale glow, like having stroked a dragon or handled the eggs of the great auk."[44] Elíasson expresses the same sentiment: "Every glacier lost reflects our inaction. Every glacier saved will be a testament to the action taken in the face of climate emergency. One day, instead of mourning the loss of more glaciers, we must be able to celebrate their survival."[45] His glacial oeuvre depicts the observable changes in the glaciers of Iceland, and it seems that the time shown in his "ice watch" is running out.

One of the first countries that will be affected by the loss of glaciers will be Iceland, for what will Iceland be when that part of its beauty is lost? Much of the country is connected with its glacial landscapes that the contemporary Icelandic poet and writer, Steinunn Sigurðardóttir, asks in her poetry collection, *Dimmumót* (*Twilight*, 2019): "What takes over then? What will we become? Named what name? Of which land will we become, the so-called Icelanders, when the glacier disappears? Not ICE-landers"[46] and associates the lack of glaciers with a "Non-Iceland" ("Ekki-Ísland"), with apprehensions that such a phenomenon will be experienced as a reality by the coming generations.[47] The phenomenon of glaciers, as seen through the aforementioned cultural encounters, bears with it an affect for their loss that concerns not only Iceland but also the rest of the world.

43. "Fegurð Íslands er kjarni ímyndar Íslands og sjálfsmyndar þjóðarinnar. Samkvæmt rannsóknum mælist hún mikilvægari en Guð og tungumálið, hjá mörgum rennur þetta í eitt. Fegurðin varð höfuðóvinur framkvæmdarinnar." *Draumalandið*, 240. Translation taken from *Dreamland*, 257.

44. "Í framtíðinni verður jökull framandi fyrirbæri, sjaldgæfir eins og bengaltígur. Að hafa lifað tíma hvítu risanna verður sveipað ævintýraljóma, eins og að hafa klappað dreka eða handleikið egg geirfuglsins." Magnason, *Um tímann og vatnið*, 183. Translation from *On Time and Water*, 183.

45. "Glacier Melt Series."

46. Sigurðardóttir, "Hvað tekur svo við?," 57. My translation.

47. Sigurðardóttir, "Hvað tekur svo við?," 38.

CONCLUSIONS: ICELAND AND ITS NATURE

It therefore becomes clear that Elíasson's glacial oeuvre reflects a culturally current presentation of Icelandic self-identity, one that in its "Icelandicness" touches upon the preservation of (Icelandic) nature through underlying political, socio-historical and artistic narratives such as those discussed in Magnason's and Sigurðardóttir's books. The *Ice watch* series, especially, invites spectators to a personal engagement with environmental issues through its displaced otherness.

The association of Iceland with glaciers as it is embedded in Elíasson's works is a product of artistic and political efforts that commenced during the Romantic period, a process of national self-identity that is still in a state of becoming in a relatively young nation. What is constant, at the very least, is the association of Iceland with its nature, whether it be rough, exotic, or pristine. The environmental challenges remain urgent, and perhaps they are more urgent nowadays than they ever were, as recent research shows the unexpectedly rapid melting of the Breiðamerkurjökull glacier.[48]

Anxieties about the disappearance of glaciers are prominent especially in Iceland where the Ok glacier died in 2019—that is, lose its status as one. Both Elíasson and Magnason participated in the revelation of its memorial.[49] Others outside of Iceland also lament the current situation of glaciers. The Canadian poet Talya Rubin, in her poem "Iceland is melting and so are you," from her poetry collection of the same name (2021), voices Sigurðardóttir's apprehensions, as the child of the speaker's dinner host "is weeping in the back seat" as he hears some devastating news from the CBC:

> We heard a report that Iceland is rising as the ice is melting. It's
> worse than they thought. When you drill a hole in the ice shelf,
> it's empty. This young boy, his body nearly collapsing from the
> grief. Feeling what we can't feel . . . [50]

QUESTIONS FOR DISCUSSION AND DEBATE

1. How can an appreciation and understanding of art aid in the education of the public in terms of the scientific facts surrounding climate change? Can art offer its own solutions?

48. Erlendsdóttir, "Hröð bráðnun Breiðamerkurjökuls."
49. Guðmundsson, "Minnast jökulsins sem hvarf."
50. Rubin, *Iceland Is Melting*, 17.

2. Is the concept of a museum space becoming irrelevant when thinking about the nature/culture dichotomy and our implications in climate change? When thinking about Elíasson's works in a public space, does the lack of physical structural boundaries aid his cause in promoting an awareness for climate change?
3. When thinking about a country such as Iceland with its natural attractions, would you agree that the country loses its essence when these attractions disappear? Would you travel to Iceland without these natural tourist destinations?
4. What role can tourism play in promoting the conservation of nature? Or do the repercussions of the tourism industry undo perhaps the efforts to reduce our carbon footprint?
5. When works of art and literature become harbingers of an endangered future, will readers and audiences be more inclined to listen and act? Or do their fictionality and artificiality diminish their influence?

BIBLIOGRAPHY

Baker, Joanne. "Big Bangs and Bronze Ice: Reflections on Olafur Eliasson." *Nature*, Jul 22, 2019. https://www.nature.com/articles/d41586-019-02228-w.

Benediktsson, Karl, et al. "Inspired by Eruptions? Eyjafjallajökull and Icelandic Tourism." *Mobilities* 6 (2011) 77–84.

Bergsson, Guðbergur. "Hugmyndir um fegurð." In *Tímarit máls og menningar* 57 (1996) 111–21.

Bjarnadóttir, Birna. *Holdið hemur andann: Um fagurfræði í skáldskap Guðbergs Bergssonar.* Reykjavík: Háskólaútgáfan, 2003.

———. *Recesses of the Mind: Aesthetics in the Work of Guðbergur Bergsson.* Montreal: McGill-Queen's University Press, 2012.

Sveinsson, Einar Ólafur, ed. *Brennu-Njáls saga.* Reykjavík: Hið íslenzka fornritafélag, 1971.

Egilsson, Sveinn Yngvi. *Náttúra ljóðsins. Umhverfi íslenskra skálda.* Reykjavík: Litlaprent, 2014.

Eriksson, Olivia. "Reaching Out! Activating Space in the Art of Olafur Eliasson." *NESCUS* 4 (2015) 287–93.

Erlendsdóttir, Ólöf Rún. "Hröð bráðnun Breiðamerkurjökuls kom á óvart." *RÚV*, November 16, 2021. https://www.ruv.is/frett/2021/11/16/hrod-bradnun-breidamerkurjokuls-kom-a-ovart.

Gavin, Francesca. "Ice and Emergency: Olafur Eliasson." *Good Trouble Magazine*, April 21, 2020. https://www.goodtroublemag.com/home/ice-and-emergency-olafur-eliasson.

Gestsdóttir, Guðrún Sóley. "It's More about the Principle—Olafur Eliasson." Hönunarmiðstöð. May 25, 2020. https://www.honnunarmidstod.is/en/ha-frettir/its-more-about-the-principle-olafur-eliasson.

"The Glacier Melt Series." https://glaciermelt.is.

Guðmundsson, Brynjólfur Þór. "Minnast jökulsins sem hvarf." *RÚV*, August 18, 2019. https://www.ruv.is/frett/minnast-jokulsins-sem-hvarf.

Gunnarsson, Gunnar. *Salige er de enfoldige*. Copenhagen: Gyldendal, 1920.

Hafsteinsson, Baldur. "'Icelandic Putridity': Colonial Thought and Icelandic Architectural Heritage." *Scandinavian Studies* 91 (2019).

Hálfdanarson, Guðmundur. "Iceland: A Peaceful Secession." *Scandinavian Journal of History* 25 (2000) 87–100.

Hancox, Simone. "The Performativity of Ice and Global Ecologies in Olafur Eliasson's Your Waste of Time." *Performance Research* 18 (2013) 54–63.

Hornby, Louise. "Appropriating the Weather: Olafur Eliasson and Climate Control." *Environmental Humanities* 9 (2017) 60–83.

"Ice Watch." https://olafureliasson.net/archive/artwork/WEK109190/ice-watch.

Kanal, Christopher. "In Conversation with Icelandic Artist Olafur Eliasson." *Lux-Mag*, Summer 2019. https://www.lux-mag.com/olafur-eliasson/.

Listasafn Íslands. "First Steps in Promoting Icelandic Art in Copenhagen." https://www.listasafn.is.

Loftsdóttir, Kristín. "'The Danes Don't Get This': The Economic Crash and Icelandic Postcolonial Engagements." *National Identities* 18 (2016) 31–52.

———. "Dualistic Colonial Experiences and the Ruins of Coloniality." *Scandinavian Studies* 91 (2019) 31–52.

———. "The Exotic North: Gender, Nation Branding and Post-Colonialism in Iceland." *NORA: Nordic Journal of Women's Studies* 23 (2015) 246–60.

———. "Iceland, Rejected by McDonald's: Desire and Anxieties in a Global Crisis." *Social Anthropology* 22 (2014) 344.

Magnason, Andri Snær. *Draumalandið: sjálfshjálparbók handa hræddri þjóð*. Reykjavík: Mál og menning, 2006.

———. *Dreamland: A Self-Help Manual for a Frightened Nation*. London: Citizen, 2008.

———. *On Time and Water*. Translated by Lytton Smith. London: Serpents Tail, 2020.

———. *Um tímann og vatnið*. Reykjavík: Mál og menning, 2019.

Magnússon, Sigurður. "Nature in Icelandic Poetry." *The Literary Review (Teaneck)* 39 (1996) 505.

May, Susan, ed. *Olafur Eliasson: The Weather Project*. London: Tate, 2003.

Obrist, Hans Ulrich, and Ólafur Elíasson. *The Conversation Series*. Cologne: Verlag der Buchhandlung Walther König, 2008.

Oslund, Karen. *Iceland Imagined: Nature, Culture, and Storytelling in the North Atlantic*. Seattle: University of Washington Press, 2011.

Reinhard, Henning. "A Saga for Dinner: Landscape and Nationality in Icelandic Literature." *Ecozon@* 2 (2011) 61–72.

Rubin, Talya. *Iceland Is Melting and So Are You*. Toronto: Book*hug, 2021.

Sigurðardóttir, Steinunn. *Dimmumót*. Reykjavík: Mál og menninng, 2019.

Sjón. *Mánasteinn: Drengurinn sem aldrei var til*. Reykjavík: JPV útgáfa, 2013.

———. *Moonstone: The Boy Who Never Was*. Translated by Victoria Cribb. New York: Farrar, Straus & Giroux, 2016.

Skidmore, Maisie. "Yes, But Why? Olafur Eliasson." https://wepresent.wetransfer.com/stories/yes-but-why-olafur-eliasson#chapter1.

Van der Liet, Henk. "Iceland: A Postcolonial Literary Landscape?" *Amsterdamer Beiträge zur älteren Germanistik* 67 (2011) 447–471.

10

Landscape Change on the Fringe of a Commuter City in the Rural-Urban Fringe of Tokyo since 1992

An Application of Repeat Photography

Tom Waldichuk

INTRODUCTION: URBANIZATION AROUND CITIES IN JAPAN, RURAL-URBAN FRINGE, TOKYO, PRESERVATION POLICIES

During the 1970s, as large urban centers in Japan became more crowded, residents started to move to suburban and rural-urban fringe communities where land was cheaper, mirroring what was happening in most large Canadian and American cities.[1] This led to much rural to urban land conversion and disappearing farm landscapes. Such was the case in the rural-urban fringe of Tokyo, where three amalgamated communities became the bedroom community of Ushiku City, which is located in Ibaraki Prefecture about 50 km northeast, or a one-hour train trip, from Ueno railway station in Tokyo (Map 1).

1. For a modern-day account of issues in the rural-urban fringe of Canada, see Beesley, *Rural-Urban Fringe*.

Authors have looked broadly at the rural-urban fringe in Japan from a land-use regulations perspective. For example, Sorensen talks about disorderly development in fringe urbanization control areas (UCA)[2] as outlined in the City Planning Law of 1968[3] that prevent development on farmland.[4] Hebbert and Nakai[5] and Nakai[6] talk about the application of this law to the rural-urban fringe of Japan with a focus on the different players, such as landowners and developers, involved in land transactions. Ishikawa focuses on this problem in her review of green space preservation legislation with reference to the rural-urban fringe—she says it is a challenge due to the different levels of government involved and the disconnected legislation that vary in enforcement.[7] Some landscapes are automatically preserved by regulations—for example, natural and farm landscapes in UCAs, where little urban development can take place.[8]

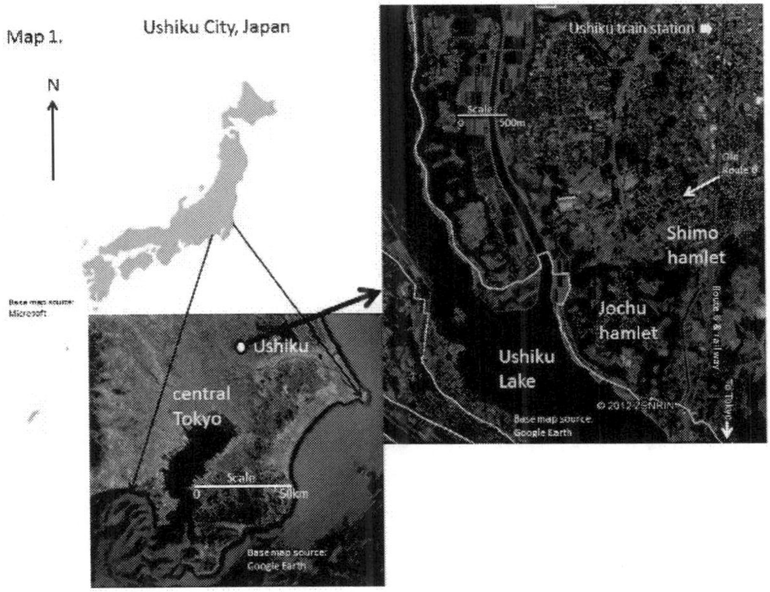

2. Sorensen, "Land Readjustment and Metropolitan Growth," 232.

3. Hasegawa, "Drafting of the Planning Law," 231–38.

4. See Japan, Ministry of Land, Infrastructure and Transportation. *Introduction of Urban Land Use.*

5. Hebbert and Nakai, *How Tokyo Grows*, chapters 3 and 4.

6. Nakai, "Urbanization Promotion and Control," 197–216.

7. Ishikawa, "Green Structure Plan," 232.

8. Sorensen, "Land Readjustment and Metropolitan Growth," 232.

Valuable Landscapes

What rural landscapes are deemed worthy of preservation in the rural-urban fringe has changed over the years. The *satoyama*, which is a traditional farm landscape made up of upland farm fields, rice paddies, and woodlots,[9] is one such landscape that has become popularized all over Japan[10] and is a landscape that exists in the rural-urban fringe of southwestern Ushiku. Yokohari and Bolthouse[11] have examined community efforts to preserve food garden and other *satoyama* landscapes in the rural-urban fringe of Tokyo, where many energetic non-farmer retirees are assisting farmers. These garden zones also exist in southwestern Ushiku, including Shimo *Machi* (town) where one can see many retirement-age and elderly people tending plots.

Urbanization and Preservation

Historic settlements and cultural landscapes within the rural-urban fringe are affected by urbanization. Although not specific to the rural-urban fringe, Hohn[12] mentions that town preservation first became a public issue in the late 1960s along with environmental protection due to rapid economic development, which impacted both the landscapes of towns while damaging the natural environment. The Cultural Properties Protection Law was first created in 1950.[13] It was then amended in 1975.[14] According to this law, groups of historically significant buildings that fit in with the surroundings and contribute to historic scenic beauty are considered valuable cultural assets. Monuments are also included under the cultural properties law, as are historic sites, places of scenic beauty, and flora and fauna. At a larger scale, rural and natural landscapes—for example, terraced rice paddies or waterways—can also be considered cultural properties.[15] Finally, groups of traditional buildings, as found in an old castle town or a post town, can become cultural properties—these are discussed below.[16] In Ushiku the

9. See Kobori and Primack, "Participatory Conservation Approaches," 307–11.

10. Chakraborty and Chakraborty, "*Satoyama*," 56. Lindstrom, "Classic and Cute," 237. Shimpo, "Urban Ecological Life," 109.

11. Yokohari and Bolthouse, "Planning for the Slow Lane," 423.

12. Hohn, "Important Preservation Districts," 150.

13. Siegenthaler, "Creation Myths," 34.

14. Hohn, "Important Preservation Districts," 150.

15. Agency for Cultural Affairs, *Our Treasure Cultural Landscapes*, 4. Agency for Cultural Affairs, *Policy of Cultural Affairs*, 38.

16. Agency for Cultural Affairs, *Policy of Cultural Affairs*, 38.

built landscape is preserved under the Cultural Properties Act or *bunkazai*. These are artifacts such as individual buildings, statues or other landmarks, and they can be designated as locally, prefecturally, or nationally important. Chateau Kamiya, which is a large multi-storey building built in 1903,[17] and located near the city hall outside the study area, is an example of an important national cultural property (*kuni no juyou bunkazai*).

Highlighting Landscape Change and Preservation

In terms of preserving built landscapes, Hohn[18] has examined the preservation of heritage landscapes in towns and cities of Japan. Hohn[19] and Sigenthaler,[20] more specifically, have examined the preservation of stop-over or post towns in rural areas of Japan—these are villages or towns with accommodation for foot travelers. They lined the ancient roads connecting feudal Tokyo (Edo) with castle towns where regional lords (or *Daimyo)* lived up until the end of the Edo Era in 1867. Old Ushiku town (composed of Kami and Shimo *Machi*) in southwestern Ushiku is one such post town on the old road (*Mitokaido*) connecting Edo with Mito City,[21] where Mito Castle is located (Map 2) (this will be discussed further below).

Repeat photography has been used for a number of years to illustrate landscape change. Meyer and Youngs[22] review the field of repeat photography—it can be used to illustrate the context of landscape change. They do this by describing historic experiences of travelers using different modes of transportation, e.g., riding horseback along a now abandoned trail encircling Yellowstone National Park in Montana, USA.[23] The two instructors and their students use repeat photography to show where the old trail used to go in comparison to the modern-day landscape. The class then discusses the context of this landscape change.

17. Ushiku Shi, *Ushiku Shi Bunkazai Gaidobukku* [Ushiku City Cultural Properties Guidebook], 10–11.

18. Hohn, "Townscape Preservation in Japanese Urban Planning," 213–55.
Hohn, "Important Preservation Districts," 150–59.

19. Hohn, "Townscape Preservation in Japanese Urban Planning," 219, 222, 224, 244, 255.

20. Siegenthaler, "Creation Myths," 29–45.

21. Koutsuushou, *Chibakokaidou Rekishi Sanpou* [Chibakokaidou historical walk].

22. Meyer and Youngs, "Historical Landscape Change," 387–409.

23. Meyer and Youngs, "Historical Landscape Change," 387–409.

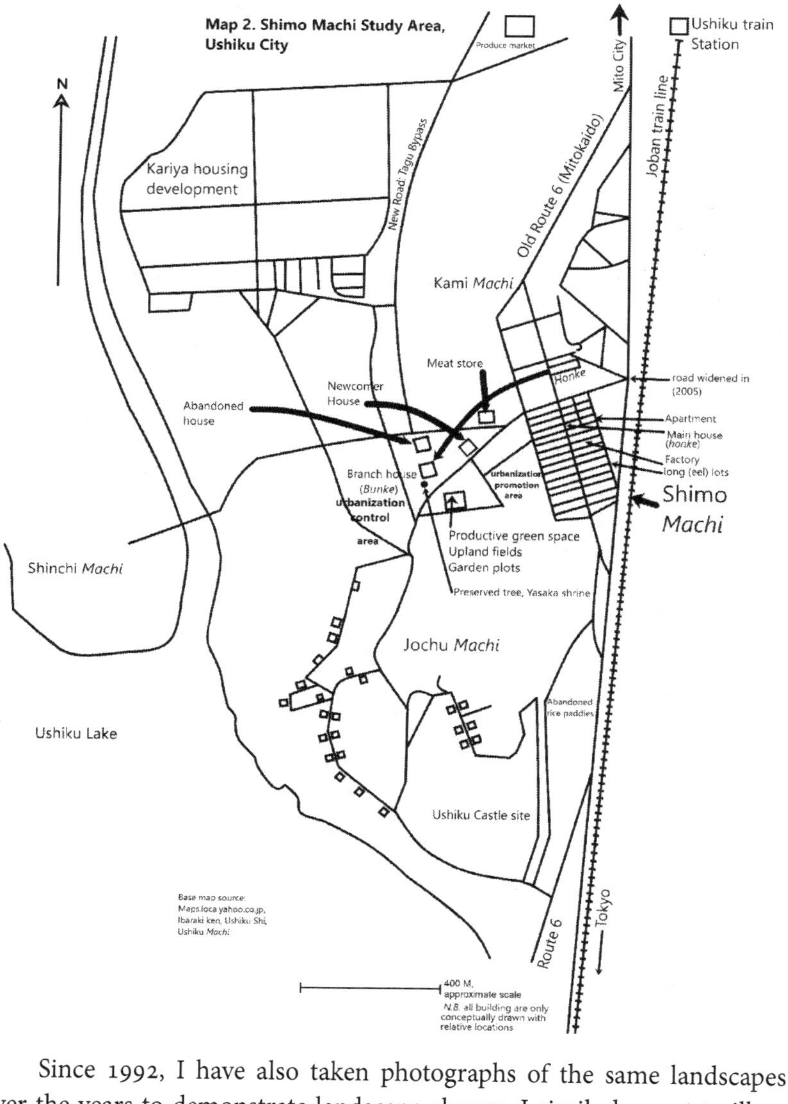

Since 1992, I have also taken photographs of the same landscapes over the years to demonstrate landscape change. I similarly want to illustrate landscape change in southwestern Ushiku using repeat photography and discuss these changes in terms of land-use policy and population in migration.

I also have referred to real estate maps (*jutaku chizu*) to record detailed landscape changes that I have observed since 1992 in the study area. I have also referred to topographical maps, air photos, and Google Earth images. Finally, since 2006 I have also talked to people informally while inventorying landscape changes, and I have interviewed city hall officials and leaders from Shimo *Machi* and Jochu wards and two members of the *Ushiku Satoyama no Kai* (Ushiku Satoyama Club). Finally, I have studied the 2011 Ushiku master plan, tourist maps, and other city documents related to landscape preservation.

Therefore, this study focuses on built and natural landscape change in the southwestern fringe of Ushiku since 1992. I focus on one ward on the outskirts of Ushiku—Shimo *Machi* ward—and I make comparisons with the adjacent and more rural Jochu ward. Of note, Shimo *Machi* ward is an old post town, and Jochu ward is an old clustered farm hamlet surrounded by traditional farm (*satoyama*) landscapes. These changes are illustrated with repeat photography.

The chapter is divided into three parts. The first part describes the evolution of southwestern Ushiku in the context of greater Ushiku City and surrounding communities, including greater Tokyo. The second part examines landscape change using repeat photography. The third part examines the context of these landscape changes, highlighting which landscape are being preserved and why.

Introduction to Southwestern Ushiku

2. *The Case Study of Ushiku: A Small City in the Rural-Urban Fringe of Tokyo*

Historic Background to Ushiku

According to records from 1841, Ushiku was a post town with lodging, public bath houses, and tea shops on the *Mitokaido* (Mito walking road) from Edo (present-day Tokyo) to Mito Castle, in present-day Mito City, east of Ushiku—for most people it took two nights and three days to walk the entire distance.[24] Ushiku village (*mura*) was the ninth post town from Nihonbashi in Edo along the *Mitokaido* where since the 1700s goods had been transported to the next post-town.[25] In 1896 the Joban railway line opened between Tokyo and Mito City, and Ushiku became a station on the line.[26] In 1889 Ushiku village consisted of the western-most appendage of present-day Ushiku city, about a quarter of the city's present size, and included the land west of the train station area, and present-day Kami Machi (also a city

24. Ushiku Shi, *Ushiku Shi Bunkazai Gaidobukku* [Ushiku City Cultural Properties Guidebook], 5.

25. Chanmiyo-TV, *Ushiku Time-Slip Journey.*

26. Hokoku Ushiku, "Shashin de miru 20 nen" [20 years in photos].

ward), Shimo Machi, Jochu, as well as areas to the west and north.[27] According to the Ushiku *Bunkazai* Guidebook,[28] Ushiku village eventually became Ushiku Town (*Machi*) after amalgamating with Okada village in 1954, and then Okuno village in 1955. It became a city in 1986 with a new combined area of about 59 square kilometers—the city's maximum east-west length is about 14.5km, and its maximum north-south distance is about 10.7 km.[29]

In the 1970s and 1980s people started to move to Ushiku and commute to their employment, usually as far as Tokyo, along Japan Railway's Joban line. The population of Ushiku, according to the *juumin kihon daichou*[30] (residents' basic register), was 16,356 in 1959. In 2019 the population started to decline to 85,076 from a maximum of 85,107 in 2018. (The 2022 population of Ushiku City is 84,478.) According to the Ushiku City Hall *jumin kihon daicho*, in 1992 the population was 62,255. Most of the growth has been related to a new housing development a few kilometers north of Ushiku railway station, where Hitachino-Ushiku railway station was built. Many of the people who I labelled as newcomers in the early 1990s now have lived in Ushiku approximately thirty years. Many of these people have reached retirement age, and some of them are in their seventies, eighties, and nineties—the population over sixty-five has almost tripled since 1992.[31] The southwestern part of Ushiku is within a 5 km walk or drive to the Ushiku railway station—many people walk, ride their bikes, or take the bus to the train station as there is little automobile parking around the station. Kami *Machi* is between Shimo *Machi* and the railway station—these wards are connected and are located along the old medieval road connecting Tokyo to Mito City. Jochu Ward is connected to Shimo *Machi* Ward on the southwest and is bordered on its far side by Ushiku Lake (Map 1).

27 *Gaikyou* [Outlook], 1. Ushiku Shi no Enkaku [Ushiku City History], 2.

28. Ushiku Shi, *Ushiku Shi Bunkazai Gaidobukku*, 1.

29. Ushiku Shi [City], *Tokei Ushiku Heisei 15 nendou* [Ushiku Statistics 2003], 13.

30 Ushiku Shi [City], *Shisei jouhou* [city administrative information], *Jumin kihon daichou jinkou* [Residents' Basic Register Population], (3 *gatsumatsu jinkou—settaisu*) [end of March population, household numbers] (2022, 4 *gatsu*, 1 *nichi koushin*) [updated 1 April 2022].

31. In 1992 the population over sixty-five years of age only accounted for 9 percent of the total population. Ushiku Shi [City], *Tokei Ushiku Heisei 15 nendou* [Ushiku Statistics 2003], 32. However, in 2022, the 65 and over population increased to 29.9 percent according to Ushiku Shi [City] Shisei Jouhou [City administrative information], *Jumin Kihon Daicho jinkou* [Citizens' basic population register] (*Choumeibetsu, Gyouseikutoubetsu, Nenreibetsu jinkou nado* [by town name, by administrative ward, etc., by age, etc.])(2022 *nen* 9 *gatsu*, 6 *nichi koushin*) [updated September 6, 2022]), *Kijunhi* [Reference date], *Reiwa* 4 *nen* 9 *gatsu* 1 *nichi genzai* [As of September 1, 2022], Ushiku Shi *Jinkou Piramiddo* [Ushiku City Population Pyramid].

Southwestern Ushiku: Jochu and Shimo Machi Wards (see Map 1)

Shimo Machi Ward Description:

I will first describe Shimo *Machi* ward, its landscape and its changes, then compare it briefly with adjacent and more Jochu ward. According to Ushiku City Hall statistics the 2022 population of Shimo ward was 1,195,[32] which is a decrease of 153 over the 2009 population of 1,355,[33] but an increase of 277 over the 1992 population of 898.[34] The old centre of Ushiku town (Ushiku M*achi)* consists of Shimo and Kami *Machis* (Map 3). These two places mean lower town (*Shimo*) and upper town (*Kami*). They are both post towns or (*shukuba machi*) on the *Mitokaido*, connecting to Mito city where the Mito lords (*daimyou*) lived in the Edo era. This ancient walking route generally follows the modern-day national Route 6, a mostly two-lane road that starts in Tokyo and goes along the Pacific coast to northern Japan. Route 6 is considered a highway; however, it travels through Ushiku and other communities with stop lights, so the speed limit is usually 50 or 60 km per hour. The current Route 6 highway bypasses Shimo and Kami *Machis*. Therefore, the traffic that currently travels along the parallel old Mito Road in Shimo and Kami Machis is generally local.

Both Shimo and Kami *Machis* have long lots facing old Route 6—sometimes referred to as eel (*unagi*) lots because they are so long[35] (Map 2). These are the properties belonging to old-time residents, who often own farmland on the outside of the hamlet, e.g., on the west side toward Jochu ward. These are the original households or *honke*. The reason for the long lots with narrow frontage along Route 6 was that the property was taxed according to the length of this frontage—the narrower the frontage, the cheaper the taxes.[36] The properties extend back about 75 m from the road. Traditionally, barns would be found in the back of these properties—many of these farm buildings have fallen apart or are in the process of doing so.

32. Ushiku *Shi* [City], *Shisei jouhou* [City administrative information], *Jumin kihon daichou jinkou (chomeibetsu, gyouseiku tou betsu, nenreibetsu jinkoutou)* (2022 *nen* 9 *gatsu* 6 *nichi, koushin* [updated September 6, 2022]) *kijunhi* [Reference date], *Reiwa* 4 *nen* 9 *gatsu* 1 *nichi genzai* [as of September 1, 2022], Gyouseikutou betsu jinkou—settaisu, https://www.city.ushiku.lg.jp/data/doc/1626231229_doc_32_0.pdf

33. Ushiku Shi [City] *Toukei Ushiku* [Ushiku Statistics] Dai 16 Hyou [Table no.16] Gyoseikubetsu Setaisuu to Jinkou no Ido [Household and Population Movement According to Ward], 28.

34. Ushiku Shi [City] *Jumin kihon daicho* [residents' basic register], 32, cited in Waldichuk, *Landscape Developments*, 139.

35. Chanmiyo-TV, *Ushiku Time-Slip Journey.*

36. Chanmiyo-TV, *Ushiku Time-Slip Journey.*

The roads crossing old Route 6 and running parallel to the long lots were also narrow, with often just enough room for one lane of automobile traffic. I noticed that one of the main roads crossing old Route 6 leading to the west side of Shimo *Machi* ward was widened in about 2005, so that two cars can easily pass by each other (Photos 1 and 2). In November 2015, I noticed that more widening of this crossroad had occurred near the meat store (Map 3) on the west side of old Route 6 in Shimo *Machi*.

Among these long-time residences are small factories (one exists near the Shimo *Machi* public hall) (Map 3). There are also shops that front many of these long lots, such as a produce store in the centre of Shimo *Machi*, a convenience store and a post office (Photo 3). The remains of a communal water well can still be seen in Shimo *Machi* along the *Mitokaido*.[37]

Branch families (known as *bunke*[38]), which are the offspring of the main household *(honke)* can be found in single detached homes on the west side of Shimo *Machi* ward, on the dry upland fields between Shimo *Machi* and Jochu wards (Map 3). Traditionally the oldest son takes over the main household in rural Japan. One or more of the siblings could build a home on the fields that the family owned nearby. Some of the other siblings would move to other locations, even Tokyo. If a family has a daughter and no sons, a man traditionally marries the daughter, takes her family name and takes over the family household. Over time the number of branch families has increased on this upland farmland to the west of old Route 6. There have also been newcomers from outside Ushiku moving to homes on this land among the *bunke*. Thus, there has been much urban development on this farmland in Shimo *Machi* next to Jochu.

37. Chanmiyo-TV, *Ushiku Time-Slip Journey*.

38. See the following article for information about *bunke-honke* relations and land inheritance: Ariga, "Family in Japan," 362–68.

Photograph 1: Narrow road crossing *Mitokaido* in Shimo *Machi*, May 1992 (T. Waldichuk photo)

Photograph 2: New apartment building and widened road, Shimo *Machi*, May 2005 (not exact location as photo 1) (T. Waldichuk photo)

Photograph 3: *Mitokaido* looking north from Shimo *Machi* to Kami *Machi*, post office and convenience store on left, approximately 1992 (Waldichuk, 1995, p.146)

Unlike Jochu ward, which is in a UCA, Shimo *Machi* ward is in an urbanization promotion zone (UPA), which has few development restrictions (which will be discussed later). Hence, some of the owners of the long eel lots along old Route 6 in Shimo hamlet have built apartment buildings in the back of the lots since about 2000 (Photo 2; Map 2). These apartment buildings are clustered near the Shimo community hall, hotel and convenience store.

Also, behind these new apartments, to the east toward Route 6, small rental houses (known as *shakuya*) surrounded by upland farm fields have been replaced by apartment buildings, and the surrounding farmland has also filled in with apartment buildings over time (Photos 4 and 5).

The line separating the urbanization promotion and control areas runs through Shimo *Machi* ward along its southwestern boundary, close to Jochu ward. This line has not changed since I first visited Ushiku in 1992, although in the north end of Ushiku the line has changed due to the development around the new Hitachino-Ushiku train station, which in the 1990s was known as *Hokubu Danchi* (meaning "Northern Area Track housing"). UPA/UCA lines are reviewed periodically to determine if growth warrants their expansion.[39]

39. Sorensen, "Land Readjustment," 2338.

Photograph 4: Shimo *Machi* Ward, April 1992 (T. Waldichuk photo)

Photograph 5: Shimo *Machi* Ward, May 2005 (T. Waldichuk photo)

In Shimo *Machi* ward there are some small areas of farmland that are preserved as "Productive green space" (*seisan ryokuchi*) which is—as mentioned above—farmland in an UPA that is preserved as farmland and is taxed at a lower rate than the surrounding urban land. Most of the farm areas are only a fraction of a hectare (minimum 500 square metres for "Productive green space"[40]), but they have existed since 1992 in Shimo *Machi* (and other parts of Ushiku).[41] The "Productive green space" law (*seisan ryokuchi ho*) was enacted in 1974.[42] Tsubota[43] outlines this law, which was revised in 1991. One has to farm their "Productive green space" land in the UPA continuously for 30 years in order to be taxed as farmland; otherwise, it is taxed at the much higher residential land.

Other Recent Changes and Trends in Shimo Machi Ward:

Not only have cross-streets been widened in Shimo *Machi*, but as mentioned previously there has also been a new road built that connects Shimo *Machi* ward with Kariya ward (Map 3). The development of this road, even the part going through Shimo *Machi*, has taken several years. This new road connects to the Route 6 bypass that will move cars from Route 6 west to the Inari R.; thus, bypassing Ushiku's downtown.[44] In addition, in front of the produce store across from the post office there was a fire tower (*hinomiyagura*) that people in the old days used to climb to ring the bell to warn of a fire in the neighborhood; however, it—like the one in Jochu—has been removed. Over the last few years, a traffic light has been installed in the intersection where the fire tower was.

The number of trees at the back of the long lots fronting old Route 6 has decreased too. There has been a notable reduction in green space in these long lots since the early 1990s, noted by comparing photos taken at the same location over time; this is especially notable where new apartments have been built on the back of the eel lots (Photos 1 and 2) and where the small rental houses have been replaced by an apartment building. This follows the trend in all of Ushiku City between 1992 and 2012 of an 18 percent reduction in forest and a 38 percent reduction in what is termed wilderness or wasteland.[45]

40. Fujie, "Summary of Review of Policies," 91.

41. See Waldichuk, "Green Space and Suburban Planning," 56–66.

42. Tsubota, *Urban Agriculture in Asia*, 4.

43. Tsubota, *Urban Agriculture in Asia*, 4–8.

44. As of March 26, 2022, the bypass now connects Jochu *machi* with Route 6 to the south (Koukudou kotsuushou (2022).

45. Ushiku Shi [City]. *Toukei Ushiku* [Ushiku Statistics], 6. *Chimokubetsu Menseki* [Area by land], 15.

Map 3. Ushiku City, Japan

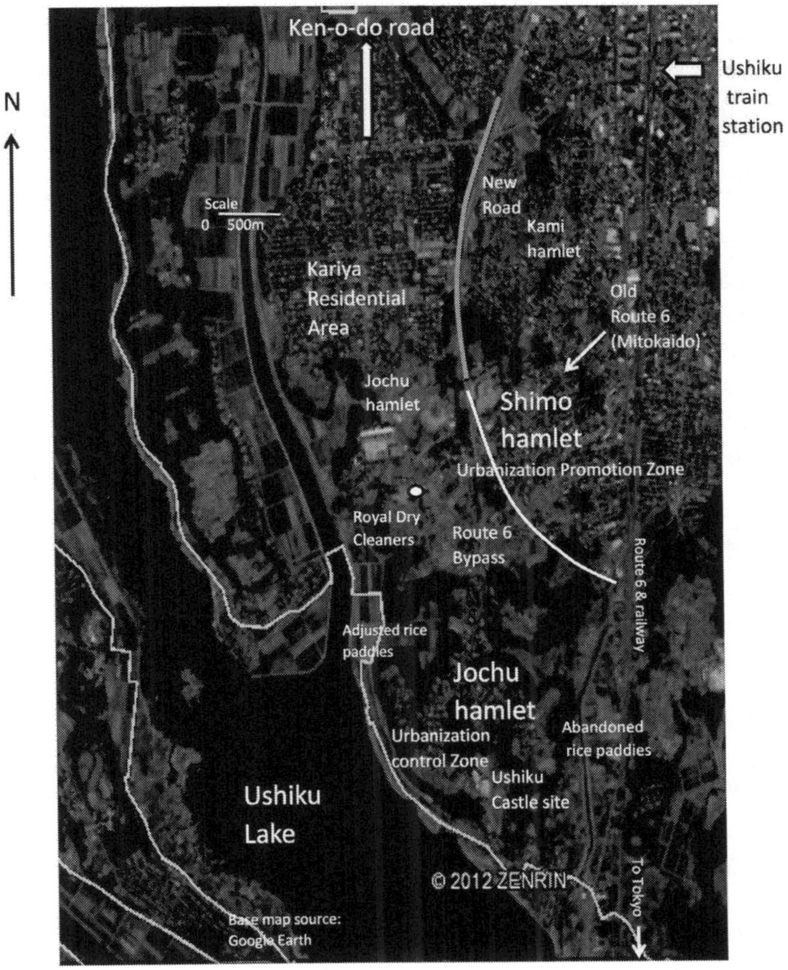

Many of the old homes along old Route 6—the *Mitokaido*—have been rebuilt. There is basically no old traditional housing left.[46] In the early 1990s I noticed one such rebuilt house, but the number of rebuilt homes has increased since then. Many of these new homes have been reconstructed without the characteristics of the previous homes. In the early 1990s there was a thatched roof house with mud walls and floors—home to two full-time farmers, which I had the honour of visiting, but it was torn down and replaced with a conventional single-detached home, which was later also torn

46. Ushiku Shi [City], *Ushiku Shi Bunkazai Gaidobukku* [Ushiku City Cultural Properties Guidebook], 5.

down. According to a carpenter in Shimo *Machi* it is hard to maintain the thatches on the roofs, as there are few skilled people to do so. In the 1970s there were several thatched roof houses, which one can see an image of in a recently released public YouTube video (at the 33:11 mark in the video).[47]

However, some buildings in Shimo *Machi* look neglected and may have been abandoned—this characteristic is more noticeable in rural Jochu. Most of the older settlements—both urban and rural—in Ushiku have abandoned housing,[48] attributed to an aging population, some of which can no longer continue to live in their homes, and a weak demand in Japan for purchasing used suburban and rural homes (people prefer to buy brand new houses[49]), which means that many of these homes sit empty. In the case of Shimo *Machi*, most of the run-down or abandoned-looking buildings are located in the back end of these long lots; however, these may be mostly out-buildings, e.g., sheds. Since about 2011, I did notice one house that was empty and for sale among the branch family and newcomer housing west of old Route 6 (map 2) toward Jochu.

DISCUSSION: CONTEXT OF LANDSCAPE CHANGE

The people who farm the landscape continue to change. In 1990 there were only four full-time farm households in Shimo *Machi*—the same number as in Jochu—but there were only twenty-four part-time farm households—much fewer than the sixty-one in Jochu ward.[50]

More people continue to use informal garden plots on upland fields west of old Route 6 between Shimo *Machi* and Jochu wards (Map 2); there is a blurring of labelling people as part-time farmers and gardeners growing produce for one's own consumption. Some of the informal garden plots are located next to productive green space (Map 2). Most of the people I have observed working this land are seniors. Some of the people who are gardening in Shimo *Machi* are newcomers who are either renting or borrowing the land from mostly aging farmers. In Jochu, some of these keen gardeners who I have talked to are retired non-farmers who have taken up gardening in earnest, exemplified by buying machinery such as rotor tillers.[51] Much of

47. Ushiku Shi [City], *Ushiku Shi no Rekishi Tanbou* [Ushiku City History Searching] (#18).

48. Kubo and Mashita, "Why the Rise," 3–22.

49. Plaza Homes, Housing Policy in Japan—Pre-owned Housing Market.

50. Ministry of Agriculture, Forestry and Fisheries, Hamlet Data Cards, cited in Waldichuk, "Green Space and Suburban Planning," 160.

51. This is similar phenomenon to what Yokohari and Bolthouse saw in terms of

the farmland that existed in the early 1990s between Shimo *Machi* and Jochu, which was in a UPA has been replaced by new housing (see repeat photography example, photos 6 and 7). There are still a few farming residents who sell their produce privately or through the Ushiku wholesale market. In terms of landscape preservation, two trees at Yasaka shrine on the west side of Shimo ward have been formally preserved and recorded with a number on a map published by the city's greenery promotion section (*Ryokka Suishinka*). Three trees have also been preserved in Jochu—these are called *shimin no ki* (city people's trees).[52] Also, starting in 1990 the beginning of a greening promotion plan for Ushiku started.[53]

More landscape change has taken place in Shimo *Machi* than Jochu *Machi* ward because it is in an UPA,[54] in which the urban development of land is permitted.[55] As mentioned in the introduction, this is part of the 1968 Urban Planning Law—farm and natural landscapes can be protected—at least indirectly—if they fall within UCAs.[56] There can be no urban development in a UCA, in which the ward of Jochu is largely located. On the other hand, Shimo *Machi* ward is in a UPA, where it is more difficult to preserve farm, forest, and other natural landscapes. Still, the 2011 Ushiku Master Plan does talk about maintaining agriculture (p. 59) and revitalizing the historical post town landscape (p. 56) in Shimo *Machi*;[57] however, I can find only one occurrence of "hozen" (the word for preservation) (p. 59) in the plan when describing a patch of green space close to the Shimo elementary school near Kami *Machi*, unlike in Jochu[58] where the plan mentions preserving natural landscapes and the remains of Ushiku castle. The master plan does mention *satoyama* landscapes, but not in Shimo *Machi*

retired white-collar workers taking up farming (Yokohari and Bolthouse, "Planning for the Slow Lane," 423).

52. Ushiku Shi [City], *Shimin no ki Gaido mappu* [Citizens' Tree Guide Map].

53. Ushiku Shi [City], *Gurin ha-moni-Ushiku* [Green Harmony Ushiku]—*Ushiku Shi Midori to Shizen no Machizukuri Ryoka Suishin Keikaku (Gaiyou)* [Ushiku City Green and Nature *Machizukuri* Greening Promotion Plan (Outline)].

54. Based on data in the Greening Promotion Plan, p. 13 (above), green space and agricultural space has declined from 92% in 1947 to 21% in 1989 in the urbanization promotion areas of Ushiku, but in the Urbanization control areas the equivalent decline is only 10% over the same time period and almost all of that is farmland.

55. See Sorensen, "Land Readjustment, Urban Planning," 2338.

56. See Sorensen, "Land Readjustment and Metropolitan Growth," 232.

57. Ushiku Shi [City], *Toshikeikaku Masuta- Puran 2011* [Urban Planning Master Plan 2011], 56, 59.

58. Ushiku Shi [City], *Toshikeikaku Masuta- Puran 2011* [Urban Planning Master Plan 2011], 70.

or Jochu.[59] Instead the plan mentions *yatsuda* landscapes in Jochu, which roughly translates as wet rice paddies in depressions or troughs.[60]

Photograph 6: Shimo Machi uplands, 1992. (Waldichuk, 1995, p.144; 1998, p. 19)

59. Examples of *satoyama* can be found on the following pages: Ushiku Shi [City], *Toshikeikaku Masuta- Puran 2011* [Urban Planning Master Plan 2011], 11, 14, 32, 36, 37, 40–42.

60. Ushiku Shi [City], *Toshikeikaku Masuta-Puran 2011* [Urban Planning Master Plan 2011], 69.

Photograph 7: New housing in same location as photograph 6, Shimo *Machi* uplands, 2006. (T. Waldichuk photo)

The lack of preservation in the post town section of Shimo *Machi* contrasts with the fact that at least seven post towns in Japan have had their landscapes preserved as "Important Preservation Districts" (IPDs); the first designation was in 1976.[61] Waley[62] mentions that the promotion of tourism has been a major incentive to apply for IPD status and points to the example of Shirakawa Village in Gifu Prefecture. In the greater Tokyo area the only IPD is located in Kawagoe City in Saitama Prefecture,[63] which adjoins Tokyo Prefecture and has many old Edo Era buildings clustered together, which I have taken a group of our TRU students to see while on a field course. Still, in Shimo *Machi* there was an English language brochure produced by NPO Corporation Chanmiyo TV titled "Ushiku Time-Slip Journey" in about 2015–17, which discusses Ushiku post-town and includes a map of *Mitokaido* going through Kami and Shimo *Machis*.[64]

In Jochu, which is mostly in an urbanization control area, the upland fields are still generally cultivated. However, most of the rice paddies close to Route 6 have been abandoned. This is because a new bypass road for Route 6 is going through this area. This national-level public development can take place in an urbanization control area.[65] Farm landscapes in Shimo *Machi* ward have not been preserved, other than areas of productive agricultural green space.

CONCLUSION

In summary, Shimo *Machi* ward contains a traditional *shukuba Machi* (post town), and it is located along the old *Mitokaido* that ends in Mito City. However, this road has not been designated as a culturally significant landscape in Ushiku. It has been highlighted by the transportation ministry where it travels through Kashiwa or Matsudo cities, closer to Tokyo.[66] There has been urban residential development in Shimo *Machi*,

61. Hohn, "Important Preservation Districts," 150. Hohn, "Townscape Preservation," 213.

62. Waley, "Who Cares about the Past," 148–66.

63. Waley, "Who Cares about the Past," 154.

64. Chanmiyo TV, *Ushiku Time-Slip Journey.*

65. Sorensen, "Land Readjustment and Metropolitan Growth: An Examination of Suburban Land Development and Urban Sprawl in the Tokyo Metropolitan Area," 234.

66. *Kokudou Koutsuushou Kantou Chiho Seibi Kyoku* [Japan Ministry of Land,

particularly on the upland fields between Shimo *Machi* and adjacent Jochu ward. Moreover, the homes of the main household families (*honke*) on the *Mitokaido*, located on eel lots, are gradually being renovated or totally redeveloped. On the east side of *Mitokaido* there are apartments in the back yards of some of these eel lots. Trees that were in the back of these long lots have gradually disappeared. On the other hand, there is still an abundance of green space in adjacent Jochu, which is protected by its designation as an urbanization control area (one could also argue that there is an increased amount of green space in the form of annual and perennial plants taking over abandoned rice paddies and some upland fields because of an aging and declining farm population). Also, according to the 2011 Ushiku master plan, these natural landscapes in Jochu are to be preserved, e.g., the basic policies related to the preservation of the water environment of Ushiku Lake and the natural environment related to farmland and green space.[67] Although these Jochu landscapes are not explicitly labeled as being related to *satoyamas*, the word *satoyama* is used throughout the master plan to describe much of the natural landscape. As mentioned previously, these *satoyama* landscapes have a positive image in Japan.[68] When I undertook a questionnaire study in 1992–93,[69] newcomer residents wanted a more urban landscape (in both Shimo *Machi* and Jochu), whereas old-timers did not want the landscape to change. Overall, most respondents wanted the landscape to remain the same. But the landscape has gradually become more urban, especially in Shimo *Machi*. Still, there are efforts to preserve small-scale garden plots, and as exemplified by a brochure and youtube videos, keen residents have been attempting to educate others about the local cultural landscapes of the past.

DISCUSSION QUESTIONS

1. Who should determine which public landscapes should be preserved?
2. What are the benefits of green space?
3. How and why do attitudes toward cultural and natural landscapes change over time?

Infrastructure, Transport and Tourism Kanto Regional Development Bureau]. *Chiba-kokaidou* [Chiba old highway] *Rekishi Sanpou* [historical walk].

67. Ushiku Shi [City], *Toshikeikaku Masuta-Puran 2011* [Urban Planning Master Plan 2011], 68.

68. See Lindstrom, "Classic and Cute," 237.

69. Waldichuk, *Landscape Developments*.

4. How might local residents' attitudes to landscape change differ from visitors? Think of examples where you live.
5. What is the relationship among landscape preservation policies and landscape attitudes?
6. What are the practical modern-day problems of trying to preserve old cultural landscapes?

BIBLIOGRAPHY

Agency for Cultural Affairs. *Our Treasure Cultural Landscapes to Future Generations, Cultural Landscape Protection in Japan.* https://www.bunka.go.jp/english/report/publication/pdf/pamphlet_en_01.pdf.

———. *Policy of Cultural Affairs.* http://www.bunka.go.jp/english/report/annual/pdf/2016_policy.pdf.

Ariga, Kizaemon. "The Family in Japan." *Marriage and Family Living* 16 (1954) 362–68. https://doi.org/10.2307/348444.

Beesley, Kenneth, ed. *The Rural-Urban Fringe in Canada: Conflict and Controversy.* Brandon, MB: Rural Development Institute, University of Brandon, 2010.

Chakraborty, Abhik, and Shamik Chakraborty. "Satoyama: A Landscape Conservation Discourse of Romantic Nostalgia and Reflexive Modernity in 'Post Growth' Japan." *Japan Studies Association Journal* 11 (2013) 46–64.

Chanmiyo-TV. *Ushiku Time-Slip Journey—Guide Map for Tourists.* NPO Corporation Chanmiyo-TV, n.d.

Fujie, Takeshi. "Summary of Review of Policies that Affect Land Mobility and/or Values in Japan." In Annex 2 Summary of Country Case Studies. OECD. Agricultural Support, Farm Land Values and Sectoral Adjustment—the Implications for Policy Reform. 2008, 89–93. https://read.oecd-ilibrary.org/agriculture-and-food/agricultural-support-farm-land-values-and-sectoral-adjustment_9789264031739-en#page1.

Gaikyou [Outlook], 1. Ushiku Shi no Enkaku [Ushiku City History], . . .9. Shimin no Kurashi [Citizen Living]. https://www.city.ushiku.lg.jp/data/doc/1528095205_doc_228_1.pdf.

Hasegawa, Junichi. "Drafting of the 1968 Japanese City Planning Law." *Planning Perspectives* 29 (2014) 23–38. https://doi.org/10.1080/02665433.2014.899921.

Hebbert, Michael, and Norihiro Nakai. *How Tokyo Grows: Land Development and Planning on the Metropolitan Fringe.* Occasional Paper No. 11. London: Suntory-Toyota International Centre for Economics and Related Disciplines, London School of Economics & Political Science, 1988.

Hohn, Uta. "Townscape Preservation in Japanese Urban Planning." *Town Planning Review* 68 (1997) 213–55. http://www.jstor.org/stable/40113818.

———. "Important preservation districts for groups of historic buildings." In *Hozon-Architectural and Urban Conservation in Japan,* edited by S. Enders, N. Gutschow, (Hg.), 150–159. Stuttgart: Edition Axel Menges GmbH. Google Books, 1998.

Hokoku Ushiku. "Shashin de miru 20 nen" [20 years in photos]. 31 May 2006. https://www.city.ushiku.lg.jp/kouhoushi/2006_06_01/p04shasin.htm.

Ishikawa, Mikiko. "Green Structure Plan for a Sustainable Urban-Rural Relationship in Japan." In *Toward Sustainable Cities: East Asian, North American and European Perspectives on Managing Urban Regions*, edited by A. Sorensen et al., 228–38. Aldershot, UK: Ashgate, 2004.

Japan Ministry of Land, Infrastructure and Transportation. *Introduction of Urban Land Use Planning System in Japan*. City Planning Division, City and Regional Development Bureau, Tokyo: Ministry of Land, Infrastructure and Transportation, January 2003. https://www.mlit.go.jp/common/001050453.pdf.

Kobori, Hiromi, and Richard B. Primack. "Participatory Conservation Approaches for *Satoyama*, the Traditional Forest and Agricultural Landscape of Japan." *AMBIO: A Journal of the Human Environment* 32 (2003) 307–11. https://doi.org/10.1579/0044-7447-32.4.307.

Kokudou Koutsuushou Kantou Chiho Seibi Kyoku [Japan Ministry of Land, Infrastructure, Transport and Tourism Kanto Regional Development Bureau]. *Chibakokaidou* [Chiba old highway] *Rekishi Sanpou* [historical walk]. http://www.ktr.mlit.go.jp/chiba/limit/rekishi/03/index.htm.

Kokudou Koutsuushou Kantou Chiho Seibi Kyoku [Japan Ministry of Land, Infrastructure, Transport and Tourism Kanto Regional Development Bureau]. *Ippan kokudou 6 gou Ushiku Tsuchiura baipasu* [General national highway 6 Ushiku Tsuchiura bypass]. May 2005. https://www.ktr.mlit.go.jp/ktr_content/content/000835931.pdf.

Kubo, Tomoko, and Michihiro Mashita. "Why the Rise in Urban Housing Vacancies Occurred and Matters in Japan." In *The Rise in Vacant Housing in Post-Growth Japan: Housing Markets, Urban Policy, and Revitalizing Aging Cities*, edited by Tomoko Kubo and Yoshimichi Yui, 3–22. Advances in Geographical and Environmental Sciences. Singapore: Springer, 2020. https://doi.org/10.1007/978-981-13-7920-8_1.

Lindstrom, Kati. "Classic and Cute: Framing Biodiversity in Japan Through Rural Landscapes and Mascot Characters." *Popular Communication* 17, no.3 (2019): 233–251. https://doi.org/10.1080/15405702.2019.1567735.

Meyer, Judith l., and Yolonda Youngs. "Historical Landscape Change in Yellowstone National Park: Demonstrating the Value of Intensive Field Observation and Repeat Photography." *Geographical Review* 108 (2018) 387–409. https://doi.org/10.1111/gere.12255.

Nakai, Norihiro. "Urbanization Promotion and Control in Metropolitan Japan." *Planning Perspectives* 3 (1988) 197–216. https://doi.org/10.1080/02665438808725659.

Plaza Homes. "Housing Policy in Japan—Pre-owned Housing Market." March 26, 2018 https://www.realestate-tokyo.com/news/pre-owned-housing-market-in-japan/.

Shimpo, Naomi. "Urban Ecological Life in a Metropolitan Area—An Insight From *Satoyama* Conservation Activities in the Greater Tokyo Area." *Landscape and Ecological Engineering* 18 (2022) 109–19. https://doi.org/10.1007/s11355-021-00484-5.

Siegenthaler, Peter. "Creation Myths for the Preservation of Tsumago Post-Town." *Planning Forum* 9 (2003) 29–45. http://www.txstate.edu/history/people/faculty/siegenthaler/contentParagraph/0/content_files/file2/creationmyth.pdf.

Sorensen, André. "Land Readjustment, Urban Planning, and Urban Sprawl in the Tokyo Metropolitan Area." *Urban Studies* 36 (1999) 2333–60. https://doi.org/10.1080/0042098992458.

Sorensen, André. "Land Readjustment and Metropolitan Growth: An Examination of Suburban Land Development and Urban Sprawl in the Tokyo Metropolitan Area." *Progress in Planning* 53 (2000) 217–330. https://doi.org/10.1016/S0305-9006(00)00002-7.

Tsubota, Kunio. "Urban Agriculture in Asia: Lessons from Japanese Experience." n.d., 1–10. https://www.fftc.org.tw/htmlarea_file/library/20110728160155/eb576.pdf.

Ushiku Shi [City]. *Gurin ha-moni- Ushiku [Green Harmony Ushiku]—Ushiku Shi Midori to Shizen no Machizukuri Ryoka Suishin Keikaku (Gaiyou)* [Ushiku City Green and Nature *Machizukuri* Greening Promotion Plan (Outline), Oct 1990.

Ushiku Shi [City]. *Shimin no ki Gaido mappu* [Citizens' Tree Guide Map], n.d.

———. *Shisei Joohou* [city administrative information], *Jumin Kihon Daicho jinkou* [Residents' basic population register] (*Chomeibetsu, Gyoseikutoubetsu, Nenreibetsujinkou nado* [by town name, by administrative ward, etc., by age, etc.]) (2022 *nen* 9 *gatsu*, 6 *nichi koushin* [updated September 6, 2022]), *Kijunhi* [Reference date], *Reiwa* 4 *nen* 9 *gatsu* 1 *nichi genzai* [As of September 1, 2022], Ushiku *Shi Jinkou Piramiddo* [Ushiku City Population Pyramid]. https://www.city.ushiku.lg.jp/data/doc/1626231221_doc_32_0.pdf.

———. *Shisei jouhou* [city administrative information], *Jumin kihon daichou jinkou* [Residents' Basic Population Register], (3 *gatsumatsu jinkou—settaisu*) [end of March population, household numbers] (2022, 4 *gatsu*, 1 *nichi koushin*), 3 *gatsumatsu no jinkou, settaisu* [End of March population, number of households]. https://www.city.ushiku.lg.jp/page/page001937.html.

———. *Tokei Ushiku Heisei 15 Nendou* [Ushiku Statistics 2003], Ushiku: *Kikakubu* [Planning Department], *Keiei kikakuka* [Corporate Planning Division], March 2004.

———. *Tokei Ushiku* [Ushiku statistics], 6. *Chimokubetsu menseki* [area by land, n.d. http://www. city.ushiku.lg.jp/scms/admin76381/data/doc/1367998670_doc_24_0.pdf.

———. *Toukei Ushiku* [Ushiku Statistics] Dai 16 Hyou [Table no.16] *Gyoseikubetsu Setaisuu to Jinkou no Ido* [Household and Population Movement According to Ward], 2012. http://www.city.ushiku.lg.jp/scms/admin76381/data/doc/1354188281_doc_24_0.pdf.

———. *Toshikeikaku Masuta- Puran 2011* [Urban Planning Master Plan 2011], Ibaraki Ken, Ushiku *Shi:* Ushiku *Shi, Kensetsubu* [Construction Division], *Toshikeikakuka* [City Planning Section], 2012.

———. *Ushiku Shi no Rekishi Tanbou* [Ushiku City History Searching] (#18), Ibaraki, Chanmiyo TV, June 19, 2022, 33:11. https://www.youtube.com/watch?v=E-19dmN73y4&list=PLqDahvltHGU494WaopvGxWUJ6whIcZ51G&index=3.

Ushiku *Shi Bunkazai Gaidobukku* [Ushiku City Cultural Properties Guidebook], 2015 Ushiku: Ushiku *Shi Bunka Isan Katsuyou Jikkou Iinkai* [Cultural Heritage Utilization Executive Committee], Ushiku *Shi Kyouiku Iinkai Bunka Geijuutsuka* [Board of Education Culture and Arts Division]. 2015.

Waldichuk, Thomas. "A Comparison of Japanese and North American Attitudes toward Residential Landscapes in the Rural-Urban Fringe." *Great Lakes Geographer* 5 (1998) 15–29.

———. *Landscape Developments on the Rural-Urban Fringe of a Commuter City Near Tokyo: Residents' Attitudes in Ushiku City, with Western Comparisons*. North York, ON: York University, Department of Geography, PhD diss., 1995.

———. "Green Space and Suburban Planning in Japan." In *Future Uncertain: Economic, Environmental, Social, and Political Challenges Facing Japan*, edited by Merran Eby and David A Welch, 56–66. Proceedings of the Annual Conference of the Japan Studies Association of Canada, October 12–17, Toronto: University of Toronto, Munk School of Global Affairs, 2018. http://buna.yorku.ca/jsac/jsac2017/jsac2017_proceedings.pdf.

Waley, Paul. "Who Cares About the Past in Today's Tokyo?" In *Urban Spaces in Japan: Cultural and Social Perspectives*, edited by Christoph Brumann and Evelyn Schulz, 148–66. Nissan Institute/Routledge Japanese Studies Series. London: Taylor & Francis, 2012.

Yokohari, Makoto, and Jay Bolthouse. "Planning for the Slow Lane: The Need to Restore Working Greenspaces in Maturing Contexts." *Landscape and Urban Planning* 100 (2011) 421–24. https://doi.org/10.1016/j.landurbplan.2011.02.024.

11

What Kind of Hero Is Greta?

The Promise and Problem of Youth Climate Activism in Swedish Opinion Journalism

JENNA COUGHLIN AND CULLEN HAUCK

INTRODUCTION

Climate change is a pressing issue facing today's children and youth,[1] yet this topic is underrepresented global school curricula. In a 2021 analysis of the education plans and curricula frameworks in forty-six member states, UNESCO found that less than half make reference to climate change.[2] Despite this, educators recognize the importance of this issue for young people: In the same UNESCO study, a majority of survey respondents (predominantly teachers and principals) reported that it was "very or somewhat common" for children and youth to participate in environmental activities outside of school, and most also indicated school support for these activities.[3] In addition to the direct impacts of climate change, one reason for

1. Lee et al., "Youth Perceptions of Climate Change"; Hickman et al., "Climate Anxiety in Children."

2. "Learn for Our Planet," 3.

3. "Learn for Our Planet," 29–31.

educators' support may be concern for the mental health of young people. Researchers have predicted that "chronic, long-term, and potentially inescapable stressors" related to climate change will adversely affect mental health.[4] When Swedish climate activist Greta Thunberg became the global face of youth climate activism in 2019, some expressed concern for her mental health, and even those supportive of her cause debated the efficacy of her bleak rhetoric.[5] Some of her most famously pointed utterances, such as "I want you to panic," and "You have taken away my dreams and my childhood,"[6] have been met with the concern that they might instill hopelessness in young listeners.

On the other hand, narratives that convey a positive version of Thunberg's story often depict her as a heroic figure.[7] Figuring Thunberg as a hero has obvious appeal: it is familiar to Western audiences, who are accustomed to stories in which a single protagonist overcomes significant odds to win the day.[8] It also presents itself as an alternative to what is perceived as "hopeless" climate discourse[9]: As Hickman et al. point out, children and young people have limited power in society; this lack of agency is associated with climate anxiety, while a restoring agency can mitigate stress.[10] Figuring young activists as heroes and encouraging other young people to follow their example is an appealing strategy for increasing their sense of agency. However, as Moriarty (2021) demonstrates, the hero narrative facilitates hopeful thinking by focusing on the actions of the individual, rather than facilitating an understanding of complex systems and how collective action can be taken to influence them.

Due to its robust welfare state and emphasis on equality, Sweden is sometimes assumed by outsiders to be a society that values the collective above the individual. However, as Brembeck et al. summarize, while "an ethos of solidarity" in Sweden has promoted the idea that no one is better

4. Hickman et al., "Climate Anxiety in Children," e871.

5. Harsanyi, "Real Tragedy of Greta Thunberg"; Kalkstein, "Sorry, Greta, But You're (Mostly) Wrong"; Russo, "Don't Dampen Graduation Joy"; Yoder, "Do We Need More"; Zraick, "Greta Thunberg"; Klein, "Your Kids Are Not Doomed."

6. Thunberg, *No One Is Too Small*, 43, 96.

7. Moriarty, "Modeling Environmental Heroes," analyzes this narrative in children's literature, but heroic figuration of Thunberg is also addressed in Martínez García, "Constructing an Activist Self"; Ryalls and Mazzarealla, "Famous, Beloved, Reviled"; Taft, "Hopeful, Harmless, and Heroic"; and Witoszek and Mueller, "Ecological Ethics of Nordic Children's Tales."

8. Moriarty, "Modeling Environmental Heroes."

9. Taft, "Hopeful, Harmless, and Heroic."

10. Hickman et al., "Climate Anxiety in Children," e863, e871.

than anyone else, "the Northerners have long regarded themselves as inviolable individuals."[11] Thus, an ambiguous "theme" runs throughout the welfare state, that of "personal freedom and collective obligation." Media responses to Thunberg's activism and rhetoric reflect this ambiguity: Rather than avoiding the "hero narrative" in favor of one that stresses collective action, opinion writing from around the time of the first global school strike tends to figure Thunberg as an almost superhuman individual worth emulating by comparing her to both fictional and historical hero figures.

In this chapter, various hero narratives identified from a selection of Swedish opinion writing will be analyzed for how they figure Thunberg as a girl activist, particularly the extent to which they emphasize individual versus shared agency and responsibility. In the conclusion, the relevance of this study will be discussed, particularly for educators who wish to teach children and youth about climate change in a way that grants them agency and promote trusting relationships with adults.

Methodology

This research was undertaken as part of a broader project entitled "Responses to Greta Thunberg in International Media," in which a faculty member (Coughlin) together with several student researchers (including Hauck) has compiled a public Zotero database of opinion journalism related to Thunberg from multiple countries.[12] The central aim of this project is to assess how different countries have responded to the global youth climate movement by examining the representation of Thunberg and the school strikes movement in opinion journalism from digital and print newspapers. Opinion journalism was chosen as the focus of inquiry because it reflects a variety of viewpoints on Thunberg's leadership and fosters public discussion on topics ranging from her individual identity to the school strikes as a whole.

This chapter focuses on Swedish opinion journalism published from August 2018 to March 2019 and is the result of collaborative research conducted by Coughlin and Hauck. This was a critical period for the expansion of youth leadership initiatives related to climate change, including Greta's first school strike and the establishment of the global #FridaysforFuture movement. Responses to the movement greatly diversified as Thunberg began traveling to give speeches at leadership conferences in Davos, Frankfurt,

11. Brembeck et al., "Introduction," 13.

12. See https://pages.stolaf.edu/responses-to-thunberg/.

and the UN, culminating with the first global climate strike held on March 15, 2019, with over 1.5 million youth participants.[13]

The texts analyzed were sourced onsite at the Stockholm University Library using Retriever Research (Mediearkivet). Articles were obtained using the search term "Greta Thunberg" and then sorted into the database as either news or opinion journalism with irrelevant entries omitted. The search was limited to *Dagens Nyheter*, *Aftonbladet*, *Expressen*, *Göteborgs-Posten*, *Sydsvenskan*, and *Svenska Dagbladet* (listed here in descending order based on their coverage of Thunberg). These newspapers have some of the widest circulation in Sweden and originate in its populous southern region between Stockholm and Malmö. The genres of Swedish opinion journalism analyzed for this chapter include leaders/editorials (*ledare*), commentaries (*krönikor*), debate columns (*debatt*), and letters to the editor (*läsarinlägg, debattinlägg*).

Students were introduced to rhetorical criticism as a methodological approach and also read peer-reviewed scholarship that analyzes either communications by or media representations of Thunberg and the school strikes movement. This scholarship has been published in various fields including media and communications, education, leadership studies, and gender studies, among others. Students also read sources about childhood and gender in a Nordic context. In tandem with these sources, feminist rhetorical criticism and ideological rhetorical criticism emerged as particularly useful approaches.[14]

The Girl Activist as Hero

This chapter focuses on one prominent rhetorical strategy observed in opinion pieces from this period—comparing Thunberg to heroic figures as they appear in history, fiction, and contemporary media. These comparisons to heroes largely align with findings by Taft (2020), a girlhood studies scholar who critiques the western liberal presentation of girls as "hopeful, harmless, and heroic." Taft reads the "girl activist" as a "figure," utilizing Claudia Castañeda's definition of the term as "the simultaneously material and semiotic effect of specific practices."[15] Among Taft's examples are Malala Yousafzai and Emma Gonzalez, both of whom are figures with whom Greta has been compared in both Swedish and international media.[16] Taft argues

13. Hazan, "Massive School Strikes Worldwide."
14. Foss, *Rhetorical Criticism*, 141–44, 237–42.
15. Cited in Taft, "Hopeful, Harmless, and Heroic," 3.
16. Cf. Wahrborg, "Någons frihet tycks alltid"; Hanson, "Greta Thunberg och

that, despite its "neoliberal and colonial logics," the "girl power" movement has nevertheless opened up a space of potential for girls to become legible as political actors.[17] However, she argues that figuring politically active girls as sources of hope "can . . . be potentially demobilizing in that it assuages public feelings of concern and returns us to a position of political comfort."[18] Likewise, figuring girls as "harmless" mitigates the anxieties raised by calls to transform political and economic systems: such calls need not be taken seriously when made by "just a girl"—a figure who is inspiring, but ultimately powerless.[19]

Similarly, Moriarty notes that children's literature about Greta Thunberg tends to depict her as an exceptional hero who must work against forces in society to inspire change. While narratives about Thunberg have the positive ecopedagogical goal of inspiring children to become ecocitizens, the hero narrative ultimately undermines this goal by "celebrating individual success positing that change comes through exceptional individuals."[20] Moriarty critiques this "idealization of the individual" for its association with the values of "neoliberal extractive capitalism."[21] She advocates instead for "environmental literature that stresses the role of 'ordinary' people who partake in community actions, and which advocates for collective action that leads to societal transformations."[22]

HERO FIGURATIONS IN SWEDISH OPINION JOURNALISM

In the first months after Thunberg's initial school strike, Swedish opinion writers portray her as a contemporary iteration of heroes from history and fiction, characterized by their unique ability to lead by challenging those in authority. In particular, these authors link her pursuit of higher ideals to that of other girls remembered for holding society accountable and protesting oppression. As Ole Andreas Kvamme articulates, Thunberg's rhetoric emphasizes the "cosmopolitan" aspect of the Paris Agreement rather than its intergovernmental aspect. Focusing on the cosmopolitan norms emphasized in the agreement, including the wellbeing of future generations,

Emma González."

17. Taft, "Hopeful, Harmless, and Heroic," 5–6.
18. Taft, "Hopeful, Harmless, and Heroic," 7–8.
19. Taft, "Hopeful, Harmless, and Heroic," 8.
20. Moriarty, "Modeling Environmental Heroes," 206.
21. Moriarty, "Modeling Environmental Heroes," 206.
22. Moriarty, "Modeling Environmental Heroes," 206.

biodiversity, and equity, allows her to appeal to these norms to support her argument, while also critiquing governments for failing to uphold them in practice.[23] This strategy gives Thunberg and other youth authority to participate in democracy, as members of the "future generations" referenced in the agreement.[24] Many of the heroes to whom Thunberg is compared share a commitment to higher ideals and aim to hold political leaders accountable. These comparisons suggest that Thunberg has taken up the mantle of responsibility that has been cast off by adults.

For example, *Aftonbladet* columnist Dick Harrison compares Greta Thunberg's push for political action on climate change to Joan of Arc's efforts to legitimize King Carl VII in an embattled fifteenth-century France. As Harrison contends, both Greta Thunberg and Joan of Arc act as "exponents of the same political . . . [and] historical phenomenon—even children and youth can play prominent roles in their own age."[25] Although Harrison points out that the religious nature of Joan's agenda differs from Greta's, the two figures are similar in carrying out "idealistic offensives that go upwind" of society. Harrison also mentions Malala Yousafzai of Pakistan and Nadia Murad of Iraq–both Nobel Peace Prize laureates–who worked to liberate children and other vulnerable people from systemic injustices. Harrison's comparison is meant to suggests that, although exceptional, Thunberg is not an unprecedented figure in world history.

In the realm of fiction, Thunberg has also been compared to the famed children's book protagonist Pippi Longstocking. This comparison has been made in Swedish and international media as well as protest art, and Thunberg herself seems amenable to this comparison, describing it as "fun."[26] According to Eva-Maria Metcalf, since the 1960s and 1970s Pippi Longstocking has fit "the model for heroes and heroines in children's literature" who are "independent, willful, strong, rebellious, and imaginative child protagonists who dared question authority even in realistic prose."[27] The product of Swedish author Astrid Lindgren's childhood dream of a person who has power but no will to abuse it,[28] she lives independent of social norms and possesses supernatural physical strength along with a keen wit, both of which she uses to protect her kid neighbors from bullying, outsmart

23. Kvamme, "School Strikes, Environmental Ethical Values," 17–19.

24. Kvamme, "School Strikes, Environmental Ethical Values," 19.

25. Harrison, "Harrisons historia." All translations from the original Swedish are by Jenna Coughlin.

26. Sörbring, "Årets Kvinna—Greta Thunberg."

27. Metcalf, "Pippi Longstocking in the United States," 22.

28. Führer, "Astrid Lindgren's World in Vimmerby," 255.

condescending adults, and resist cultural expectations imposed upon herself. Per Svensson compares the adults who uphold the social order in Pippi's adventures, such as teachers and police officers, to Thunberg's conservative critics.[29] He characterizes them as laughable "villains" who present incoherent arguments and ultimately lose their credibility. In one instance, a policeman assumes Pippi does not know the capital of Portugal and uses this to demonstrate that she should be in school; when her reply implies that she not only knows the answer but has been to Lisbon herself, the officer looks foolish for having underestimated her. Svensson compares this to critics who tell Thunberg to go back to school to learn more about climate change, even though her speech and actions make it clear that her knowledge surpasses that of many adults. For Svensson, the exchange reveals the faulty logic in conservatives' arguments about who has the legitimacy to speak—youth and lack of power do not necessarily imply a lack of authority on an issue.[30]

Knutsen identifies a similar representation of Thunberg in Norwegian opinion journalism, which she terms "the young girl against the crabby old men."[31] Norwegian opinion writers adopt this discourse when rising to defend Thunberg from older, white men in proximity to power, whom studies suggest tend to be skeptical toward climate science.[32] In pointing to Pippi's encounter with the police officer, Svensson aligns Thunberg's critics with older men in power. Since the police officer is made to look ridiculous in the scene, Svensson's comparison suggests that Thunberg makes her older, male critics seem ridiculous for feeling threatened by a little girl. A similar humorous comparison that mocks Thunberg's critics while casting her as a hero from popular culture is Larsson, who suggests that "if climate collapse were a space opera, Greta Thunberg would be a Jedi and the climate deniers Darth Vader."[33] Unlike Pippi, who playfully subverts social norms, this tongue-in-cheek comparison frames Thunberg's struggle against older men in power as a clear-cut struggle between good and evil.

In addition to raising questions about authority, columnists regularly associate Greta Thunberg's prominence with her ability to subvert gender norms. In this hero figuration, Thunberg is admired for thwarting her own fate, creating new potential for how society might regard girls. *Aftonbladet*

29. Svensson, "Högern har pippi på Greta."

30. For other readings of Pippi as a figure who promotes particular Swedish/Nordic values, see Berggren and Trägårdh (2010) and Witozsek and Mueller (2021).

31. Knutsen, "Den polariserende klimaheltinnen," 49–54.

32. Knutsen, "Den polariserende klimaheltinnen," 77.

33. Larsson, "Domedagsklockan gör Greta."

columnist Caroline Ringskog Ferrada-Noli highlights how Thunberg challenges the norms for how girls should act. As she puts it, the fundamental "ticket to exist" for girls is being judged by their appearance, and this expectation can be interpreted as society's way of upholding a gendered order.[34] In light of this, Ferrada-Noli finds it remarkable that Thunberg is not judged by her appearance, but instead on her ability to raise alarm about the climate crisis. Ferrada-Noli mentions that the *New York Times* has called Thunberg a "Cassandra figure," a truth-teller who is not believed. However, she argues instead that Thunberg's rejection of typical gender roles calls to mind ancient Greek heroes such as Icarus, Odysseus, and Oedipus, who fought against their fate. By comparing Thunberg to masculine mythological heroes, Ferrada-Noli argues against those who interpret the reception of Thunberg as conforming to gender norms (i.e., the woman who is not believed) and argues instead that Thunberg is "smashing" them.[35]

These hero figurations emphasize Thunberg's agency as something adults should take seriously. However, they focus on Thunberg as an individual and tend to represent her as exceptional, if not entirely unique, and they also tend to depict her activism as a struggle against adult opponents.

THUNBERG'S "DEFENDERS": CRITIQUES OF HERO FIGURATIONS

While these comparisons have been relatively uncontroversial, others have been judged by the public as going too far. For example, in December 2018 Linhamn Church tweeted, "Jesus of Nazareth has now appointed one of his successors, Greta Thunberg"; this was met with great distaste by scholars, politicians, and media figures alike.[36] In a comment that echoes Taft's critique of "girl power," Ann Heberlein, doctor of Ethics at Lund University, stated, "Greta is a fifteen- year-old with tremendous passion, and that should be encouraged. But to appoint her as one of Jesus' successors who is going to save the world is to put a very heavy responsibility on her."[37]

The response to this tweet is one of many examples in which adult enthusiasm for Greta has been critiqued for assigning too much responsibility to a young person. Particularly when coming from elected officials, this enthusiasm has been critiqued for serving as a substitute for action and therefore an abdication of responsibility. Opinion writers such as Ingrid Rusten

34. Ferrada-Noli, "Greta krossar normen."
35. Ferrada-Noli, "Greta krossar normen."
36. Vickhoff, "Hårda kritiken."
37. Vickhoff, "Hårda kritiken."

have pointed out the irony of such abdication, since Greta's own rhetoric emphasizes the need for adults to assume responsibility for the climate crisis rather than pass it on to future generations. Rusten declares that local politicians are "wrongheaded in pointing to youth demonstrators as sources of hope—on the contrary, youth demonstrators are putting their hope in politicians to fulfill their own responsibilities."[38] Heidi Avellan displays similar thinking when stating that Thunberg "isn't the hope or the answer, just a reminder that we need answers."[39] Some of these writers use the rhetoric of "savior" or "Saint Greta" ironically to characterize these politicians as hypocritical. In Håkan Engström's critique, published under the headline, "Can Saint Greta Bear All our Guilt?," the author takes the comparison to Jesus to an extreme conclusion: Imagining children as incorruptible, he argues, is a way of forcing them to atone for the "sins" of adults who have lost their innocence with age. "Not even Jesus," he writes, "managed to walk the short path to Golgatha, he collapsed along the way. And then he was sacrificed."[40] Engström's text is a particularly bleak example of a common critique of heroizing activist youth: By seeing Thunberg as a source of hope, decision-makers absolve themselves of their own responsibility for effecting change. Such critiques tend to figure the opinion writer (and those who agree with them) as Thunberg's defender, restoring what they perceive as the proper degree of agency to adults.

These opinion writers attempt to counteract the moves that render girl activists harmless by pointing out that when politicians figure youth activists as sources of hope, they are either failing to hear, or willfully disregarding, activists' core message about the urgency of action. They suggest that failing to listen while simultaneously praising the activists for their commitment is ultimately patronizing. By figuring themselves as "defenders" of Greta, these opinion writers try to articulate the ways girl activists are rendered "harmless" in order to prevent this.

Other "defenders" of Thunberg focus on the impact of including a child in political debate: For example, Johan Hakelius paints a picture of the Swedish political arena as an adults-only zone, where those who contribute their opinions should expect to be subject to backlash. Given this, he considers it unethical to place an opinionated child in "problematic situations that children should not be put into."[41] He reiterates that bullying is the only foreseeable outcome of exposing her to the political fray, as it encourages

38. Rusten, "Änsliga politiker."
39. Avellan, "Att hänga med Greta."
40. Engström, "Kan Sankta Greta."
41. Hakelius, "Oetiskt att använda."

adults to "rant and rave against children." Ultimately, he contends that the big-name "journalists, columnists, prize juries, and celebrities" are using her unjustly by making her a figurehead of the climate movement. Even if the media were to treat her with the respect due a child, this would censor the conversation and stall people from asking critical questions.

Columnist Cecilia Blomberg levels a similar critique: Writing about a Q&A session for the Swedish Center Party think tank Fores, Blomberg expresses distaste for the questions Thunberg fielded: many questions were too technical for Thunberg to answer, resulting in a superficial conversation. Blomberg argues that "the big questions of our time" are too important to be addressed only in venues with "padded walls and soft cushions."[42] Had the guest for the Q&A been a politician or climate change authority, she believes more important questions would have been asked and truthfully answered, unimpeded by the vulnerability of children like Thunberg being present. This, she contends, is not Thunberg's fault but rather evidence that she is being used by those in power to avoid the most difficult questions raised by climate change. Blomberg contends that children deserve to be respected and treated with dignity rather than used "to distort the debate." Blomberg and Hakelius articulate one way that girl activists are rendered "harmless": society deems that they should be treated with care. However, purported concern for the vulnerability of youth becomes an excuse to address the issue in a non-threatening and superficial manner.

CONCLUSION

Swedish opinion writing about Greta Thunberg is largely written by well-meaning adults who support her cause, even if they disagree with how she is being represented or received. These texts can thus serve as useful examples for educators, many of whom take climate change and its impact on young people seriously. Hickman et al. argue that "current narratives" about eco-anxiety tend to individualize this phenomenon "with suggestions that the best response is for the individual to take action."[43] Swedish "hero narratives" about Thunberg have a similar effect, framing her activism as a unique struggle against insurmountable odds. Although well-intentioned, figuring children and youth as sources of hope is unhelpful when it becomes an excuse for adult complacency. Critics of this hero narrative, however, argue that "the responsibility to act lies with those in power."[44] Critiques of

42. Blomberg, "Är exploatering av barn."
43. Hickman et al., "Climate Anxiety," e871.
44. Hickman et al., "Climate Anxiety," e871.

hero figurations from Swedish media often urge Swedes to take seriously their roles as "ecocitizens," which differ depending on age and status, rather than assigning responsibility to others, especially children. This reproduces a Swedish national self-conception of autonomous individuals who must balance their personal freedom with responsibility toward others. However, some of these defenses may go too far, suggesting that youth are too vulnerable to participate in climate activism and seeking to transfer agency back to adults. Given that a sense of betrayal by those in power accompanies young people's feelings of anxiety, children and youth would be better served by narratives that emphasize the ways in which all members of society can act as ecocitizens, using their particular abilities and spheres of influence to address environmental degradation and injustice.

Rather than figuring young people as heroes who can save the day, "having one's feelings and views heard, validated, respected, and acted upon, particularly by those in positions of power and upon whom we are dependent" can help protect the mental health of children and young adults.[45] One way to avoid a simplified narrative in which youth figure as heroes who will "save the day" is to expose them to multiple viewpoints on Thunberg and youth activism and provide them with the space to process and express their own views. Educators should equip students to think critically about how this narrative represents the efficacy of individual versus collective action and should also reflect themselves on the importance of their own actions in establishing a trusting relationship with students.

REFLECTION QUESTIONS

1. How might the impacts of climate change on mental health pose challenges for children and youth in an educational setting?
2. Why is it important to equip students with a sense of agency and trust in adults as it relates to climate change or other major social and/or environmental challenges?
3. Think of another influential figure in history or contemporary society who is often portrayed as a "hero" in educational media or literature for children and youth. How might you encourage students to think critically about this narrative strategy? What resources would you need to teach a version of these events that includes the efforts of other people and communities in this figure's success?

45. Hickman et al., "Climate Anxiety," e871.

4. Think of other challenges (local, national, or global) that impact the students in your own school context: How might you provide students with a sense of agency in relationship to these problems? How might you avoid the two pitfalls mentioned in this chapter of either overburdening or overprotecting them?
5. Reflect on the extent to which you incorporate current events of concern to your students into your teaching. How might you equip students to participate in debate or social action by introducing differing viewpoints on these events?

BIBLIOGRAPHY

Avellan, Heidi. "Att hänga med Greta räcker inte." *Sydsvenskan*, Mar 12, 2019.

Blomberg, Cecilia. "Är exploatering av barn det nya liberala, Fores?" *Göteborgs-Posten*, Dec 4, 2018.

Brembeck, Helene, et al. "Introduction." In *Beyond the Competent Child: Exploring Contemporary Childhoods in the Nordic Welfare Societies*, 7–30. Frederiksberg, DK: Roskilde University Press, 2004.

Engström, Håkan. "Kan Sankta Greta bära all vår skuld?" *Sydsvenskan*, Dec 5, 2018.

Ferrada-Noli, Caroline Ringskog. "Greta krossar normen för hur flickor ska vara." *Aftonbladet*, Feb 26, 2019.

Foss, Sonja K. *Rhetorical Criticism: Exploration and Practice*. 5th ed. Long Grove, IL: Waveland, 2018.

Führer, Heidrun. "Astrid Lindgren's World in Vimmerby: A 'Total Work of Art'?" In *Beyond Pippi Longstocking: Intermedial and International Aspects of Astrid Lindgren's Works*, edited by Bettina Kummerling-Meibauer and Astrid Surmatz, 239–57. Children's Literature and Culture 77. New York: Routledge, 2011.

Hakelius, Johan. "Oetiskt att använda sig av barn i opinionsbildning." *Expressen*, Nov 17, 2018.

Hanson, Matilda E. "Greta Thunberg och Emma González vet hur en rörelse byggs." *Dagens Nyheter Lördagsmagasinet*, Dec 1, 2018.

Harrison, Dick. "Harrisons historia: Är Greta Thunberg vår tids Jeanne D'Arc?" *Svenska Dagbladet*, December 16, 2018.

Harsanyi, David. "The Real Tragedy of Greta Thunberg." *Detroit News*, Oct 2, 2019. https://www.detroitnews.com/story/opinion/columnists/2019/10/03/opinion-real-tragedy-greta-thunberg/3830224002/.

Hazan, Louise. "Massive School Strikes Worldwide." *350.Org* (blog), Mar 16, 2019. https://350.org/massive-school-strikes-worldwide/.

Hickman, Caroline, et al. "Climate Anxiety in Children and Young People and Their Beliefs about Government Responses to Climate Change: A Global Survey." *The Lancet Planetary Health* 5 (2021) e863–73. https://doi.org/10.1016/S2542-5196(21)00278-3.

Kalkstein, Adam. "Sorry, Greta, But You're (Mostly) Wrong." *New York Daily News*, Sep 24, 2019. https://www.nydailynews.com/opinion/ny-oped-sorry-greta-youre-mostly-wrong-20190924-t7depfksqnfmhpjgcwv6iyfesm-story.html.

Klein, Ezra. "Your Kids Are Not Doomed." *New York Times*, Jun 5, 2022. https://www.nytimes.com/2022/06/05/opinion/climate-change-should-you-have-kids.html.

Knutsen, K. S. "Den polariserende klimaheltinnen : En kritisk diskursanalyse av fremstillinger av Greta Thunberg i meningsytringer i norske papiraviser." Master's thesis, University of Agder, 2020. https://uia.brage.unit.no/uia-xmlui/bitstream/handle/11250/2681374/KOM501%20Kristin%20Stavseth%20Knutsen.pdf?sequence=1&isAllowed=y.

Kvamme, Ole Andreas. "School Strikes, Environmental Ethical Values, and Democracy." *Studier i Pædagogisk Filosofi* 8 (2019) 6–27. https://doi.org/10.7146/spf.v8i1.117967.

Larsson, Markus. "Domedagsklockan gör Greta till popstjärna." *Aftonbladet*, Jan 27, 2019.

"Learn for Our Planet: A Global Review of How Environmental Issues Are Integrated in Education—UNESCO Digital Library." https://unesdoc.unesco.org/ark:/48223/pf0000377362.

Lee, Katharine, et al. "Youth Perceptions of Climate Change: A Narrative Synthesis." *WIREs Climate Change* 11 (2020) e641. https://doi.org/10.1002/wcc.641.

Martínez García, Ana Belén. "Constructing an Activist Self: Greta Thunberg's Climate Activism as Life Writing." *Prose Studies* 41 (2020) 349–66. https://doi.org/10.1080/01440357.2020.1808923.

Metcalf, Eva-Maria. "Pippi Longstocking in the United States." In *Beyond Pippi Longstocking: Intermedial and International Aspects of Astrid Lindgren's Works*, 15–34. Children's Literature and Culture 77. New York: Routledge, 2011.

Moriarty, Sinéad. "Modeling Environmental Heroes in Literature for Children: Stories of Youth Climate Activist Greta Thunberg." *The Lion and the Unicorn* 45 (2021) 192–210. https://doi.org/10.1353/uni.2021.0015.

Peter Währborg. "Någons frihet tycks alltid vara någon annans ofrihet." *Göteborgs-Posten*, Mar 19, 2019.

Russo, Michael P. "Don't Dampen Graduation Joy with Climate Worries (Your Letters)." *Syracuse*, Jun 17, 2022. https://www.syracuse.com/opinion/2022/06/dont-dampen-graduation-joy-with-climate-worries-your-letters.html.

Rusten, Ingrid. "Änsliga politiker försöker gömma sig bakom Greta." *Sydsvenskan*, March 13, 2019.

Ryalls, Emily D., and Sharon R. Mazzarella. "'Famous, Beloved, Reviled, Respected, Feared, Celebrated': Media Construction of Greta Thunberg." *Communication, Culture and Critique* 14 (2021) 438–53. https://doi.org/10.1093/ccc/tcab006.

Sörbring, Karin. "Årets Kvinna—Greta Thunberg." *Expressen*, Mar 8, 2019.

Svensson, Per. "Högern har pippi på Greta." *Dagens Nyheter*, Mar 16, 2019.

Taft, Jessica K. "Hopeful, Harmless, and Heroic: Figuring the Girl Activist as Global Savior." *Girlhood Studies* 13 (2020) 1–17. https://doi.org/10.3167/ghs.2020.130203.

Thunberg, Greta. *No One Is Too Small to Make a Difference*. 2nd ed. New York: Penguin Random House, 2019.

Vickhoff, Alexander. "Hårda kritiken efter Limhamnskyrkans ord om Jesus: Greta är en av hans efterträdare." *Expressen Kvällsposten*, Dec 5, 2018.

Witoszek, Nina, and Martin Lee Mueller. "The Ecological Ethics of Nordic Children's Tales: From Pippi Longstocking to Greta Thunberg." *Environmental Ethics* 43 (2021) 61–78. https://doi.org/10.5840/enviroethics20215725.

Yoder, Kate. "Do We Need More Scary Climate Change Articles? Maybe." *Grist*, Feb 16, 2021. https://grist.org/climate/do-we-need-more-scary-climate-change-articles-maybe/.

Zraick, Karen. "Greta Thunberg, After Pointed U.N. Speech, Faces Attacks From the Right." *New York Times*, Sep 24, 2019. https://www.nytimes.com/2019/09/24/climate/greta-thunberg-un.html.

12

Eyes Wide Open

Towards an Ecological Education of Faith, Wonder and Love[1]

KIMBERLY FRANKLIN

Whenever I have meditated upon You
I have acquired a veritable treasure from You;
Whatever aspect of You I have contemplated,
A stream has flowed from You.
There is no way in which I can contain it:

Your fountain, Lord, is hidden
From the person who does not thirst for You;
Your treasury seems empty
To the person who rejects You.

1. St. Ephrem the Syrian (Ephrem, *Hymns on Faith*), a monk who lived in the fourth century and wrote theology in poetic form, used these three virtues to characterize how one can come to know God's hiddenness. The prerequisite is faith, and the proper attitude is wonder and love. Although he was speaking specifically about Eastern Orthodox faith in God, our experience of grace-filled glimpses of something beyond what is visible or something eternal can invite us into this faith. See Brock, *Luminous Eye*; Brummelen, *Walking with God*; Brummelen, *Steppingstone to Curriculum* for an in-depth exploration of his spiritual vision.

Love is the treasurer
Of Your heavenly treasure store.

—ST. EPHREM THE SYRIAN (HYMNS ON FAITH 32:2–3)

BEGINNING TO SEE

I began my teaching career in the mid-1980s. Concern for the environment was increasing and making its way into curriculum and the school year through environmentally focused educational events.[2] As a teacher first, and then principal, I believed in helping learners understand their care-taking role in the world, and I believed in the importance of weaving together educational experiences and holistic encounters with the created world as a way of nurturing that role. I was also beginning a personal journey of understanding creation as a gift of revelation, a second Scripture.

The world, through my first exposure to the rich Christian Reformed tradition of Christian education, was becoming vibrant with meaning and wonder, and I wanted to share that world with my students.[3] We went on field trips to places of natural beauty and created a butterfly garden on the school grounds so that our classroom caterpillars would have a home once they had metamorphosized. We had classroom pets, painted fish signs on drains, taught the three Rs (reduce, reuse, recycle), celebrated Earth Day, planted flowers in window boxes outside each classroom, and did projects to raise awareness of water consumption and endangered animals and ecosystems. We learned poems about nature, we sang about nature, we read about nature, we wrote about nature, we created artistic representations of nature. As much as possible, the curriculum was an integrated whole and had room for their questions and wonder and, since it was a Christian school, much room for praise of the creator.

2. Although the more common term is "environmental education," I prefer "ecological education" because the term "environment" implies a possible separation between an object or person or thing and that which surrounds it. The word "ecological," on the other hand, implies interdependence, hierarchies of relationships and dependence on something greater than us, conveying a sense that we are small but important parts of a whole—a whole we cannot fully see or comprehend—but a whole that is a great and continuing wonder, and that our choices matter because we are the ones who can choose.

3. Dr. Harro Van Brummelen (*Walking with God*, *Steppingstone to Curriculum*) was my first introduction to this richer view of the created world. He later became a mentor and colleague, and I am eternally grateful to him.

I can't be sure how students were impacted by these efforts. I hope they had glimpses of the invisible hidden in the visible. I hope they learned a little to gaze with faith and wonder and then to respond to the world around them with loving care and reverence. I'm grateful that the generous Holy Spirit was present amid our bright and joyful busyness. The grace of the Holy Spirit is needed to gaze with reverence and attention.[4] I think it is likely that my students suffered from this busyness and my own inability to gaze—to pray with my eyes open, to be a true teacher of ecology, to create a truly unified ethos of love and care for the world. My eyes needed healing.

While I taught my students to love God as creator and to wonder at his creation, and to even consider their role as "stewards" of creation,[5] I didn't have a fully sacramental understanding of the world yet or clarity around my role in creation as a personal image-bearer called to be a priest. Through me, they would have caught the sense that the world was still an object, still needed by egocentric me but not something that needed me to receive it as gift and then offer it back in an imitation of God's self-emptying love for us. I didn't know that part of my being was to exist *for* the life of the world. I didn't know that hidden within each aspect of creation was a spark of divine reality, an incarnate word or logos, that God was all and in all and sustaining all, that loving and choosing to care for the created world was loving God and participating in an eschatological movement towards fulfillment in Christ.[6] I didn't know that the most important ecological

4 *"It is the Holy Spirit who makes us find joy in each flower and gives to us the joy of gazing at it with our eyes."* This is a line from a beloved prayer in the Orthodox tradition called "Glory to God for All Things." The prayer is attributed to Metropolitan Tryphon of Turkestan and was found in the effects of a priest, Protopresbyter Gregory Petrov, imprisoned and later martyred in a Soviet Gulag. It is a remarkable witness of seeing God's presence in the most brutal of places, and the power of poetry to convey deep symbolic connections. This prayer can be retrieved at http://ww1.antiochian.org/orthodox-prayers/akathist-of-thanksgiving.

5. Stewardship is a common Protestant understanding of our responsibility towards creation, but although it highlights the need to care for the world, it also can denote ownership and control and utilitarian use. An Orthodox understanding would emphasize humanity's priestly role as a more appropriate response to a sacramental cosmology. A priest receives the world as gift and offers it back to God with love, often in a transformed manner and in a way that imitates the giver (see Ware, *Through the Creation*). For rich descriptions of this understanding, see Theokritoff (*Living in God's Creation*) and Schmemann (1973).

6. The doctrine of Logos/Logoi was consolidated and developed comprehensively by St. Maximus the Confessor (*On the Cosmic Mystery*; *On the Ecclesiastical Mystagogy*), an Early Church Father of the seventh century. For Maximus and for the Orthodox Christian tradition, the ontological distinction between Creator and created remains. The creation is not the creator except in the incarnation when God became man for our sakes. This is a profound mystery. Yet because God spoke the creation into existence, the original logoi

move I could make was an inner one of repentance, to see, first, my own sin—the sin of not gathering only what I need, of not gathering with Christ on behalf of all—with the kind of sorrow that turns me toward a better way of being through the practice of virtue that becomes so habituated I cannot imagine treating the world any other way. I often wonder how I would have taught my young students to have a more profound ecological vision with that repentance.[7]

WIDENING EYES

When I entered the Eastern Orthodox Church in 2007, one of the most enlightening and profound practices of this beautiful and sacramental tradition was learning to pray with my eyes open. My cradle to adulthood experience had been to close my eyes as a first step of prayer, blocking out the world around me and somehow, through my imagination, emotion, and words, projecting myself into a heaven of "just me and Jesus." The consequences of praying with my eyes closed and the accompanying theology were profound and deeply fragmenting, creating a disconnect between heaven and earth, between body and mind/spirit, between creation and creator, between belief and practice.[8]

But then, by God's grace, I was invited to "come and see." As an Orthodox Christian, I was invited to draw near to Christ's self-offering in the Eucharist with fear/awe, faith, and love. I was encouraged to widen my eyes in prayer and attention, to reverently experience the immanence *and* transcendence of the Trinitarian God and the communion of his saints in the liturgy, to pour my heart and mind into the given symbolic words of beautiful hymns, prayers and psalms, to see every person as an icon of Christ and to see the world as full of his glory, every aspect a "burning bush," every place "holy ground" because all was a gift of revelation and encounter with the eternal—if I only had eyes to see.[9]

of creation remain in what is created, revealing through a veil God in creation. Maximus likens God's presence in creation to God's presence in Scripture. Elizabeth Theokritoff's (*Living in God's Creation*, 188) discussion of St. Maximus and the logos/logoi, explains the logoi as "principles of connection: they point us to dialogue with the Creator and with his purpose for all the creations with which we share the world."

7. Chryssavgis, *Beyond the Shattered Image*.

8. I recently saw a similar fragmentation in a young friend, who told me that she was so overcome by the devastation and brokenness around her that she could no longer read books that took place in the real world. She could only read fantasy. Her loss of agency as a human being with the capacity to receive the world as gift and participate in the healing and transformation of the world was heartbreaking.

9. See Metropolitan Kallistos Ware (*Through the Creation*) for a beautiful meditation on all of creation as a "burning bush." He relates Moses' removal of his shoes to

Praying with my eyes open in the Orthodox Church was a constant weaving together of the visible and invisible. It was lighting a candle as a symbol of ceaseless prayer, breathing in the fragrant clouds of incense carrying my prayers to the altar in heaven, venerating a cross or icon beckoning me to a cruciform yet joy-filled life, standing with others in stillness, prostrating in reverence, holding a child in preparation for baptism, receiving the holy sacraments, being anointed with oil, sprinkled with holy water, sharing blessed bread, flowers, fruit, eggs, and honey. It was and always is a feast of tasting and seeing, touching and seeing, smelling and seeing, hearing and seeing. My eyes were being healed by a cosmology of incarnation. I was taught to see glimpses of the divine logoi or ideas or principles given flesh or enlivened, taught that God is both hidden and revealed in the infinite myriad ways he veils himself in creation, taught that he wants to reveal himself to me in all of the ways I can bear him, taught that the eternal is always breaking through the created if I see with faith, wonder and love. I was also taught how to respond to the gift, recognizing that a gift reveals relationship, and I desired to honour the gift through being like the giver, one who also gives sacrificially for the life of the world.

WIDENED AND FOCUSED EYES

The Orthodox tradition also provided holy encounters with "living epistles," the kinds of teachers we all need. Once a year I visit an Orthodox hermitage deep in the mountains of British Columbia, and I have a glimpse of heaven, a paradisiacal place where it seems true harmony between humanity and nature has been created, a place of wild beauty, a place of simplicity and justice, a place of wonder and reverence and luminous life. The life is so luminous that one glimpse a year is enough to shine through the many days between my visits, transforming the way I view the world around me and making me long for a different way of being in the places I inhabit. Thankfully, one glimpse a year ensures my longing is filled with hope in the possibility of that way of being, rather than despair at how far away I am. One glimpse a year illumines a path I can follow.

If you were to come with me to this place, heaven may seem initially hidden. So often the divine is initially hidden, until our eyes are ready to see, until we truly seek. This heavenly place is in a lonely wilderness, next to a marsh, in the middle of a pine forest on the top of a mountainous plateau. The summers are very hot and the winters long and frigid. At times, when I visit in July, the mosquitos seem as large as hummingbirds, and I dash from

removing our worldly ways of seeing in order to stand on "holy ground."

my car to the cabin door as quickly as possible. At other times the alternating threats of fires and floods are real and present. Nature is groaning with us, groaning because of us.

In the midst of this wilderness are three monks dedicated to a life of prayer for the world, dedicated to offering back to God, with love, reverence and care, all that has been given to them. The love they have for God and for each other naturally flows out to the world around them. They take only what they need and make or transform in accordance with God's will. They gather with Christ. Any abundance is shared generously.

Their dedication to this place is as evident as their devotion to God and each other. With simple organic materials they have fashioned a small cabin with small individual "cells," a small living area and kitchen, a wood burning stove, overflowing bookshelves, and a beautiful chapel fragrant with incense and filled with a holy stillness.[10] Eating utensils and plates are carved out of wood, guests are served carefully prepared and nourishing vegetarian food, crumbs are gently swept off the table and composted or burned in the stove or eaten because all food served has been blessed and therefore would never be considered garbage. A small vegetable garden and greenhouse provide for many of their needs, a small workshop and gazebo overlooking the pond reveal the balance of work and prayer. Walks after lunch might take you up a hill to a cross that borders their property, a cross placed on the highest point of their property continually orienting them to a cruciform life, a cross that has protected them from fire during one particularly difficult fire season. As we walk, every step is an opportunity for new revelations and the brothers teach me to see, to gaze with attention, faith, and wonder, to walk reverently with awareness—because this attention and careful walking is key to seeing how closely heaven and earth are united, key to loving responses and ethical caring. I am introduced to all the plants and asked to consider their uniqueness and uses. I am told stories about the wildlife and how they seek to live harmoniously with their wild visitors. In this heavenly place, I am a guest of the monks who teach me to be a guest of God with all my brother and sister creatures.

My eyes (and my hands and feet) needed healing and I am still healing. When I am encouraged, at the end of the liturgy, to "go forth in peace" or, in other words, to go into the world in the same dynamic way that I am in the liturgy, I am still a beginner. It is easy to forget, and my eyes start to glance, bounce, and consume rather than gaze with compassion,

10. Eastern Orthodox monasticism refers to individual sleeping rooms as "cells." These rooms are places of personal prayer and contemplation. They are a place of inner struggle to discover the true self in communion with Christ and in that discovery, come into proper relationship with God and all others.

stillness, and reverence. What wouldn't be possible in the liturgy suddenly becomes possible in my daily life. I am caught up once again in the artificial separation of heaven and earth, my eyes are closed to the unity and interdependence I have with all other creatures, being one of the "little ones," the created ones, a created "word," sharing in the gift of creation, owing my gift of being to the love and will of God. I am wasteful and inconsiderate of the people and creatures around me, I take from this world more than I need, and I easily forget to sacrificially share what I have been so generously given. Sometimes, I am also overwhelmed by the devastation and brokenness I see around me, overwhelmed by my part in that brokenness, and unsure of my personal agency in making any kind of difference. Sometimes I err on the other side, refusing to accept the limitations of nature and controlling my environment for my own needs. I am like the blind man who needed Christ to touch his eyes twice to see (Mark 8:22), but my blindness is deeper, and I need his touch again and again.

Fifteen years after the initial invitation to "come and see," I am even more convinced that learning to keep our eyes wide open with attention and reverence and a love that is self-emptying and self-offering is the only path of restoration for ourselves and our world. I am also convinced that any education leading to an ecological vision of care, harmony and hope and away from a culture of controlling, consuming or despairing, depends on this way of seeing, this attention that becomes prayer, communion, and revelation, leading to mindfulness of all creation and an ethical, loving and just way of being in the world.[11] Christ called this way of seeing, having a "single eye" so that our whole bodies would be full of light (Matt 6:22). St. Ephrem, one who could easily be named the patron saint of ecology, called it seeing with a luminous eye, an eye that is first purified from our unnatural ways of seeing and therefore able to see with the inner eye of faith.[12]

To see in this way is a grace, and I am convinced of the generosity of God's love for all, that we are all being drawn by his design and providence to long for this way of seeing. I also believe that the path towards this way of seeing is an ancient one and well-travelled. In other words, we are created to see this way, endlessly invited to see this way, and given the grace to become the way we see.

11. See Simone Weil's essay, "School Studies and the Love of God" in *Awaiting God* for an inspiring meditation of attention and study as prayer.

12. Brock, *Luminous Eye.*

TOWARDS A WIDE-EYED EDUCATIONAL ECOLOGICAL VISION

As an educator, my greatest joy and most important task is to participate in this image of God as the one who gives us light to see and the grace or "fountain of life" to be like him, to help my students open their eyes to this light, to nurture their natural faith that there *is* infinitely more to see hidden in the world around them, nurture their affinity with all they see, nurture their freedom from enslaving and destructive ways of being. I want them to see the world as transparent to God, to know that God did not make anything that he is not, that everything is a "bond of unity" with him and with all else.[13] In essence, offering them an ecological vision is offering them a cosmological vision. I want them to see how they are image bearers, to see themselves as "bonds of unity," microcosms of the universe, active agents in holding heaven and earth together in harmony and justice, participating in its transformation and offering it back to God with gratitude and praise.

The "bond of unity" pattern is a fascinating one for educators to explore since forming bonds of unity is an essential aspect of teaching. We are always seeking ways to weave together what is still separate or divided for our students: what they know and don't know; the visible and the invisible; symbol and the object; fact and concept; part and whole; knowing and doing; the who, the what, and the how and the why; and the good, the beautiful, and the true. The bonds of unity we offer in ourselves, and our teaching and our curriculum are small incarnations and potent revelations, light that enables seeing and points to ways of well-being.

As I consider practices that foster this "eyes wide open" ecological education in the classroom, I am aware that I am pulling at a thread with a thousand connections. I cannot pull the thread of curriculum without pulling the thread of pedagogy or educational space design, or axiology or epistemology. What is true about the Orthodox tradition, that every part reveals and leads to the whole, is also true about education. Beliefs about teachers, learners, learning, knowing are embedded or veiled in practices, practices our students experience holistically, practices requiring ongoing reflection and refinement—we can't get to the end of unity. So, the two questions offered below for educators are ones that I think could lead most potently to

13. St. Maximus the Confessor (*On the Ecclesiastical Mystagogy*, 65) highlights the unifying nature of humanity as being microcosms of the world and image bearers of the incarnate one who is 'bound together'. "*. . . every soul is able, through the grace of the Holy Spirit and its own hard work and diligence, to join and weave these things to one another—that is, reason to the mind, prudence to wisdom, practice to contemplation, virtue to knowledge, and faith to 'ceaseless knowledge' . . . then the soul is also made one with the true and good and one and only God.*"

helping our students widen their eyes in faith, wonder, and love. They are focal points or ways of reflecting on practice rather than a to-do list. They are intended to pull in a thousand ways, in ways that become living expressions in personal/particular contexts. I am also aware that these focal points are not necessarily new educational ideas, but it is my hope that my words can come alongside of other incarnate words, reminding, or recalling what is already deeply known.

Are You a Wide-Eyed Teacher?

The most significant "bond of unity" we can offer our students is ourselves. We cannot teach our students to see each other and the world with faith, wonder, and love if we have not at least begun to see that way ourselves. We and our students are image bearers, created to learn through observation and imitation, models, examples and guides. Our students learn more from our way of being than our words. In essence, we are the curriculum, or we are the ones who gather ways to incarnate patterns that are true, good and beautiful. Therefore, our main task as teachers is to become our words or illustrate our words holistically, or to curate holistic encounters for our students and to model responses to those encounters, keeping in mind that learning is a highly organic/social process.[14]

While the responsibility of the "teacher as curriculum" can be overwhelming given Christ's warning about leading little ones astray (Matt 18), this responsibility does not mean that we must be perfect. In fact, it is much better for us to think of ourselves as beginners and learners like our students, to come alongside them with humility and friendship, always preserving their freedom and independence as much as possible. What is most important is that they see how their souls are in their own hands (Ps 119:109). We, as teachers, may be a little further on the path, but still companions on a common trajectory, still failing and learning from our failures, still needing to repent. We invite, inspire, point, see our own contradictions, encourage, share opinions and fresh perspectives or new ways to connect their thinking, and we continue to learn with them. We also show them that the inner world of thoughts and motivations has a direct impact on the outer world, and therefore are worth our attention and struggle for virtue.

14. Another word for this kind of teaching and learning is Mimetic, see Christoph Wulf ("Mimetic Learning"). Mimetic teaching and learning are also deeply rooted in the Orthodox tradition of catechism and spiritual direction. New catechumens are told to immerse themselves in the tradition and with a community as the best way to begin to understand.

We show them how to create their own "bonds of unity," to find integral ways of being in the world.

By providing strong incarnations or models or types, we also provide standards, enabling students to assess themselves in relation to those standards. Their ability to do this independently preserves their freedom and provides ongoing inspiration for growth. We also introduce them to other teachers who have shown the way, the ones who have taught us. These teachers can be encountered personally as well as through text, story, and image. Our students, like us, need "living epistles" and incarnations that both ground them and inspire them.

How Are You Encouraging a Wide-Eyed Ecological Ethos?

An ecological education of the type I'm envisioning is not a four-week unit study in a science block on the timetable, although it may have an intensified focus for a period of time. It would also not focus too much on all that is wrong with our ecology, on problems so large and overwhelming, and demanding so much activism and righteous anger, eyes may shut with despair rather than widen with hope. Although, of course, the world's groaning and our part in it would not be ignored. An ecological ethos would be more about the spirit of the classroom or the "air" students are breathing in an overall approach to the world around them and to their learning. This air would need to be breathed throughout each day and in relation to all aspects of the classroom, for it to become a part of who they are. Elizabeth Theokritoff describes such an ethos as

> taking part in the celebration . . . a way of living that is liturgical, eucharistic and ascetic. Our actions and work are to glorify God as part of a cosmic liturgy, a world in which every creature glorifies its Creator in its own way. Our use of the world is to be an offering of thanks to its Creator, recognizing that everything we have the use of is his; it is by his mercy that it is available for our needs and the needs of others. And we are to handle the good things of earth with ascetic detachment, not making them idols to which we are enslaved.[15]

This ethos or "air" would be reflected in the classroom in how materials are used and shared, how space is arranged and oriented, how time is arranged and oriented, how life and learning are experienced in community and in solitude and stillness, how knowing is understood and assessed, how

15. Theokritoff, *Living in God's Creation.*

virtue is connected to knowing, how the classroom weaves together the beautiful, good and true, and how all of the arts create opportunities for unique expressions of wide-eyed perception, gratitude and offering.

To encourage an ethos sounds somewhat abstract. Having been a teacher-educator, I'm aware that most teachers (especially new teachers) would prefer a list of things to do, but I believe an ecological educational ethos is more dynamic, thoughtful, and emergent than that. It is a concelebration of a way of being that is unique to persons and contexts. Teacher and students gather around what it is to know with humility and a shared desire to truly see and Christ hears their prayer, Christ is in their midst, the ethos is a grace.[16] What characterizes this ethos most, as noted above by Theokritoff, is a spirit of gratitude and asceticism—a willingness to say no to ourselves, to refuse to gather more than we need, in small but meaningful acts of ecological kindness, and a participation in the making and giving of gifts on behalf of all and for all.

Such wide-eyed teaching in a wide-eyed ethos concelebrated with intentionality and infused with grace, would, I believe, nurture young people to walk more gently in this world and to know the good they can do, the small steps they can take, towards being an ongoing "bond of unity" for the life of the world.

QUESTIONS FOR REFLECTION AND DISCUSSION

1. When have you had an experience of seeing the hidden in the visible, or through creation to the creator? How would you characterize this kind of seeing? How did this experience impact you and your educational practice? How can you nurture this way of seeing in your life?
2. The author describes educational practice as flowing from a "bond of unity" pattern. Describe how your educational experience has or has not been a "bond of unity." What are some practices in education that encourage fragmentation rather than unity? How could educational practices move toward this pattern?

16. Parker Palmer (*To Know*) builds on early desert monastic understandings of knowing and discusses how the subject or truth we want to know "sits in the center and knows." We as teachers and learners come around what we want to know with an attitude of humility, compassion, and care recognizing that we all "see through a glass darkly," that we can't get to the end of knowing when approached in such a relational manner. He compares this way of knowing with more modern notions of knowing stemming from motivations of power and ownership.

3. How might an ecological educational ethos be reflected in the way schools and classrooms are designed and inhabited?
4. Why do you think the arts (story, myth, poetry, visual arts) are so important in developing this way of seeing?
5. An important emphasis in this chapter is the connection between virtue and knowledge. This is an ancient connection noted as far back as Plato and Aristotle. Do you think this connection is as evident in education contexts today? Which virtues are taught implicitly or explicitly? Which virtues are missing? Which vices are implicitly taught through current educational practices?

BIBLIOGRAPHY

Brock, Sebastian. *The Luminous Eye: The Spiritual World Vision of Saint Ephrem.* Kalamazoo, MI: Cistercian, 1985.

Brummelen, Harro Van. *Steppingstones to Curriculum.* 2nd ed. Colorado Springs, CO: ACSI, 2006.

———. *Walking with God in the Classroom.* 2nd ed. Dubuque, IA: Alta Vista College Press, 1998.

Chryssavgis, John. *Beyond the Shattered Image.* Minneapolis: Light and Life, 1999.

Ephrem. *Hymns on Faith.* Washington, DC: Catholic University Press, 2017.

Maximus the Confessor. *On the Cosmic Mystery of Christ: Selected Writings from St. Maximus the Confessor.* Translated by Paul M. Blowers and Robert Louis Wilken. Yonkers, NY: St. Vladimir's Seminary Press, 2003.

———. *On the Ecclesiastical Mystagogy: A Theological Vision of the Liturgy.* Translated by Johnathan Armstrong. Yonkers, NY: St. Vladimir's Seminary Press, 2019.

Palmer, Parker. *To Know as We Are Known: Education as a Spiritual Journey.* San Francisco: HarperOne, 1993.

Theokritoff, Elizabeth. *Living in God's Creation: Orthodox Perspectives on Theology.* Yonkers, NY: St Vladimir's Seminary Press, 2009.

Ware, Kallistos. *Through the Creation to the Creator.* London: Friends of the Centre, 1996.

Weil, Simone. *Awaiting God.* Translated by Brad Jersak. Altona: Friesen, 2012.

Wulf, Christoph. "Mimetic Learning." *Designs for Learning* 1 (2008) 56.

13

How Does War Damage the Environment?

The Main Ways that Wars and Militarism Harm the Environment[1]

Doug Weir

We're often asked how armed conflicts harm the environment. In this chapter we try to provide as many different examples of harms as we can. It's intended as a non-exhaustive introduction that follows the cycle of conflicts and has links for further reading. Critically, environmental damage has implications for people, as well as ecosystems. This means that protecting civilians first requires that we protect the environment that they depend upon.

ENVIRONMENTAL DAMAGE BEFORE CONFLICTS

The environmental impact of wars begins long before they do. Building and sustaining military forces consumes vast quantities of resources. These might be common metals or rare earth elements, water, or hydrocarbons. Maintaining military readiness means training, and training consumes

1. This article by Doug Weir was originally published on the website *Conflict and Environment Observatory* at https://ceobs.org/how-does-war-damage-the-environment/. The author gave permission to have this article published in this book.

resources. Military vehicles, aircraft, vessels, buildings, and infrastructure all require energy, and more often than not that energy is oil, and energy efficiency is low. The CO_2 emissions of the largest militaries are greater than many of the world's countries combined.

Militaries also need large areas of land and sea, whether for bases and facilities, or for testing and training. Military lands are believed to cover between 1–6 percent of the global land surface. In many cases these are ecologically important areas. While excluding public development from these areas can benefit biodiversity, the question of whether they could be better managed as civil protected areas is rarely discussed. Military training creates emissions, disruption to landscapes and terrestrial and marine habitats, and creates chemical and noise pollution from the use of weapons, aircraft, and vehicles.

A UK battle group training on the British Army Training Area Suffield (BATUS), Alberta Canada.
Much of what we know about the potential health and environmental risks from the residues of weapons come from training ranges, with very little data from conflict contexts. Now commonly used explosives are under increasing scrutiny thanks to civil chemicals legislation. Credit: Ministry of Defense

Sustaining and renewing military equipment and material means ongoing disposal costs, with implications for the environment. It is not just the most hazardous nuclear and chemical weapons that create environmental problems throughout their lifecycle. The same is also true for conventional weapons, particularly where they are disposed of through open burning or detonation. Historically, vast quantities of surplus munitions were also dumped at sea.

A history of weak environmental oversight has left many countries with serious environmental legacies linked to military pollution, with impacts on public health and vast costs for environmental remediation. These continue to grow as emerging pollutants like PFAS are identified. These legacies are also a problem around overseas bases where one-sided agreements with host nations can reduce environmental oversight.

Indirectly, high levels of military spending diverts resources away from solving environmental problems and away from sustainable development. International tensions stoked by high levels of military spending also reduce opportunities for international cooperation on global environmental threats, such as the climate emergency. It is also important to consider how security policies and militarism are tailored to ensuring access to, and control of, natural resources like oil, gas, water, and metals.

ENVIRONMENTAL DAMAGE DURING CONFLICTS

The environmental impact of conflicts themselves vary greatly. Some international armed conflicts may be brief but highly destructive. Some civil wars may last for decades but are fought at low intensity. Many contemporary conflicts have blurred the lines, lasting years but with sustained periods of high intensity warfare. Who is fighting, where they're fighting, and how they're fighting all strongly influence the environmental impact of a conflict.

High intensity conflicts require and consume vast quantities of fuel, leading to massive CO_2 emissions and contributing to climate change. Large-scale vehicle movements can lead to widespread physical damage to sensitive landscapes and geodiversity, as can the intensive use of explosive ordnance. The use of explosive weapons in urban areas creates vast quantities of debris and rubble, which can cause air and soil pollution. Pollution can also be caused by damage to light industry and environmentally sensitive infrastructure such as water treatment plants. The loss of energy supplies can have reverberating effects that are detrimental to the environment, shutting down treatment plants or pumping systems, or can lead to the use of more polluting fuels or domestic generators.

Severe pollution incidents can be caused when industrial, oil, or energy facilities are deliberately attacked, inadvertently damaged, or disrupted. In some cases, deliberate attacks on oil or industrial facilities are used as a weapon of war, to pollute large areas and spread terror. Other scorched earth techniques include the destruction of agricultural infrastructure like canals, wells and pumps and the burning of crops. Tactics like these threaten food security and livelihoods, increasing the vulnerability of rural communities. Whether unintended or deliberate, these large-scale pollution incidents can lead to transboundary impacts from air pollution or through the contamination of rivers, aquifers, or the sea. In some instances, these even have the potential to affect weather or the global climate.

Weapons and military material used during conflicts also leave environmental legacies. Land mines, cluster munitions and other explosive remnants of war can restrict access to agricultural land and pollute soils and water sources with metals and toxic energetic materials. In major conflicts, large volumes of military scrap may be produced or abandoned; this can contain a range of polluting materials, contaminating soils, and groundwater, whilst exposing those who work on it to acute and chronic health risks. Wrecked or damaged ships, submarines, and offshore oil infrastructure can cause marine pollution.

Many conventional weapons have toxic constituents; others such as depleted uranium are also radioactive. Incendiary weapons such as white phosphorous are not only toxic but can also damage habitats through fire. While now restricted, the widespread use of chemical defoliants damaged public and ecological health across large areas of Vietnam.

Easy access to small arms and light weapons can harm wildlife through facilitating increased hunting and poaching, and the ungoverned spaces created by conflict create the ideal conditions for wildlife crime. Weapons used in wildlife crime have been found to have been sourced from countries affected by conflict. Scientists and researchers may be unable to access areas due to security problems, harming conservation programs. While national parks and protected areas may lose what protection they had or protecting them may be made more difficult when poachers are armed. These situations can encourage more militarized conservation, which can have negative effects on relationships with local communities.

Deforestation often increases during conflicts. Much of the time this is due to overharvesting by communities who are suddenly reliant on wood and charcoal for fuel and heating. But it can also be as a result of armed or criminal gangs taking advantage of the collapse of management systems. Civilian coping strategies can also lead to the overharvesting of other natural resources or to environmentally damaging practices such as artisanal oil refining. And in some cases, community systems of sustainable resource management may be disrupted.

Environmental damage and degradation can also stem from resource extraction used to finance conflicts. In many conflicts, armed groups vie for control over oil, mineral resources, or timber. Processing methods, such as the use of mercury in gold mining, can pollute water bodies. In addition to armed groups and artisanal workers, private companies may also be active in areas affected by conflict, often operating with minimal environmental oversight.

Human displacement is common to many conflicts. Camps for refugees and internally displaced peoples can have large environmental footprints, particularly where they are unplanned or lack essential services, like water, sanitation, and waste management. Their location is also important, as camp residents may be compelled to use local resources such as firewood, which can place local resources under pressure. People displaced by conflict may also move internally to urban areas, swelling the population and placing local environmental services under strain.

In some cases, the areas where displaced people move through may be placed under pressure, for example herders moving their livestock through sensitive ecosystems. Large-scale refugee movements can also create transboundary environmental impacts, when areas in neighboring countries struggle to cope with the influx of people and with meeting their basic needs.

One basic need common to displacement camps and to urban areas experiencing conflict is waste management. Systems often break down during conflict leading to increased rates of waste dumping and burning, improper management and less waste segregation. Waste management systems are just one element of environmental governance that may collapse during conflicts. Local environmental laws and regulations may be ignored, and local and national administrations may lose their capacity to monitor, assess or respond to environmental problems. New administrations may also emerge in areas that are held by non-state actors and whose approach to environmental governance may differ markedly from that of the government. In recent years there has been a growing trend towards the weaponization of environmental information during conflicts, leading to the increased politicization of environmental risks.

Governments may be unable to meet their international environmental obligations, particularly because projects and programs supported by the international community may be curtailed. In this way a localized conflict may harm the environment nationally by impacting governance and projects countrywide. The existence of a conflict can also create serious technological risks from industrial infrastructure, and then hamper the international cooperation required to address them.

These diverse impacts on the environment mean that conflicts are often viewed as sustainable development in reverse and may set countries back years. Not just because of new damage, but in the development that would have taken place were it not for the existence of a conflict. But is it all negative? There are times where the existence of conflict can confer protection to areas, for example by slowing unsustainable development that would otherwise have taken place in areas that are insecure, or by excluding human activities due to the presence of explosive remnants of war. But overall, and particularly because of the disruption conflicts cause to societies and to governance, the harms far outweigh the benefits.

ENVIRONMENTAL DAMAGE DURING OCCUPATIONS

Occupations may be relatively short-lived or can last decades. While states have an obligation to protect the occupied population, their environmental obligations are less well defined. As with conflicts, occupations can hold back sustainable development, for example by limiting access to materials or technologies, or by acting as a barrier to investment. Pre-existing environmental programs and projects may be curtailed or replaced by a new incoming administration.

A lack of investment and development can lead to the slow collapse of critical environmental infrastructure, infrastructure that may be damaged or degraded by periods of violence. Measures taken by the occupied population to oppose the occupier can also lead to environmental harm. The increased military presence can impact landscapes by vehicle movements or training areas, or by the building of walls and fences that can disrupt wildlife movements, or separate people from the resources they are dependent on. Poor waste management at military bases, whether operated by states or private contractors, can harm public health and the environment. Meanwhile, militarized responses to security issues can create more serious environmental harm than civil responses would.

Inequitable resource management is common to occupations, with resource grabs and over-extraction common, whether of water or minerals. Environmental oversight can be limited or preferential, facilitating environmental degradation. The occupied population may be unable to enjoy the same environmental human rights as those of the occupier and be forced to live with limited resources, poorer environmental services, and higher levels of pollution.

Politically focused development is common as the occupying power seeks to make its mark on a territory. In this way major infrastructure works may be undertaken with little environmental oversight.

ENVIRONMENTAL DAMAGE AFTER CONFLICTS

It is rare these days for conflicts to conclude cleanly with a peace agreement and a ceasefire. Low level conflict and insecurity can continue for long periods. In this respect many of the forms of harm that occur during conflicts are also applicable to this phase, particularly in its early stages.

Transitions to peace are typified by weak state control. This means that environmental governance, and the capacity to provide it, is often absent. Attention to environmental issues in the face of many competing social and economic priorities is usually limited. These conditions are key to many post-conflict environmental problems. In some instances, peace and power sharing agreements have impeded governance by creating fragmented political systems.

In the immediate aftermath of conflicts, states and international actors may be faced with immediate legacies, such as vast quantities of rubble and debris. If managed poorly, for example through informal dumping, disposal can create new environmental risks. There have been instances where the looting of industrial sites has exposed communities to pollutants, and many of the environmentally harmful coping strategies that people used to survive during conflicts may continue well beyond their end.

In conflicts with high levels of displacement, land rights and ownership issues are common, particularly when returnees move home. Influxes of people can increase environmental pressures in areas from which they have been absent, particularly through agricultural conversion or expansion. This can lead to increased rates of deforestation. Research has shown a sharp increase in deforestation rates in many post-conflict countries, with clearance outpacing the state's ability to control it.

The presence of military forces can extend well into the post-conflict phase. The operation and ultimate closure or handover of bases are associated with pollution issues, particularly where the host nation may be unable to enforce environmental standards. The use of practices like burn pits has exposed military personnel and communities to hazardous pollution, leaving veterans with ongoing health problems. The post-conflict clearance of landmines and explosive remnants of war can lead to soil degradation, localized pollution, and negative changes in land use when areas are released back to communities.

The damage that conflicts do to environmental governance can have implications for environmental protection for years. This can set back progress on issues as diverse as pollution control, resource and protected area management, climate change adaptation, and biodiversity protection.

Finally, the environmental costs of recovery may be significant. Massive urban rebuilding projects can require huge volumes of resources.

CONCLUSION: ENVIRONMENTAL OPPORTUNITIES

While armed conflicts and military activities can cause or facilitate many different forms of environmental harm, addressing the environment during and after conflicts can also create opportunities for building and sustaining peace, and for helping to transform societies through sustainable recovery.

Shared natural resources can provide the basis for dialogue between warring parties, as can common environmental threats that extend across human boundaries and borders. Unpredictable energy supplies during conflicts can encourage a transition to solar power, while the devastation conflicts cause can be an opportunity to build back greener, or to create new domestic legal frameworks to sustainably manage resources.

However, these opportunities are dependent on more attention being paid to the environment before, during, and after conflicts. If we fail to call for greater protection before and during conflicts, damage will be seen as acceptable. And if we ignore the environment after conflicts, we will not only miss out on opportunities to encourage sustainable recovery; we may also be setting states up for future resource conflicts.

QUESTIONS FOR DISCUSSION AND DISCUSSION

1. Doug Weir explains that military lands cover between 1–6 percent of the global land surface, and in many cases, these are ecologically important areas. While excluding public development from these areas can benefit biodiversity, Weir suggests that the question of whether they could be better managed as civil protected areas is rarely discussed. Should military lands be managed and protected and if so, how?
2. Can you describe other ways in which war harms the environment?
3. The1868 St. Petersburg Declaration states "the necessities of war ought to yield to the requirements of humanity." Does this relate to the environment too?
4. Explore the current international laws of war that protect natural resources and the environment in the context of civil war or local conflicts. Are they inadequate?

5. In 2022 it is expected that governments will adopt a UN General Assembly resolution containing a new normative PERAC framework. PERAC stands for the Protection of the Environment in Relation to Armed Conflicts. The framework will address how the environment should be protected across the cycle of armed conflicts. This will see the most significant advance in the legal framework intended to prevent and remedy environmental damage from war since the 1970s. Read the twenty-seven principles outlining how the environment should be protected before, during, and after armed conflicts. Ecocide is not addressed, and climate change does not feature. What are your thoughts in relation to these two missing principles? What are the strengths of this framework?

BIBLIOGRAPHY

"The PERAC Legal Framework, Frequently Asked Questions." https://ceobs.org/perac-principles-frequently-asked-questions.

"States to Adopt New Legal Framework on War and the Environment." https://ceobs.org/states-to-adopt-new-legal-framework-on-war-and-the-environment.

Weir, Doug. "How Does War Damage the Environment?" https://ceobs.org/how-does-war-damage-the-environment/.

14

Expanding Language Opportunities for Deaf Learners through Intentional Field Trips into the Natural World

Tips for Classroom Teachers, Special Educators, and Teachers of the Deaf

MELANIE SIMPSON

INTRODUCTION

Deafness is a low-incidence exceptionality and most estimates suggest that overall, childhood deafness constitutes approximately one percent of the entire school population.[1] Deaf students are adept learners who, like their hearing peers, come from diverse backgrounds, demonstrate a variety of interests and talents, and have a range of specific learning strengths and needs. In 2022, due to both the introduction of Universal Newborn Hearing Screening (UNHS) during the early 2000s[2] and improvements in hearing technologies (including cochlear implants), the language development of

1. Schein, "Demography of Deafness"; Hutchinson and Martin, "Special Education in Ontario."

2. World Health Organization, "Newborn and Infant Hearing Screening."

most deaf children follows a similar trajectory to that of hearing students.[3] When deaf students are provided with good access to the auditory signal and early intervention, most develop age-appropriate language and literacy skills.[4] Communication decisions made by parents and caregivers in the first years of life impact the language and modality that deaf students use to communicate. Currently, the majority of deaf students use spoken language and are being educated in inclusive mainstream settings alongside their hearing peers while receiving varying support from teachers of the deaf.[5] Only a small minority of deaf learners who do not attend a school for the deaf communicate in a native sign language (i.e., American Sign Language [ASL]) or use a combination of sign and spoken language accessing the curriculum through an educational interpreter. As such, general education teachers play a major role in the education of deaf students by partnering with teachers of the deaf to learn how to provide the appropriate accommodations and educational supports.[6]

All children are born hard-wired to build their expressive and receptive language through free play or planned activities that occur with their caregivers and with their peers.[7] Most typically developing children have access to four language acquisition conditions: (i) quantity and quality of exposure (ii) to accessible language (iii) through meaningful interactions (iv) with capable users.[8] Language acquisition is a lifetime endeavor which impacts literacy skills and cognitive development. Teachers should be acutely aware that the foremost issue facing deaf students is that clear access to linguistic input and communicative exchanges cannot be assumed.[9] Busy (and therefore noisy) classroom environments, unstructured discussions occurring during collaborative learning, comments made during classroom discussions by students sitting behind them or across the room, and overhearing speech, can be out of reach when strategies and accommodations are not intentionally implemented. For all deaf students, the above-mentioned scenarios occur daily, and therefore, intentional vocabulary development is often required to mitigate the lost opportunity for language expansion.

Teachers of the deaf, available for consultation or support, can provide practical counsel to classroom teachers, resource teachers and other

3. Edwards and Isquith, "Cognitive Development."
4. Fulcher et al., "Listen Up"; Mayer et al., "Reading Achievement of Deaf Students."
5. Millett, "Collaborating for Student Success."
6. Knoors and Hermans, "Effective Instruction."
7. Moore and Linthicum, "Human Auditory System."
8. Mayer, "What Really Matters."
9. Tomblin et al., "Comparison of Language Achievement."

educational support staff throughout a deaf learner's educational journey.[10] Classroom teachers may have had access to in-service presentations or video-recorded modules on topics such as remote microphone troubleshooting, captioning of video recordings, and reducing background noise.[11] As such, the information that follows will not be exhaustive, in terms of strategies and scenarios, for supporting language development and educational programming for deaf learners.

The primary goal of this chapter is to excite teachers towards implementing strategies and intervention approaches which will enable language expansion in deaf learners while in a specific learning environment: nature. While the primary student profile will be that of a deaf learner who uses spoken language exclusively, educators will notice that the accommodations and strategies are of a universal design; all learners benefit from optimizing teaching and learning in nature. It is important to note that in this chapter, the term "deaf" will be used to refer to any individual identified with a hearing loss, from mild to profound, irrespective of the use of amplification (i.e., individuals with cochlear implants are deaf). The principles illustrated in this chapter can be used in any language of instruction (e.g., American Sign Language or English) but it should be noted that instructional strategies mentioned may differ for different modalities. Some strategies will be more useful than others, depending on a child's learning needs. Classroom teachers, resource teachers, and teachers of the deaf should work together to ensure that deaf students are accessing the full range of the curriculum. Prior to setting out into the outdoor learning environment, teachers should consider: a) student centered planning by consulting language and listening profiles (i.e., audiograms), b) universal design for learning and integration of alternative curriculum topics, c) specific strategies for language development and d) gathering data to enhance your balanced assessment practices.

WHAT DOES THE NATURAL ENVIRONMENT HAVE TO OFFER DEAF STUDENTS?

For school-aged children, meaningful interactions taking place in the right context will increase vocabulary learning and retention[12] and impact the quality of teacher conversational input while increasing curiosity.[13] Extending classroom learning into the natural environment provides the

10. Millett, "Collaborating for Student Success."
11. Millett, "Collaborating for Student Success."
12. Bobzien et al., "Using Repeated Reading."
13. Duncan and Lederberg, "Relations between Teacher Talk Characteristics."

perfect backdrop for language development conditions (i.e., meaningful interactions in quality and quantity) and could be considered imperative for children's development. Vocabulary development—a key focus with deaf students—is least successful when done in isolation through word lists or drills. New vocabulary words are not learned after being heard only once; with multiple experiences and practice using and hearing a word, students move new vocabulary from their receptive lexical bank to their expressive language.[14]

Vygotsky[15] wrote about the importance of play, theorizing that children develop rules and practice mature experiences through imaginative role-playing. Natural environments provide interesting backdrops for imaginative play with forested paths and interesting tree trunks igniting stories or kindling creative scenarios. Cross-curricular connections can be made between math and science; for example, students could be sent off to make an estimation of a tree's age by counting the rings visible on the stump, or using the same tree stump, students could measure the distance between the rings to establish various growing conditions over the decades. More than just a play-space, nature offers seasonal experiences and a plethora of artifacts to discover. Inviting students to be still and listen for bird calls could be the beginning stages of an interesting unit where students learn to identify birds by their song. With just a bit of careful planning, teachers can bring any learning objective into the natural environment crafting lesson plans that cater to all types of learners. All subjects can be taught in nature when teachers allow their creativity to run freely. For example, how would a music class echo in the forest, or how would an art lesson be enhanced through a walk in the woods? School spaces often have designated Snoezelen Rooms for a sensory reorganizing experience,[16] but why not take that idea into the natural world where you listen to the wind in the trees, smell the forest scents and tickle your toes with the moss on the ground?

Outdoors excursions will require a few special procedures, and teachers should connect with school administrators to discuss their destination and plans. Parent permission forms are typically required when students leave the indoor sanctuary of the classroom and teachers should forewarn caregivers providing lists of suggested outerwear which will help mitigate varying weather patterns. Every outdoor learning environment will present with different listening opportunities and challenges, but overall, the

14. Strassman et al., "Teaching Academic Language."
15. Vygotsky, *Mind in Society*.
16. Alberta Teachers' Association, "Snoezelen Room."

benefits are great, and teachers can develop strategies to assure communication, comfort, and learning expectations are met while journeying into nature.

STUDENT-CENTERED PLANNING

School-aged deaf children receive varying levels of support for language development depending on their individual learning profile. Teachers of the deaf can partner with classroom teachers and resource teachers to determine the strengths and needs of deaf learners through a variety of assessment measures. In some jurisdictions, Individual Education Plans (IEPs) are developed to record the strengths and needs of the learner, to identify audiological specifications (e.g. severe-to-profound hearing loss), to outline any modified expectations implemented varying the current grade level expectation, and to list the necessary accommodations.[17]

For the success of any programming, wise teachers consider access to communication their number one priority during all hours of the school day by carefully implementing the access-related accommodations listed in the IEP.

It is the role of the teacher of the deaf to maintain strong liaisons with their collaborative partners (i.e., classroom teachers, special education teachers, educational assistants) and to advocate for the implementation of appropriate accommodations in all learning environments.[18] Accommodations range from the use of specific teaching strategies, such as repeating student responses in conversations, to making the learning more visual. Simple attention-getting strategies can be used prior to providing instructions which will help signal the deaf student to get close enough to read lips while listening, greatly reducing their struggle to understand your spoken language.

Remote microphone systems, such as Soundfield systems or personal Frequency Modulated systems (FM systems), paired with speechreading can be very important keys to a child's access to conversations. Cochlear implants and hearing aids have microphones on the external ear-level piece; these microphones pick up speech signals best within a 3-foot radius. Any distance from the speech signal will significantly impact its strength; the outdoor environment causes additional challenges for microphones because without a contained space, the combined effect of distance and lack of

17. Hutchinson and Martin, "Special Education in Ontario."

18. Knoors and Hermans, "Effective Instruction"; Millett, "Collaborating for Student Success."

reverberation of sound waves causes speech signals to seemingly "disappear into the air." To better illustrate the challenge of listening through cochlear implants and hearing aid microphones in the outdoor environment, consider what it would be like to have a conversation using the speakerphone of your smartphone: how would distance from the phone, wind noise, and the direction you are facing challenge the conversational exchange? In the outdoor environment, intentionally using an RM system will provide access to conversations, directions, and warnings, mitigating that which would otherwise be lost. The pass-around microphone or a second transmitter can be given to a deaf learner's immediate peer group so that the shared learning experiences are also accessible. As in the classroom, teachers must remember to mute the transmitter when the student is not intended to hear the conversation. Consistent access to spoken language while outdoors can be achieved through fully functioning, well maintained, appropriate listening technology and teachers should not leave the classroom without it!

Student-centered planning also involves developing fluency in the language of the natural environment. Becoming "fluent" in the language of nature can be done by exploring print resources and digital resources which are widely available prior to engaging in the outdoor experiential learning. Governments across the world have been developing frameworks for educators to support the learning of green and sustainable development through interactions with nature. For example, both the Ministry of Education in British Columbia and the Ministry of Education in Ontario[19] have released curriculum documents providing cross-curricular connections for relevant topics across grade levels. The European Commission offers recommendations for educators to support students of all ages.[20] Consulting other resources such as the Project Learning Tree: Pre-K-8 Environmental Education Activity Guide[21] or the Ontario Society for Environmental Education[22] will allow teachers to become "fluent" and capable users in the language of the natural environment.

While it may be easiest to simply step outside and explore the tiny red spiders on the sidewalk closest to the school door, developing strong lesson plans which identify student strengths and needs paired with learning objectives will allow an outing to go from basic to high level while also meeting pedagogical requirements. Teachers who model the language of the

19. British Columbia Ministry of Education, "Environmental Learning and Experience"; Ontario Ministry of Education, *Ontario Curriculum.*

20. European Commission, "Learning for Environmental Sustainability."

21. Project Learning Tree Canada, *Project Learning Tree.*

22. Ontario Society for Environmental Education, "Nature Connections."

natural world need to know their subject area and learning objectives well to be able to guide students, scaffold appropriately, and enhance their students' learning through critical questioning and dialogue. In the same way that educators would prepare a dialogic reading lesson, outdoor educators need to be prepared to challenge students' thinking, elaborate on students' thoughts, and provide clear, appropriate, and precise Tier 3 (subject specific) vocabulary.[23]

UNIVERSAL DESIGN FOR LEARNING AND INTEGRATION OF ALTERNATIVE CURRICULUM TOPICS

Not only is the teacher of the deaf responsible for ensuring that appropriate accommodations are implemented, they are also responsible for the identification, assessment, and instruction of alternative curriculum goals specific to each deaf student which include topics such as: listening and spoken language development, self-determination and advocacy, audiological understanding and management, and pragmatics and social interactions.[24] For some deaf students, weekly withdrawal sessions will occur to practice specific alternative curriculum goals, and when possible, teachers of the deaf will remain in the classroom to facilitate group learning experiences or provide incidental modeling of appropriate communication strategies to the deaf student's peers. In the outdoor environment, teachers of the deaf may join their student on an outing by partnering with their colleagues and implementing team-teaching strategies. For example, prior to the excursion, the colleagues meet to develop specific learning targets for the deaf student. Pre-teaching of concepts may occur in the one-to-one setting or directly in the classroom with peers while using various pedagogical materials. Activities which can occur prior to the excursion include: i) planning a route, ii) putting together an excursion kit, iii) preparing an Experience Book,[25] iv) exploring images, v) reading about the targeted learning vi) and pre-teaching vocabulary. Spiralling back to the content after the excursion and throughout the year is an important added step that teachers of the deaf will provide for repeated experience with novel words; the increased deliberate exposure will allow for better recall and deeper understanding.[26]

23. Beck et al., *Bringing Words to Life.*
24. Millett, "Collaborating for Student Success."
25. Alsop and Watkins, *SKI-HI Curriculum.*
26. Pearce et al., "Complete Guide."

In terms of the alternative curriculum goals, the outdoor environment offers unique opportunities for developing metacognition and self-awareness of their individual listening and spoken language skills, and in the development of self-advocacy skills. Here are some ideas that teachers could use with all students to highlight the variety of listening conditions in the natural world:

1. After conducting a listening check to ensure that the deaf student's listening technology is functioning correctly, teachers can ask students to pause and strain to listen. As students listen, they can begin to list the sounds that can be identified. Some sounds may or may not be heard and teachers can use this opportunity to highlight softer sounds to see if students can hear them. With a focus on self-determination and self-advocacy, students can be directed to consider possible adjustments that could be made to access the sound such as, moving closer to the sound source or deliberately eliminating background noise. Depending on the age and maturity of the deaf student, they can be guided to consider whether their listening technology is working optimally. Changing batteries in hearing aids or changing the cochlear implant battery becomes an independent responsibility for some students as young as eight or nine years old.
2. Second, sounds change in the natural environment. Students can put their heads on a log and listen as a voice travels the length of the log. Students can be directed to consider how the sound changes when a stick is knocked on a log versus a rock. Teachers can direct students to consider how the wind sounds in one area of the woods compared to another and how the varieties of trees might influence this. Which sounds could be considered "soft sounds" and which sounds are "loud" (e.g., birds chirping vs. a waterfall)? To practice personal communication or listening and spoken language skills, students can be directed to participate in a "Think-Pair-Share" moment with their peers about this topic.
3. What strategies can students use in the natural environment to be sure they are alerted to danger and acting safely? Localization strategies, or locating sounds in the environment, are important skills. Students with a unilateral hearing loss have more difficulty with localization and students with differing listening configurations in each ear will also find localization more challenging. Conversations for awareness about how listening and localization changes in the outdoors are more

meaningful with the real-life experience of it and can be beneficial to all students.

4. Social interactions can change in the natural environment due to various listening challenges, and reliance on the RM system, especially for access to conversations, should be consistently modeled. Excitement during outdoor adventures inevitably ignites many conversations between students as they flit about exploring the woods or examining nature; the teacher can facilitate group interactions by repeating student comments through the transmitter. Smaller group interactions are easier to negotiate and teachers might consider dividing students into pairs or groups of three. Requiring the students to use the pass-around mic encourages turn-taking which is part of a universal design for learning. Classroom teachers who are aware of these strategies can make communication among peers more productive in an outdoor session.
5. Typical attention-getting strategies will not work outdoors; it is virtually impossible to flicker the lights or stomp your feet to create vibrations—two culturally acceptable attention-getting strategies used among the members of the Deaf community. For the entire group's safety, various visual signals could be established before venturing outdoors. For example, hands crossed above the head could mean "you've gone too far, come back," or a red cloth tied to a tree could signify a meeting place. Establishing one or two predetermined directives will provide freedom within a safe boundary.
6. Once access to the speech signal has been addressed, outdoor environments provide an excellent alternative setting for increasing vocabulary by enhancing children's knowledge of and experience with cross-curricular topics.[27] While outdoors, teachers should move among their students to scaffold and elevate the learning from basic knowledge and comprehension to advanced evaluation and creation (see Blooms Taxonomy[28]).

The success of a universally designed lesson is in the fact that all students benefit from a teacher's mindful individualization of curriculum topics.

27. Antia et al., "Explicit and Contextual Vocabulary Intervention"; Fisher and Blachowicz, "Vocabulary Instruction in a Remedial Setting"; Zucker et al., "Going Nuts for Words."

28. Anderson et al., *Taxonomy for Learning.*

SPECIFIC STRATEGIES FOR LANGUAGE DEVELOPMENT

With consistent use of listening technology, (e.g., hearing aids or cochlear implants)[29] teachers can use specific evidence-based techniques to intentionally target vocabulary expansion.[30] Most incidental learning opportunities are not accessible to the deaf learner. Overhearing conversations can be a rich source of language development for typically-hearing children but is challenging and rare for deaf students, therefore, most vocabulary and world knowledge must be learned through intentional face-to-face interactions.

Teachers can use the remote microphones to *repeat conversations* that are occurring increasing the opportunity for incidental learning. For example, when students are exploring small mushrooms just steps off the path, teachers will overhear them as they make observations: "I can see mushrooms on this tree trunk!" or "I found a huge toad-stool like the one in the *Frog and Toad* books." The teacher can intentionally repeat their comments: "Sarah sees mushrooms on a tree trunk and Todd found a huge toadstool that he thinks looks like the one in the *Frog and Toad* books." Repeating student utterances provides a better access to the deaf student working to follow the group interaction.

Acoustic highlighting is a strategy for emphasizing the key words or phrases in a sentence making them more noticeable and is most commonly used with younger students. This strategy is done by changing the rate of your speech, elongating and pausing before and after a word, using the intonation of a sing-song pattern, or changing the volume of a target word or phrase. Acoustic highlighting is often used in conjunction with other strategies such as *repeating* a phrase for emphasis, *recasting* a phrase so that it makes more sense or becomes more manageable to the hearer, and *reframing* a phrase so that there is better contextual information. When outdoors, once assured that you have the student's attention, use acoustic highlighting and these other strategies to emphasize the key vocabulary and concepts.[31] Additionally, pre-laminated vocabulary words or printing text on a portable whiteboard can increase exposure to novel vocabulary and concepts.

Many teacher-student interactions are delivered through imperative language where the teacher presents a question or a comment which demands a response.[32] Guiding a group of students into the outdoor en-

29. Pisoni et al., "Efficacy and Effectiveness."
30. Strassman et al., "Teaching Academic Language."
31. Gallagher et al., "Academic Vocabulary."
32. Murphy, *Declarative Language Handbook.*

vironment may evoke more imperative statements from the teacher but it would be most beneficial if *declarative language* and *commenting strategies* are used. Declarative statements and comments invite children to observe the environment, absorb contextualized clues, and make self-determining actions based on higher-level thinking. For example, rather than telling a child to join the classmates at the fallen tree, consider making a string of comments carefully positioned between deliberate 15-second pauses. "I wonder where the other kids are exploring."—pause—"I see them over by the fallen tree."—pause—"I can see they are collecting small objects for their Experience Book."—pause—"I wonder if you are ready to join them."

Language modeling techniques can also be used as children and teachers explore the outdoor environment.[33] The teacher can *infuse specific vocabulary into comments* and *demonstrate wonder*: "I wonder if the mushrooms that your group is finding are in *damp* or *parched* areas of the forest." When posing questions and making wondering statements, teachers can be intentional about implementing the "*wait time*" technique. *Wait time*, simply stated, allows students to listen and ponder the question or comment without being overloaded with information. Oftentimes, students will respond to the question or comment with a more mature response when teachers pause for fifteen to twenty seconds prior to making any other statements. Teachers are encouraged to count quietly to themselves to ensure that the pause is long enough for student contemplation and organization of a response.

GATHERING DATA FOR ENHANCING A BALANCED ASSESSMENT

Learning in the outdoor environment offers fresh opportunities for teachers to engage in formative and summative assessment. Teachers can lean on triangulation of data from three specific assessment measure groupings[34]: i) consideration of process, ii) consideration of product, iii) student-student or student-teacher conversations. Overall evaluation of student learning should come from more than one experience and should occur over time.

Connected to the universal design for learning, assessment for learning allows teachers to make observations and design tasks that provide students *with a variety of ways to demonstrate* their learning process. As students engage in the outdoor environment, teachers can make *observation of process* their first outdoor assessment measure by observing how students

33. Fisher and Blachowicz, "Vocabulary Instruction in a Remedial Setting."

34. Ontario Teachers Federation, *Assessment for Outdoor Learning.*

apply their background knowledge to activities. Students can make oral or written self-reflections as they engage their meta-cognition for assessment as learning. It is important for students to know the purpose of any outing. Developing student-friendly learning targets using "I can" language will guide engagement and student responsibility of learning.

Teachers should take advantage of the individual connections made with students while they explore the natural environment. The *conversations that occur between teacher and student* can be used to assess a students' level of comprehension while also guiding them towards deeper learning. Throughout the various excursions, teachers can be prepared with language development checklists, pragmatics checklists, or other anecdotal observational tools. Teachers of the deaf regularly make video recordings to capture language samples which they transcribed to identify areas of need in language development. To capture group interactions, teachers can encourage students to record their group discussions using the camera on a tablet. Interactions among students and responses to prompting questions can be useful tools for evaluating students' grasp of vocabulary and concepts. For younger students, teachers may observe that the mean length of utterances (MLU) increases while in nature and interesting comments can be recorded anecdotally.

Consideration of product can include building challenging structures with natural materials, creating a piece of art, or producing a piece of writing while resting under a shaded tree. Creativity and expressive language may find fresh life when well-removed from traditional classroom spaces. Teachers can include charts and graphs in their pre-planning for outings guiding students to engage and observe elements of the natural world. Various graphic organizers readily available online can facilitate conversations upon return to the classroom and provide assessments of learning. In *The Book of Nature Connection*, Jacob Rodenburg encourages teachers to make use of worksheets such as those found in his free resource: "Leaf Shape Bingo cards."[35] Manipulating and observing various objects of all sizes that represent, for example, bilateral symmetry, allows students to increase their understanding of the concept and remember the term more easily.[36] Teachers can have students bring their notebooks outdoors for tracing found objects, making leaf rubbings, or writing notes. Students can adhere small, gathered items, draw or take pictures from their field trip, and write journal entries recording their thoughts or memories from the activity in an Experience Book. The Experience Book entries can be used to track learning and

35. Rodenburg, *Book of Nature Connection*, 64.

36. Antia et al., "Explicit and Contextual Vocabulary Intervention."

be revisited after the outing (i.e., spiralling). The vocabulary or concepts can be discussed in greater detail each consecutive time that the book is opened.

Rubrics and curriculum-based checklists can be consulted as students demonstrate their language and concept development over time. Teachers should remember to consult any captured videos of students, written journal reflections, and Experience Books as an assessment of learning. A simple cloze procedure can be made by taking a text and eliminating every nth word. Cloze procedures created to assess certain areas of language and literacy skills can assist in evaluating recall of procedural knowledge or consolidation of learning.

The multiple sources of assessment available to teachers in the natural environment should make assessment for, as, and of learning more enjoyable for everyone!

CONCLUSION

Moving the learning environment into the natural world does not have to involve significant extra planning. There are benefits to releasing children into free play in nature without agendas. Children who struggle to focus indoors may work more efficiently after a walk in nature or with the promise to go out after the required activity is fulfilled. Even so, purposeful planning with alternative curriculum topics and cross-curriculum learning objectives in mind make learning in nature very productive towards teachers' pedagogical responsibilities.

The ideas portrayed in this chapter will contribute to how teachers can ensure successful integration practices specifically for deaf students while on outdoor adventures. When goals for an outing are established (i.e., free-play or curriculum-based learning), collaboration among team members and student-centered planning will ensure that deaf students engage meaningfully with their peers to discover a whole new world of learning. Even when team-teaching and direct support is not part of the student's learning plan, it is always a good idea to seek the support from a teacher of the deaf colleague who can help ensure that curriculum content is being presented in the most readily accessible way. Whether venturing out for free play or with a pedagogical purpose, teachers should feel confident that they can facilitate good communication outdoors by implementing these suggested strategies and accommodations for all learners.

QUESTIONS FOR DISCUSSION AND DEBATE

1. What are the four conditions for language acquisition and how can teachers encourage language expansion in light of these conditions?
2. How can classroom teachers and teachers of the deaf work together to ensure deaf students have access to spoken language while on outings in the natural environment? What additional measures can be taken beyond that which is already occurring in the classroom environment?
3. Select one curriculum topic that you could cover while venturing into the natural environment. Identify the learning objectives that you would target, and write them out in student-friendly language.
4. Think about the concept of universal design, and imagine how you would apply the strategies from the chapter with students that you have worked with who may or may not be deaf.
5. Think about some of the possibilities for assessment while sojourning into nature with your students. What types of assessment measures/activities could you implement over the course of three or four visits outdoors?

BIBLIOGRAPHY

Alberta Teachers' Association. "The Snoezelen Room: A Special Place That Both Stimulates and Relaxes [Capilano School]." *ATA News* 34 (2000).

Alsop, Linda, and Sue Watkins. *SKI-HI Curriculum: Family-Centered Programming for Infants and Young Children with Hearing Loss.* Logan, UT: Ski-Hi Institute, 2004.

Anderson, Lorin W., et al. *A Taxonomy for Learning, Teaching, and Assessing: A Revision of Bloom's.* Essex, UK: Pearson, 2001.

Antia, Shirin D., et al. "Explicit and Contextual Vocabulary Intervention: Effects on Word and Definition Learning." *Journal of Deaf Studies and Deaf Education* (2021) 1–14. https://doi.org/doi: 10.1093/deafed/enab002.

Beck, Isabel L., et al. *Bringing Words to Life: Robust Vocabulary Instruction.* 2nd ed. New York: Guilford, 2013.

Bobzien, Jonna L., et al. "Using Repeated Reading and Explicit Instruction to Teach Vocabulary to Preschoolers with Hearing Loss." *Infants & Young Children* 28 (2015) 262–80. https://doi.org/10.1097/iyc.0000000000000039.

British Columbia Ministry of Education. "Environmental Learning and Experience an Interdisciplinary Guide for Teachers." https://www2.gov.bc.ca/assets/gov/education/kindergarten-to-grade-12/teach/teaching-tools/environmental-learning/environ_learning_exper.pdf.

Duncan, Molly K., and Amy R. Lederberg. "Relations between Teacher Talk Characteristics and Child Language in Spoken-Language Deaf and Hard-of-

Hearing Classrooms." *Journal of Speech, Language, and Hearing Research* 61 (2018) 2977–95. https://doi.org/10.1044/2018_JSLHR-L-17-0475.
Edwards, Lindsey C., and Peter K. Isquith. "Cognitive Development: The Impact of Cochlear Implantation." In *The Oxford Handbook of Deaf Studies in Learning and Cognition*. Oxford: Oxford University Press, 2020. https://doi.org/10.1093/oxfordhb/9780190054045.013.7.
European Commission. "Learning for Environmental Sustainability | European Education Area." https://education.ec.europa.eu/focus-topics/green-education/learning-for-environmental-sustainability.
Fisher, Peter J., and Camille L. Z. Blachowicz. "Vocabulary Instruction in a Remedial Setting." *Reading & Writing Quarterly* 21 (2005) 281–300. https://doi.org/10.1080/10573560590949386.
Fulcher, Anne, et al. "Listen Up: Children with Early Identified Hearing Loss Achieve Age-Appropriate Speech/Language Outcomes by 3 Years-of-Age." *International Journal of Pediatric Otorhinolaryngology* 76 (2012) 1785–94. https://doi.org/10.1016/j.ijporl.2012.09.001.
Gallagher, Melissa A., et al. "Academic Vocabulary: Explicit and Incidental Instruction for Students of Diverse Language Backgrounds." *Reading & Writing Quarterly* 35 (2019) 84–102. https://doi.org/10.1080/10573569.2018.1510796.
Hutchinson, Nancy L., and Andrea K. Martin. "Special Education in Ontario: Where We Are Now." In *Inclusive Classrooms in Ontario Schools*, edited by Ky Pruesse, 8. Toronto: Pearson Canada, 2012.
Knoors, H., and D. Hermans. "Effective Instruction for Deaf and Hard of Hearing Students: Teaching Strategies, School Settings, and Student Characteristics." In *The Oxford Handbook of Deaf Studies, Language and Education*, 57–71. New York: Oxford University Press, 2010.
Mayer, Connie C. "What Really Matters in the Early Literacy Development of Deaf Children." *Journal of Deaf Studies and Deaf Education* 12 (2007) 411–31. https://doi.org/10.1093/deafed/enm020.
Mayer, Connie C., et al. "Reading Achievement of Deaf Students: Challenging the Fourth Grade Ceiling." *Journal of Deaf Studies and Deaf Education* 26 (2021) 427–37.
Millett, Pam. "Collaborating for Student Success: Teachers of the Deaf and Hard of Hearing." *Canadian Audiologist* 8 (2021) n.p. https://canadianaudiologist.ca/issue/volume-8-issue-3-2021/column/in-the-classrooms/.
Moore, J. K., and F. H. Linthicum. "The Human Auditory System: A Timeline of Development." *International Journal of Audiology* 46 (2007) 460–78. https://doi.org/10.1080/14992020701383019.
Murphy, Linda K. *Declarative Language Handbook: Using a Thoughtful Language Style to Help Kids with Social Learning Challenges Feel Competent, Connected, and Understood*. N.p., 2020.
Ontario Society for Environmental Education. "Nature Connections—Ontario Society for Environmental Education." https://home.osee.ca/nature-connections/.
Ontario Ministry of Education. *The Ontario Curriculum Grades 1–8 and Kindergarten Program Environmental Education: Scope and Sequences of Expectations, 2017 Edition*. Toronto: Ministry of Education, 2017.

Pearce, Kyle, et al. "The Complete Guide to Spiralling Your Math Curriculum." *Making Math Moments That Matter*, Jan 13, 2021. https://makemathmoments.com/spiralling-guide/.

Pisoni, David B., et al. "Efficacy and Effectiveness of Cochlear Implants in Deaf Children." In *Deaf Cognition: Foundations and Outcomes*, 52–101. Oxford: Oxford University Press, 2008. https://doi.org/10.1093/acprof:oso/9780195368673.003.0003.

Project Learning Tree Canada. *Project Learning Tree: Pre-K-8 Environmental Education Activity Guide. Project Learning Tree Canada.* Project Learning Tree, 2008. https://pltcanada.org.

Rodenburg, Jacob. *The Book of Nature Connection: 70 Sensory Activities for All Ages.* Gabriola, BC: New Society, 2022.

Schein, J. D. "The Demography of Deafness." In *Understanding Deafness Socially: Continuities in Research and Theory*, edited by J. E. Nash, 21–43. Springfield, IL: Thomas, 1996.

Strassman, Barbara K., et al. "Teaching Academic Language to d/Deaf Students: Does Research Offer Evidence for Practice?" *American Annals of the Deaf* 163 (2019) 501–33. https://doi.org/10.1353/aad.2019.0001.

Tomblin, J. B., et al. "A Comparison of Language Achievement in Children with Cochlear Implants and Children Using Hearing Aids." *Journal of Speech, Language, and Hearing Research* 42 (1999) 497–509. https://doi.org/10.1044/jslhr.4202.497.

Vygotsky, Lev Semenovich. *Mind in Society: The Development of Higher Psychological Processes.* Cambridge: Harvard University Press, 1978.

World Health Organization. "Newborn and Infant Hearing Screening." https://apps.who.int/iris/bitstream/handle/10665/339288/9789241599496-eng.pdf.

15

Meditative Thinking and the Naturalist Current of Environmental Education

Principles Informing a Philosophy of Reclaiming Mystery

Douglas D. Karrow[1] and Sharon R. Harvey[2]

MEDITATIVE THINKING AND THE NATURALIST CURRENT OF ENVIRONMENTAL EDUCATION

Principles Informing a Philosophy of Reclaiming Mystery

In this chapter, we welcome the reader to the philosophical work of Martin Heidegger, an original thinker of the twentieth century, who implores us to consider a different way of thinking, a rethinking that will transform our

1. Department of Educational Studies, Brock University

2. General Studies Education, Arizona State University at Lake Havasu. The authors would like to acknowledge the contribution of Dr. Holly Tsun Haggarty, who provided an invaluable critique of the manuscript and assistance with manuscript editing. Correspondence concerning this article may be addressed to Douglas D. Karrow, 1842 King St. E., Hamilton, Ontario, Canada, L8K 1V7. Email: Doug.Karrow@Brocku.ca

relationship with nature and, in turn, our understanding and practice of environmental education.

Our work consists of four parts. In Part I, we begin by describing *calculative thinking*, a mode of thinking, which preoccupies modern Western society, and which has prompted a deleterious relationship with nature. In Part II, we introduce Heidegger's *meditative thinking* as an antidote to calculative thinking, in an effort to re-think our essential relationship with nature and environmental education. Meditative thinking can move us beyond the modern human tendency to believe all our environmental problems can be technologically solved. Acknowledging the brief history of practical and theoretical propositions of environmental education, herein referred to as "currents of environmental education," we make the case that meditative thinking is epistemically coherent with the *naturalist current*.[3] We provide Lucie Sauvé's description of this current, but then offer further exegesis, reclaiming its ancient etymological meaning—nature as *physis*. However, we note that meditative thinking is destined to flounder unless we extend a worldview[4] that supports it. In Part III, we outline the manner a *doctrine of mystery*[5] serves as an alternative worldview foundational to meditative thinking. This sets the stage for an alternative philosophy (a philosophy of education)[6] of *reclaiming mystery*. We entertain the principles that inform a philosophy of reclaiming mystery and how these may influence the thought and practice of environmental education. Lastly, in Part IV, we summarize our argument and pose questions for further discussion.

3. Sauvé, Lucie, "Currents in Environmental Education: Mapping a Complex and Evolving Pedagogical Field," *Canadian Journal of Environmental Education, 10*, no. 1 (Spring, 2005): 11–37.

4. Worldview here means a general orientation to the world where a "basic set of beliefs guide action." Guba, *The Alternative Paradigm Dialogue*, 17.

5. Cooper, David E., *The Measure of Things: Humanism, Humility, and Mystery* (Oxford: Clarendon Press, 2007). Cooper's use of the word "doctrine" implies a belief or set of beliefs held by a cultural institution (e.g., Church, political party or group).

6. The context for considering a "philosophy" is the field of education (philosophy of education).

PART I: CALCULATIVE THINKING AND OUR ENVIRONMENTAL PREDICAMENT

Heidegger, lamenting the destructiveness of our current era, sourced the problem to metaphysics,[7] to the modern understanding of Being.[8] Heidegger noted that while the ancient Greek name for, and understanding of, metaphysics was nature qua *Physis*,[9] modern metaphysics is one of Technicity.[10]

Physis, during ancient Greek times, referred to a two-fold movement, inherent in each living thing, be it a flower, a butterfly, or a human being. Heidegger explicated this term as that which "emerges from itself . . . the unfolding that opens itself up, the coming-into-appearance in such unfolding, and holding itself and persisting in appearance—in short, the emerging-abiding sway."[11] So, an entity arises out of concealment, yet reclines into concealment even in its rising. Thus, a thing may grow and while preserving its potential.[12]

In contrast to ancient Greek metaphysics, Heidegger interpreted Nietzsche's encapsulation of modern metaphysics as will-to-power[13] through

7. Metaphysics, originally from the Greek (*ta meta ta physika*—to begin with the things beyond physics), "is that branch of philosophy that studies the nature of being and knowing." *Collins Dictionary of the English Language, s.v. metaphysics, n.*"

8. The capitalized form of "Being" refers to the "living web within which all relations emerge," whereas the lowercase form of "being" refers to entities, or things themselves. Bigwood, Carol, *Earth Muse: Feminism, Nature, and Art* (Philadelphia: Temple University Press, 1993), 3.

9. Physis is the ancient Greek word for nature. Aristotle, *Physics*, trans. C. D. C. Reeve (Cambridge: Hackett Publishing Company, 2018).

10 Heidegger, Martin, *Nietzsche, vol. 1: The Will to Power as Art*, trans. David Farrell Krell (London: Routledge, 1981); Heidegger, Martin, *Nietzsche, vol. 4: Nihilism*, ed. David Farrell Krell. Translated by F. A. Capuzzi. New York: Harper & Row, , 1982). Also, Karrow, Douglas D., *Educating-with-place: Recovering from Metaphysics as Technicity* (Saarbrücken: Lambert Academic Publishing, 2010); Franklin, Ursula, *The Real World of Technology* (Toronto: House of Anansi, 1999); Postman, Neil, *Technopoly: The Surrender of Culture to Technology* (New York: Vintage Books, 1993).

11. Heidegger, Martin, *Introduction to Metaphysics*, trans. Gregory Fried and Richard Polt (New Haven: Yale University Press, 2000), 5.

12. Bigwood, *Earth Muse*.

13. Will-to-power is a doctrine put forth by Nietzsche (1883–85/1993). It posits that everything that exists does so fundamentally on an underlying basis of *power centers* whose activity and interactions are explained by a principle that they pursue the expansion of their power. Nietzsche, Friedrich Wilhelm, *Thus Spake Zarathustra*, trans. Thomas Common (New York: Prometheus Books, 1993). See also Anderson, R. Lanier, "Friedrich Nietzsche," in The Stanford Encyclopedia of Philosophy, ed. Edward N. Zalta (Metaphysics Research Lab, Stanford University, 2017), https://plato.stanford.edu/archives/sum2017/entries/nietzsche/.

the unique lens of the character of technology, which he referred to as *enframing*.[14] Heidegger suggested that modern technology has become a gathering force itself and that we humans are caught up in this larger process that is shaping and determining our being. We are "enframed" by this essence of technology. In contrast with ancient Being as Physis, today, Being as Technicity "has been radically transformed" as Physis is pushed to create beyond its limit, "to overcome, expose, resist, and compel, for its character is now nothing else but will-to-power."[15]

Heidegger indicated that our technical relation to nature is based primarily on what he called *calculative thinking*, which consigns nature as something "other" to be manipulated, managed, used, and classified.[16] The scientific method has led the way for people to delineate, classify, demarcate, reduce, and categorize entities, oblivious to the inherent, insidious domination that this separatism implies. The subject-over-against-an-object mindset has prevailed in Western approaches toward nature to the point that this thrust has been backfiring on the very project, of environmental education, of saving nature.

Calculative thinking comprises the current values our present educational system has come to cherish, despite their complicity in the ruinous consequences of a world system driven by such ends. Specifically, in the realm of environmental education, calculative thinking manifests through the habit of conceiving the aim of environmental education in instrumental terms—a cause to achieve an effect, as stated in the proposition that through "environmental education," future generations of teachers and their students are prepared to understand certain environmental problems, develop key skills necessary to their resolution, and develop the attitudes or dispositions shaping moral and ethical development .[17] Historically, the "problems-to-be solved" aimed to conserve and preserve nature. As the understanding of human's complex relationship with nature evolved, "problems" expanded to consider nature and humans through a variety of socio-cultural-political lenses (e.g., race, gender, ethnicity, class, culture, etc.). The topic of the problem to be solved shifted from nature alone, to nature *and* humans. Regardless, the overall structure of our attitude toward nature (and environmental education) was construed in problem-solving terms. Put in

14. Heidegger, Martin, *The Question Concerning Technology and Other Essays*, trans. William Lovitt (New York: Harper & Row, 1977).

15. Bigwood, *Earth Muse*, 88.

16. Heidegger, *Introduction to Metaphysics*.

17. Karrow, Douglas D., Xavier Fazio, and David Zandvliet, *Nomenclature and Discourse of Environmental and Sustainability Education in Teacher Education*, ed. Michael Peters (Singapore: Springer, 2022).

terms of the subject-object relation, humans (subjects) seek technological solutions to environmental problems (objects). This preoccupation with "problem-solving" (whether it be focused on nature and/or humans and nature) is a recurrent theme in most currents of environmental education, in contrast to the naturalist current of environmental education with its focus on human/nature relationship, as construed by Sauvé.[18]

PART II: MEDITATIVE THINKING AS ANTIDOTE TO OUR ENVIRONMENTAL CRISIS

Meditative Thinking

A different relation to nature, and by extension environmental education, is needed to meet the challenges of global environmental demise—we cannot simply problem-solve our way out of environmental catastrophe. Heidegger proposes an antidote to our environmental crisis—meditative thinking, and his related notion of Gelassenheit, or "letting-be."[19]
Heidegger describes the comportment of Gelassenheit (our human disposition toward things, e.g., nature), as "releasement toward things and openness to the mystery."[20] His meditative thinking (or receptivity) is a shift that reverses the subject-object relation, bringing a change in posture for the human—a humble stance with things, a fertile approach to being-in-the-world.

This new subject-object relationship is crucial for our time. Now, the object is recognized as having the capacity to disclose itself and call forth a response. Gelassenheit is an occasion where the altered disposition of the human subject allows the revelatory character of nature to be received and experienced in fresh ways. As we shall show, this has implications for environmental education.

Letting-be implies much more than celebrating mere aesthetics of the natural world and promoting the inherent or intrinsic value of nature. It speaks more fundamentally about a novel relationship between self and other. Some have interpreted Heidegger's thought more from Eastern

18. Sauvé, "Currents in Environmental Education."

19. Heidegger, Martin, *Discourse on Thinking*, trans. John M. Anderson and E. Hans Freund, (New York: Harper & Row, 1966). For an analysis of the term "Gelassenheit" see Harvey, *Heidegger and Eco-phenomenology: Gelassenheit as Practice* (Saarbrücken: Lambert Academic Publishing, 2009). The English translation means "calmness" or "composure"; Cambridge *German-English Dictionary, s.v. "Gelassenheit, n.,"* accessed January 20, 2022, http://dictionary.cambridge.org/dictionary/german-english/gelassenheit. Heidegger conceived of it in terms of "letting be."

20. Heidegger, *Discourse on Thinking*, 55.

influences, or even as a type of holism, such as in Indigenous experience.[21] While these may be possible applications of Heidegger's thought, our primary focus and understanding on Gelassenheit is to follow Heidegger's claim that the subject and object are always with us. We do not collapse or neutralize the subject-object relation, we merely need a new subject-object relationship, an ethics of non-objectification.[22]

Currents of Environmental Education

Environmental education first appeared in Europe early during the twentieth century as a movement to re-connect humans with nature (i.e., "nature education").[23] In this way, "nature" was the environment. Over time, though, other "environments" (specified as resource, problem, system, Being, etc.) have inspired other dedicated currents of intervention. In her seminal work characterizing the field of environmental education, Sauvé provides a cartography of "different practical and theoretical propositions . . . in the form of 15 currents of intervention, enabling a mapping of the pedagogical landscape of environmental education."[24]

Of Sauvé's currents of intervention, we wish to reclaim nature as the focus of the environment, through the naturalist current of environmental education. Sauvé characterizes the naturalist current as follows:

- it is an ancient tradition;
- its core focus is human relationships with nature;
- it proposes that nature has inherent value regardless of the instrumental value that humans ascribe;
- it suggests that the key aim of environmental education is the reconstruction of human relationships with nature.[25]

Meditative thinking is epistemically consistent with the natural current of environmental education. Meditative thinking and the naturalist current of environmental education emanate from a common history (i.e., metaphysics as Physis), they focus on human relationships with nature, and

21. Mika, Carl, *Indigenous Education and the Metaphysics of Presence: A Worlded Philosophy* (New York: Routledge, 2017).

22. Harvey, *Heidegger and Eco-phenomenology.*

23. Neal, Philip, and Joy Palmer, *The Handbook of Environmental Education* (London: Routledge, 1994).

24. Sauvé, "Currents in Environmental Education," 11.

25. Sauvé, "Currents in Environmental Education."

the character of that human/nature relationship elevates the inherent value of nature, independent of humans. However, reclaiming the naturalist current through meditative thinking is bound to fail until we examine worldview, which to this point has remained tacit. Meditative thinking cannot be realized until the traditional Western worldview is redressed.

PART III: RECLAIMING MYSTERY

A Doctrine of Mystery

Over-simplistically, there are two general schemes of reality: *absolutism,* which posits that reality is in every way "out there," and *humanism,* which contra-posits that reality is what we humans make of it. The former accepts the universe as full of mystery, whereas the latter believes humans have the control to conquer the mysteries of their world.[26] As we previously related, metaphysics as Technicity[27] is the ultimate manifestation of humanism in our lives. A doctrine of mystery attempts to synthesize the two views of reality. It recognizes the truth in the thesis of "the human-world" while acknowledging an *undiscursable,* mysterious reality—there are aspects about the world we, as humans, simply may not understand though they exist.

We anticipate that a doctrine of mystery necessitates an alternative metaphysics, perhaps metaphysics as *Neophysis*: an acute self-awareness of our subjectivity and its historical relationship with objects and objectification. Neophysis would entail a humility in the presence of the object, so that the object reveals itself to us. Nature would be viewed differently through a doctrine of mystery, with meditative thinking not objectifying nature. This has profound implications for environmental education: it entails accepting the premise that environmental education is to be wholly oriented to "nature," letting nature exist for nature's sake. In contrast to calculative thinking, which posits an instrumental aim for environmental education (problem-solving), meditative thinking conjures a different aim for environmental education, that of revelation.

26. Cooper, *The Measure of Things.*

27. Metaphysics as Technicity (calculative thinking and the modern enterprise of science), is a product of humanity. Yet, it has been appropriated by absolutist and humanist worldviews. See Verkamp, Bernard, J., *The Senses of Mystery: Religious and Non-Religious* (New York: Fordham University Press, 1997).

Reclaiming Mystery: Environmental Education as Revelation

A doctrine of mystery brings together humanist and absolutist worldviews. In the field of education, with environmental education as our focus, it establishes a foundation from which to advance a different philosophy. We are interested in sketching out the principles of such a philosophy here.

According to Ornstein and Levine, a philosophy consists of three categories: ontology, epistemology, and axiology.[28] How might each of these categories be articulated in a philosophy of reclaiming mystery?

Ontology is the study or conception of the nature of being. Through meditative thinking, we are now receptive to other ways of being that preserve a being's phenomenological possibility (we do not exhaust other beings through the character of calculative thinking). The comportments of Gelassenheit—releasement toward things and openness to the mystery—are meditative thinking's prerequisites. *Thus, the first principle of our philosophy is that of being's ontological possibility and diversity* (Table 1).

Epistemology is that branch of philosophy concerned with what counts as knowledge and how knowledge is derived. Epistemology is derived from one's ontological position. Given that the ontological category of our philosophy preserves ontological possibility and diversity, a fair appraisal of its epistemology would acknowledge that some degree of mystery in our lives is not only ineluctable, but that this mystery enhances, makes *more* meaningful, the knowledge we are able to glean and the manner we go about acquiring such knowledge. This consideration of epistemology, then, is not so much an examination of knowledge and how we come to know, as it is about our knowing relationship with mystery. Mystery *and* knowledge "complicate each other" in a deconstructive sense rather than "oppose each other" as in a structuralist understanding.[29] We are arguing that knowledge *and* mystery share a vital and essential dynamic in structuring reality. This is distinct from the common and prevailing attitude toward mystery, which is generally expressed as distain.[30] A doctrine of mystery, through our comportment toward Gelassenheit, remains open to the mystery. While acknowledging the importance of knowledge, we also pay homage to the mystery of this knowledge. The practice of reclaiming mystery celebrates the great achievements of humanity, while appreciating and acknowledging the original mysteries behind such knowledge. But it is more than this. The practice of reclaiming mystery recognizes that we

28. Ornstein, and Levine. *Foundations of Education*.

29. Moran, Dermot, *Introduction to Phenomenology* (London: Routledge, 2000), 451.

30. Jones, Richard H., *Curing the Philosopher's Disease: Reinstating Mystery in the Heart of Philosophy* (Landham: University Press of America, 2009).

cannot know all that the universe is. We must accept humility in the face of reality. The delicate balance between the knowledge-mystery continuum is to be preserved through this principle of a philosophy reclaiming mystery. *The second principle behind our philosophy is that of epistemological limitation and tentativeness* (Table 1).

The remaining category of our philosophy is axiology. We define "axiology" as the essential values important to us as educators. What values support the previous ontological and epistemological categories? First is the value of humility, necessary to correct the hubris that underlies calculative thinking. Hubris can be overcome through an attitude of humility—"a selfless respect for reality"[31]—a value we argue requires some cultivation through education. According to Murdoch there are two discernable components of humility: respect for the integrity of things and *unselfing*, the latter of which she describes as "the abandonment of hubristic claims on behalf of human beings' capacities to know how things are, plan and control the future, and dominate the world."[32] Furthermore, there are certain stances, according to Heidegger, ways of being-in-the-world, which can nurture and cultivate humility.[33] Gelassenheit, or letting-be, is one of these ways of being.[34] To take such a stance is to experience and treat things as "that they are" and not as they figure in some reductionist vision suiting human purposes .[35] Another comportment we can adopt is respect for "little things," the inconspicuous, unglamorous activities we engage in daily in our lives seemingly without noticing. We have become incapable of celebrating anything but the "gigantic" or the "striking"; instead we should be more adept at noticing and celebrating the "ordinary aspects of life," or the "simpler and more 'local' forms of community."[36] A second value important to us is the cultivation of wonder. Wonder can help us become aesthetically attuned to the natural world about us,[37] to appreciate, through the ontological and epistemological categories of our philosophy, their beauty, fragility, ephemera, limit, precarity, and danger. *Thus, the third principle behind our philosophy is that of an axiology valuing humility and wonder* (Table 1).

31. Murdoch, Iris, *Existentialists and Mystics: Writings on Philosophy and Literature* (London: Penguin, 1997), 387.

32. Murdoch, 385.

33. Heidegger, Martin, *Being and Time*, trans. John Macquarrie and Edward Robinson (San Francisco: Harper & Row, 1962).

34. Heidegger, *Discourse on Thinking*, 55.

35. Cooper, *The Measure of Things*, 4.

36. Cooper, 363.

37. Harvey, *Heidegger and Eco-phenomenology*.

Table 1

A Philosophy Reclaiming Mystery: Philosophical Categories, Principles and Implications for the Naturalist Current of Environmental Education.

Philosophical Categories	Principles	Implications for the Naturalist Current of Environmental Education
Ontology	• *ontological possibility and diversity*	Nature reveals itself and has value apart from the valuing subject, thus bringing ontological possibility and diversity.
Epistemology	• *epistemological limitation and tentativeness*	There is limitation and tentativeness to what we can know. This limitation and tentativeness evoke humility and wonder toward nature.
Axiology	• *valuing humility and wonder*	As nature is experienced as non-objectified, value for humility and wonder is instilled, which, in turn, opens the human subject to both the mystery and the revelation of nature.

A doctrine of mystery provides an outlook and stance on a worldview recognizing the truth in the thesis of the human-world while acknowledging an undiscursable, mysterious reality. Such a worldview is the foundation for meditative thinking and supports reclaiming the naturalist current of environmental education and its aim of revelation. Environmental education is revelational when the practice of reclaiming mystery considers the three principles summarized in Table 1.

PART IV: SUMMARY AND DISCUSSION QUESTIONS

Meditative thinking as an antidote to calculative thinking is an effort to rethink our relationship with nature and, by extension, environmental education. Our current trajectory of being-in-the-world is proving cataclysmic. Our wholesale inability to recognize this is an example of human hubris at its worst. We offer meditative thinking as reclaiming the naturalist current of environmental education. Founded upon a doctrine of mystery, this alternative philosophy and its practice of reclaiming mystery supports and nurtures an aim for environmental education that is revelational.

Arguing that environmental education, through the naturalistic current, be guided by meditative thinking rather than calculative thinking is going to be challenging. It will be met with skepticism and doubt. Our instrumental relation with nature calls to question a metaphysics most of us are unaware is shaping our lives, let alone the way we are interacting with the natural environment. Our preoccupation with the naturalistic current of environmental education may seem romantic and impractical. And yet, our modern tendency to problem-solve our way out of our environmental demise is not working. As nature reveals itself and lives are transformed by the displacement of the self, what opens up is a realm of "response" ability.

DISCUSSION QUESTIONS

1. Contrast the ways in which you may have experienced the influences of calculative and meditative thinking on the aims of environmental education?
2. Meditative thinking entails Gelassenheit, or letting-be, and comportments toward Gelassenheit are described as releasement toward things and openness to the mystery. What does this mean to you?
3. What does a doctrine of mystery offer to competing claims of reality, namely, the absolutist versus humanist?
4. How might you practice a philosophy of reclaiming mystery? In your professional/academic context, what might this consist of?
5. Meditative thinking and reclaiming the naturalist current of environmental education might be met with skepticism. How might this be countered? Why should it be?

BIBLIOGRAPHY

Anderson, R. Lanier. "Friedrich Nietzsche." In The Stanford Encyclopedia of Philosophy, edited by Edward N. Zalta. Metaphysics Research Lab, Stanford University, 2017. https://plato.stanford.edu/archives/sum2017/entries/nietzsche/.

Aristotle. *Physics*. Translated by C. D. C. Reeve. Cambridge: Hackett Publishing Company, 2018.

Bigwood, Carol. *Earth Muse: Feminism, Nature, and Art*. Philadelphia: Temple University Press, 1993.

Cooper, David E. *The Measure of Things: Humanism, Humility, and Mystery*. Oxford: Clarendon Press, 2007.

Franklin, Ursula. *The Real World of Technology*. Toronto: House of Anansi, 1999.

Guba, E. G. *The Alternative Paradigm Dialog*. Newbury Park: Sage, 1990.

Harvey, Sharon. *Heidegger and Eco-phenomenology: Gelassenheit as Practice*. Saarbrücken: Lambert Academic Publishing, 2009.

Heidegger, Martin. *Being and Time*. Translated by John Macquarrie and Edward Robinson. San Francisco: Harper & Row, 1962.

Heidegger, Martin. *Discourse on Thinking*. Translated by John M. Anderson and E. Hans Freund. New York: Harper & Row, 1966.

Heidegger, Martin. *The Question Concerning Technology and Other Essays*. Translated by William Lovitt. New York: Harper & Row, 1977.

Heidegger, Martin. *Nietzsche, vol. 1: The Will to Power as Art*. Translated by David Farrell Krell. London: Routledge, 1981.

Heidegger, Martin. *Nietzsche, vol. 4: Nihilism*. Edited by David Farrell Krell. Translated by F. A. Capuzzi. New York: Harper& Row, 1982.

Heidegger, Martin. *Introduction to Metaphysics*. Translated by Gregory Fried and Richard Polt. New Haven: Yale University Press, 2000.

Jones, Richard H. *Curing the Philosopher's Disease: Reinstating Mystery in the Heart of Philosophy*. Landham: University Press of America, 2009.

Karrow, Douglas D. *Educating-with-place: Recovering from Metaphysics as Technicity*. Saarbrücken: Lambert Academic Publishing, 2010.

Karrow, Douglas D., Xavier Fazio, and David Zandvliet. *Nomenclature and Discourse of Environmental and Sustainability Education in Teacher Education*. Edited by Michael Peters. Singapore: Springer, 2022.

Mika, Carl. *Indigenous Education and the Metaphysics of Presence: A Worlded Philosophy*. New York: Routledge, 2017.

Moran, Dermot. *Introduction to Phenomenology*. London: Routledge, 2000.

Murdoch, Iris. *Existentialists and Mystics: Writings on Philosophy and Literature*. London: Penguin, 1997.

Nietzsche, Friedrich Wilhelm. *Thus Spake Zarathustra*. Translated by Thomas Common. New York: Prometheus Books, 1993.

Ornstein, Allan C., and Daniel U. Levine. *Foundations of Education*. 10th ed. Boston: Houghton-Mifflin, Harcourt, 2008.

Neal, Philip, and Joy Palmer. *The Handbook of Environmental Education*. London: Routledge, 1994.

Postman, Neil. *Technopoly: The Surrender of Culture to Technology*. New York: Vintage Books, 1993.

Sauvé, Lucie. "Currents in Environmental Education: Mapping a Complex and Evolving Pedagogical Field." *Canadian Journal of Environmental Education, 10*, no. 1 (Spring, 2005): 11–37.

Verkamp, Bernard, J. *The Senses of Mystery: Religious and Non-Religious*. New York: Fordham University Press, 1997.

Made in the USA
Columbia, SC
26 October 2023

24998123R00130